BUREAUCRATS, TECHNOCRATS, FEMOCRATS

BUREAUCRATS, TECHNOCRATS, FEMOCRATS

Essays on the Contemporary Australian State

Anna Yeatman

ALLEN & UNWIN
Sydney   Wellington   London   Boston

for my parents

© Anna Yeatman, 1990
This book is copyright under the Berne Convention
No reproduction without permission. All rights reserved.

First published in 1990
Allen & Unwin Australia Pty Ltd
An Unwin Hyman company
8 Napier Street, North Sydney, NSW 2060 Australia

Allen & Unwin New Zealand Limited
75 Ghuznee Street, Wellington, New Zealand

Unwin Hyman Limited
15–17 Broadwick Street, London W1V 1FP England

Unwin Hyman Inc.
8 Winchester Place, Winchester, Mass 01890 USA

National Library of Australia
Cataloguing-in-Publication entry:
Yeatman, Anna.
  Bureaucrats, technocrats, femocrats.

  Bibliography.
  Includes index.
  ISBN 0 04 442103 6.

  1. Public administration—Australia. 2. Political sociology—Australia. 3. Welfare state. 4. Feminism—Australia. I. Title.

354.94

Set in 10/11 pt Sabon by Graphicraft Typesetters Ltd., Hong Kong
Printed by SRM Production Services SDN BHD, Malaysia

Contents

	Acknowledgements	vii
	Introduction	ix
Part I	ADMINISTRATIVE REFORM AND THE AUSTRALIAN STATE IN THE 1980S	
1	Administrative reform and management improvement	1
2	The concept of public management	13
3	Democratisation and the administrative state	36
Part II	FEMOCRATS AND THE AUSTRALIAN STATE	
4	Are femocrats a class of their own?	61
5	Dilemmas for femocracy	80
Part III	RESTRUCTURING AND THE CRISIS OF THE WELFARE STATE	
6	Restructuring and Australian public policy	101
7	Feminism and the 'crisis' of the welfare state	119
8	The politics of discourse and the politics of the state	149
	Appendix A	175
	Appendix B	179
	Bibliography	180
	Index	192

Acknowledgements

There are a number of people I would like to thank, although I hasten to exempt them from any responsibility for how I have used their stimulus, help or encouragement. For their inspiration to become creatively involved in development of democratic public policy in Australian society: Hugh Stretton, Jean Blackburn, Anne Deveson, Peter Wilenski, Colin Power, Bettina Cass, Denise Bradley and Beryl Radin; for their inspiration and encouragement to become involved in the complicated business of public management practices that are oriented both democratically and in the direction of good service-delivery outcomes: Bill Cossey, Gael Fraser, Cathy McMahon, Louise Denley, Meredith Smith and Lois Bryson. For introducing me into theoretical ways of thinking that have proved very fruitful for understanding some of my own ideas and ways of seeing: Ivan Szelenyi, David Levine, Judy Stacey, Terry Threadgold and Cate Poynton. For specific intellectual insight, encouragement and/or assistance: Staffan Marklund, Clare Burton, Peta Tancred-Sheriff, Sue Sheridan, John Browett, Riaz Hassan, Colin Power, Martin Painter and Lois Bryson. For their technical assistance and generous support: Sue Manser, the librarians on the Circulation Desk at Flinders University, John Iremonger; and, for her intelligent editing, Venetia Nelson.

Chapter 1 has appeared in a different form as an article in the *Canberra Bulletin of Public Administration* 50, 1986, pp. 357–62; and also in *Flinders Studies in Policy and Administration* 3, 1987. Chapter 2 is the revised version of an article which was published in the *Australian Journal of Public Administration*, 46, 1987.

Introduction

This is a book of theoretical essays in political sociology and Australian public administration. They contest some of the fundamental features of mainstream structures and cultures of the Australian state, especially as it has been led in the 1980s by the Labor Party, an apolitical party with a statist orientation.

In these essays I am concerned with several themes. One is the development of the complex interventionist state. The complexity of the late-twentieth-century state in advanced capitalist societies arises from several factors. The first is the proliferation of interests and movements which make claims on the state and its power to distribute social goods and values. Their claims variously shape the agendas of public policy and the character of social programs. Because these claims involve differently positioned interests they often conflict, and these conflicts politicise the construction of policies and programs. The symbolic politics of such contests becomes critically important because it is in linguistic practices that certain claims, and not others, are valorised.

The second factor is the increasingly complex differentiation of the state's activities. As the state has grown to encompass virtually every feature of the everyday lives of its subjects, it has had to enter into a vastly extended repertoire of exchanges and relationships with the different organisations of civil society: 'capitalist economies and households; social movements and voluntary public spheres (churches, organizations of professionals and independent communications media and cultural institutions); political parties, electoral associations and other 'gatekeepers' of the state-civil society division; as well as 'disciplinary' institutions such as schools, hospitals, asylums and prisons' (Keane, 1988:19–20). This extended repertoire of exchanges and relationships requires of the state increasingly differentiated and specialised capacities in policy and administration. This is expressed not only in the horizontal division of state business into different departments (e.g. Department of Community Services and Health, Department of Social Security) and into different sections or programs within these departments, but in the vertical differentiation of state business into distinct levels of government: national, provincial and local. Each level becomes a distinct protagonist with its own specialised view of these relationships, and some programs—e.g. Home and Community Care—depend on the relatively close cooperation of all three levels, while others—e.g. the Australian Development Assistance Bureau—do not.

To the extent that the state has developed this degree of internal differentiation, and become entwined in complex ways with the agents and organisations of civil society, the state's agency, or sovereignty, has become a widely dispersed field of activity. For example, this field of activity includes: the executive politics of central, national government agencies like Prime Minister's and Cabinet, the Department of Finance, and Treasury; the commercialising activities of a statutory body such as Telecom; the visits of a social worker to a mildly demented 75-year-old woman who still lives in her own home; the creative activities of local community theatre groups which depend on government subsidies; the participation of parents in the management committee of a government-funded childcare centre; the industrial and professional politics of public service unions; and the efforts of ethnic organisations and advocates of multiculturalism to extend government policy and the capacities of Australian employers and educational institutions to recognise overseas qualifications of individuals who have migrated to Australia.

This dispersion of activity within the borders of the state's jurisdiction corresponds to the increasing permeability of these borders to global traffic (in persons and goods), global politics, and global issues. The politics and management of this degree of social complexity are not containable within the conceptions of the state that we have inherited. Just as the business of the state is no longer containable in formal legislative enactments, the simple decisionist models of the state that make it appear as the public umpire of social contests and judge of wrongdoing, or as the executive committee of the bourgeoisie, are no longer relevant.

A second and related theme I am concerned with is the proposition that we need to learn to live with a complex interventionist state because it is unlikely to go away. Learning to live with it means accepting that it is a central site of social, political, cultural and economic struggle over the distribution of social, political, cultural and economic resources. It is also a site of struggle about how top-down or bottom-up the direction of such struggles over distribution should be. Accordingly, this is a book about the 'politics of the state'.

A third theme, also related to the development of the complex, interventionist state, is the argument that this politics of the state involves struggles for democratisation of the state. This theme has two aspects. The first concerns the importance of developing democratic theory so that it provides some theoretical guidance and models for the democratisation of what I and others have called 'the administrative state' (see chapter 3). The second aspect concerns the importance of developing the politics of democratisation that is associated with the so-called new social movements. These movements—the women's movement, the various multiracial and multicultural movements, gay rights movements, and the environmentalist movement—represent new political claims on the democratising of the distribution of economic, political, cultural and social resources, and these claims are directed to the state. It is the multiplication of these claims, and the inability of the traditional institutions of political compromise between the claims of capital and labour to contain them, that is one of the current pressures prompting top-down styles of state management. In chapter 7, I argue that there is a current crisis of the *ideal* welfare state and that this is driven in part by a counterrevolution in response to the democratising claims of the new social movements.

A fourth theme is the relative lack of a tradition of citizenship in the Australian state–civil society system. This lack has not been challenged by the corporatist politics of the Hawke Labor Government which came into power in 1983, and which may enter a fourth term in 1990. While government discourse has incorporated the multicultural and feminist politics of the new social movements it has done so in a way which reproduces their marginality to the traditional tripartite structures of capital, labour and the state. This is evident particularly in the reinstatement of a more selective and often income-tested approach to provision of welfare (see chapters 5 and 7) and in the cultural orientation of this government to the challenges of 'restructuring' (see chapter 6).

This is inevitable given the political-cultural traditions of the Labor Party and the Australian state, but it is also contestable by Australians who are marginalised by these traditions. My critique is an invitation to develop this contest further, to challenge the patriarchal Labor corporatist structures of inclusion and exclusion. In chapter 6, I propose that the traditionally placed and privileged adherents of white, Anglo-Australian cultural traditions are defining the agendas of the restructuring of the Australian economy. However, they are not likely to prove adequate to the task of generating an ethos of economic activity that is relevant to Australia's post-colonial position and multicultural population. Whether this ethos is developed will depend on who assumes leadership in the contemporary cultural politics of restructuring.

It is my view, expressed in a number of different ways in chapter 6, that the new social movements in Australia must develop the affinities between their struggles so that they can provide a more sustained and coherent challenge to the white, Anglo masculinist institutions which by their dominance have precluded a shared culture of Australian citizenship. In particular, it is important that the feminist, multicultural and multiracial movements within Australia develop their mutual affinities. If this is to be done with potency it has to be a politics of affinity which is both domestically and globally oriented. For example, this means that Australian feminism needs to de-centre itself as the white, Anglo movement it has been, and to link up with Aboriginal women and women of non-English-speaking backgrounds within Australia. The leverage of such a movement of affinities is not likely to be very much in relation to the increasingly global character of Australia's political economy unless it is also directed at linking up with feminists and women's organisations within the various societies within the Pacific–Asian Basin region. Such a politics of affinity is not particularly developed in Australia at this time, the late 1980s, although there are increasing signs that feminists are ready to consider the directions it implies.

A fifth theme is the significance of the tendency of the Labor state to make femocrats responsible for representing the claims of the new social movements within the policy and administrative activities of the state. These claims are symbolically corralled as those of 'the disadvantaged groups'. Femocrats have participated in these agendas of symbolic pacification, but they are also positioned to contest them. Whether they do so or not will depend on where they are positioned within the state, and, among other things, on whether they adopt top-down or bottom-up approaches. In short, there is no unitary femocratic politics, but one that is structured by the politics of the state itself where different actors adopt different value perspectives, and assume different allegiances. If feminist ideology orients femocrats to bottom-up approaches and democratising agendas for state activity, there is no reason why a femocrat might not have other kinds of allegiance, not least being the specific kind of professional training and culture within which a particular femocrat may be oriented. For example, a femocrat who has been trained by the economically rationalist models of economics or business administration may find these more compelling than the ideological commitments of feminism.

A sixth theme is the importance of developing public debate and dialogue about the practices of the complex interventionist state. There is a distinction to be made in political debate about public values between the public domain on the one hand, and the modern interventionist state on the other. The business of the latter is not necessarily oriented publicly or oriented to the maintenance and development of public values. Publicly accountable state practices which are oriented to the maintenance and development of public values are contingent on struggles within civil society to make them so. To the degree that the state and civil society now interpenetrate, as in the innumerable ways in which state activities rely on the participation of, or consultation with, particular interests and lobby groups, these are struggles that are undertaken within this zone of interpenetration. The vitality of these struggles depends, among other things, on a critical tradition of writing and analysis in public administration.

It has seemed to me clear that a central challenge to white, Anglo, metropolitan identifications here in Australia as elsewhere is in the combined impact of post-colonial, post-racist, post-patriarchal social movements as these are entwined with the pressures for economic restructuring that arise from the new terms of competition in a global economy in recession. This challenge or rather challenges have led to a combination of counterrevolution and nostalgia in state-societies such as the United States of America, the United Kingdom and Australia. Each has thrown up the image of itself as it was in its heyday to manage and to deflect the challenges of 'restructuring' in this post-colonial, post-racist and post-patriarchal era.

This is one reason, and certainly not the only one, why the party associated with the Australian traditions of egalitarianism, mateship and state-sponsored collectivism has been selected for the role of mediating the Australian state-society's responses to the current challenges of economic and cultural restructuring. The Labor Party is not only associated with those traditions, but the 'new-classing' of its branches and of its leadership (see chapters 1 and 2) permits the discourse of mateship to take on the cadences of management and economic rationalism. From the point of view of social democratic values Australia may have been more fortunate than the USA or United Kingdom in the way its dramatic traditions cast the central player, but it is important to consider the costs implied in its particular version of counterrevolution and nostalgia.

PART I
Administrative Reform and the Australian State in the 1980s

1 Administrative reform and management improvement

The rhetoric and practices of administrative reform and management improvement in Australian public bureaucracies in the early to mid-1980s deserve critical scrutiny not least because of the virtually universal legitimacy accorded to them. The very language of administrative reform and management improvement invites immediate approbation and the willing suspension of disbelief. How could we not applaud 'strong efforts ... being made to change and improve public sector operations across Australia' (Guerin, 1985a:384)? I would suggest that any rhetoric which works like this has a central relationship to claims of legitimacy made on behalf of existing or emergent systems of domination.

In hindsight, and from the vantage point of the late 1980s, it is possible to appreciate the inevitability of the Labor-led governments in the Commonwealth and four of the States adopting this rhetoric of administrative reform and management improvement in the first half of the 1980s. These governments espoused a state-centric mode of managing the significant challenges of that time to the business of government and public administration. Thus, they sought to manage neo-conservative and New Right demands for smaller government by turning them into demands for more efficient government. Moreover, they sought to manage the increasing alienation of ordinary people with respect to the over-bureaucratisation of the delivery of public goods and services by making this delivery more responsive to users' needs and more open to public participation. At the same time the necessity of managing a no-growth public revenue base in a context of increasing demands on the social security and welfare system (see Cass, 1986a) has meant that these governments have emphasised cost-effectiveness and 'doing more with less' as the essential attributes of good public administration.

If there have been also social and political administrative reform agendas of these Labor governments which have led to the adoption of social justice strategies, equal opportunity legislation and increased emphases on the rights of citizens to participate in decisions about how public services are provided, these agendas have been overwhelmed by and subjugated to the managerialist administrative reform agendas of these governments. This managerialist orientation borrows, and adapts to public sector requirements, the culture of management which has been developed by modern, twentieth-century capitalist firms. This is, of course, an economistic culture, where the business of public administration is viewed as the more or less effective and efficient instrument of producing goods and services (see Considine, 1988). The political character of these goods and services which demands processes of participation in debate about what they should be and how they are produced is subordinated to an economistic bottom line: cost efficiency. Since there is often no market principle to sanction the economic performance of public agencies it becomes meaningful in this context to view cutbacks to their budgets as enforcing more efficient performance. Where it is possible to introduce something that looks like the market principle, effort is made to do so. Accordingly, agencies are permitted, if not encouraged, to cross-charge each other for their services, and to commercialise their services in the open market. At the same time citizens are redefined as consumers, customers, or clients in relation to publicly provided goods and services. This permits a focus on whether they might not do better by looking to private, market provision of these goods and services, and introduces an emphasis on the right of consumers to 'choose' what they want. The effect of this reasoning is that the 'consumers' of public goods and services are atomised in relation to each other, and the assumption is made that they can understand and express their preferences independent of any collectively oriented and/or political dialogue about how best to explore, express, and meet their needs in relation to publicly provided goods and services. They are no longer members of a public community of citizens, but become instead private, self-interested actors.

In what follows I discuss the tension between the social-political and the managerialist agendas of administrative reform in the Labor-led Australian state of the 1980s. This tension has been shaped by the increasing predominance of the managerialist agendas over the others. It is important to appreciate that the tension between these agendas can be carried over into the managerialist rhetoric itself. For example, managerialist metaphors can be used to emphasise and legitimise public services which are *client*-oriented rather than determined, as is usually the case, by the needs and work practices of the service *providers*. This is an emphasis which may be seen as requiring emphases on access, equity, and participation, where these values are practically applied to the real-life situations of Australians who need public services. Here then is an example where the application of managerialist agendas to public service means that they converge with the social and political agendas of administrative reform.

The extent of divergence, convergence, tension or conflict between these different administrative reform agendas depends on the politics of those who are leading and implementing the agendas. It is clear that how administrative reform is expressed and implemented at any one time depends on the delicate balances of power-brokering between different players with different commitments within the ministries and the senior levels of the public bureaucracies concerned. These balances are in turn influenced by the different kinds of pressures coming up the line into the executive domains of public bureaucratic politics, where these pressures emanate from public sector unions, direct providers of public services and from citizen-clients either as individuals or as organised lobbies and social movements.

My concern in this chapter is with how conflicting agendas of administrative reform have been shaped by competing or conflicting interests within public bureaucracies. The indisputable and apparently apolitical virtues of managerialist agendas have been an effective trojan horse by which the democratising agendas of the new social movements and their advocates within public bureaucracies have been subordinated to a process of the effective reinstatement of hierarchical controls and administrative elite rule within public bureaucracies. A newly rationalised administrative elite has learnt a repertoire of symbolic gestures in the direction of consumer consultation, social justice and client rights, but has been barred effectively from more serious conversion to these values by being rewarded or sanctioned for conformity to managerialist-economic rationalist administrative agendas. In this context the new social movements and their advocates within public bureaucracies have been placed on the defensive.

THE DIFFERENT AGENDAS OF ADMINISTRATIVE REFORM IN THE 1980S

Wilenski (1987:167–69) classifies the three strands of administrative reform in the first part of the 1980s as follows: 1. reforms for a more *efficient* administration, which is the context in which the rhetorics of management improvement finds its place; 2. reforms for a more *democratic* administration; 3. reforms for a more *equitable* administration. 'Efficiency', 'democracy' and 'equity' are different types of claims of legitimacy, as Wilenski's (1985:3) definitions of the three types of administrative reform bring out:

> *a more efficient administration*: an administration which is capable of effectively and creatively meeting the tasks of modern government with as little waste and misuse as possible of resources, both human and financial.
>
> *a more democratic administration*: an administration in which the major policy decisions and the allocation of resources are made by

ministers as the elected representatives of the people; and secondly (since ministers cannot take or supervise all decisions), a more representative and diverse bureaucracy whose decisions are more open to public influence, to public scrutiny and to appeal.

a more equitable administration: an administration which is just and fair in dealing with its own employees and applicants for employment, and with individual citizens and groups relying on the services it provides.

It is important to review briefly the context in which these claims to legitimacy have been pushed onto the political and administrative agendas of not only the Australian but other modern, liberal-democratic states. The demands that state administrations become more efficient, democratic and equitable reflect the enormously increased salience of the state in our everyday lives and the growth of the state's spheres of operation over the course of this century. These demands have become articulated clearly and forcefully only in the last twenty years or so, and they reflect both contestation between different interests as to who will control the agendas of liberal-democratic state administrations and debate on the legitimate boundaries of state activity.

The demands for a more democratic and equitable administration reflect the shift away from the public's acquiescence in decisions made by officials, professionals and other experts toward increasing insistence on consumer rights to participate in these processes of decision-making and to share in the information needed for that participation to be effective. These demands reflect also the emergence of a plurality of social movements, pressure groups and single-issue groups which are no longer containable within the old established party system and its reach into types of representation within the bureaucratic modes of public decision-making. The very development of the welfare state has generated client groups and new interests which make demands of state administrations. Further, the widening scope of state administrative activities has led to increased concern about how subject they are to public scrutiny, appeal and evaluation in accordance with standards of equity and fairness. As John Keane (Introduction to Offe, 1984:30) represents Claus Offe's reading of these trends, they have signalled 'a marked increase in the social character of politics' and of, we may add, state administration.

It is in this context, then, that such administrative reforms as the following are to be placed: equal opportunity, affirmative action, freedom of information legislation (at the Commonwealth level in Australia), administrative appeals tribunals and the establishment of ombudsmen. Further administrative support for such reforms has been afforded by the establishment of administrative sections or agencies which have as part of their brief the advocacy and development of a more responsive and representative state administration. In Australia examples of these would be: the various equal opportunity and women's adviser units in both line departments and central agencies; such entities as the Commonwealth Government Office of Multicultural Affairs, and the various State Government Ethnic Affairs Commissions; and a variety of modes for building 'community participation' into structures of administrative decision-making. These developments coopt and reshape demands from the new social movements and pressure groups as much as they serve to legitimise these demands at the level of official culture and to provide significant responses to those demands.

The other set of demands for administrative reform which focus on making state administration more effective and efficient quickly assume a technical appearance and import, but they need also to be assessed against the wider backdrop of debate concerning the legitimate ambit of state activity. There is, at present, a general political debate which centres on the public sector and its legitimacy and which is framing almost all other aspects of political debate. This debate concerns whether the state is the appropriate instrumental and/or normative mechanism through which to arbitrate and allocate claims by individuals and groups. Set against a public principle of allocation of claims is a private, market-oriented principle. Necessarily, given the ideological hegemony of market-oriented individualism in our own as in most other western liberal-democratic societies, the consequence of this debate has been to put the public sector on the defensive. This has become part of a general scrutiny of how much or which parts of the public sector can be or should be privatised.

The significance of this debate is that it has displayed for such scrutiny the types of activities in which the public sector engages and has enabled a clearer understanding of public sector types of objectives. To a certain extent, this has prompted a sophisticated and positive defence of what it is that the public sector can do for the commonweal and private firms cannot (see Wilenski, 1986).

More often, the rationalisation of public sector administrative activities in the form of calculable means–ends relationships has led to what Weber would have called a defence couched in the terms of a formal, rather than a substantive, rationality. It has led to the adoption of rhetoric and measures which are designed to show that we have a cost-effective and efficient public sector. Here the point is to show that the public sector can be as well managed as private firms and that it can be made subject to similar performance and output criteria even though it lacks the final test of success in the marketplace. It is in this context that the recent substitution of the language of 'management' for that of 'administration' among the upper public bureaucratic echelons is to be understood (see Pratt, 1985:362–67), as is also the emergence of a managerialist view of training for high-level public bureaucrats (see Hughes, 1986:106–7; and Bryson, 1986).

What we may call the managerialist defence of the public sector has come to prevail over a philosophically grounded defence of public sector goods and values. As Hughes (1986:107) remarks: 'Much is missing from the managerial agenda ... there is little recognition of the differences between private management and public management, insufficient regard to the political environment in which public managers operate and a lack of detail on how managerial or analytical skills are to be combined with actual policy work.'

In many cases, it has become clear that managerialist agendas do not necessarily lead to cost-effectiveness or to improved services since they inflate the technical requirements of bureaucratic performance (see Wade, 1985; Bryson, 1986). In these instances, we can only conclude that it is the *political* functions of the managerialist approach to administrative reform which need to be emphasised. This approach represents a clear accommodation to the wider political rhetoric of small government (see Wilenski, 1983), and it ties in negatively with the social demands for a more equitable and democratic administration by making them appear undesirable contributors to an inflation of expectations with regard to state administrations and budgets.

Thus, the two sets of demands for administrative reform—for an equitable and democratic state administration on the one hand, for efficient and effective administration on the other—seem to lead in different and conflicting directions. They entail distinct political agendas and thus attract to themselves distinct and opposed constituencies, or interests. While the emphasis of the former set of demands is on openness and responsiveness of bureaucratic processes to individuals and communities and thus lends itself to a politics of community representation and consultation, the emphasis of the latter is on rationalised techniques of controlling human and material resources within strict and centrally provided guidelines. While the former emphasises qualitative change and raises important questions about the structures of authority which govern the decisions affecting our lives (see Hawker, 1981), the latter emphasises calculable outcomes and processes, which necessarily need to be able to take existing authority structures as *givens*. While the former focuses on new issues of democratisation, new because they concern this newly evolved state apparatus reaching into every aspect of our lives, the latter requires strict hierarchical divisions because it requires calculable and predictable lines of authority. While the former emphasises 'representative' principles of public bureaucracy—the value of bringing all significant social groups into the administration of the state—the latter emphasises control of the troops by a trained managerial elite within the public service. While the former is congruent with democratic cultures of people management and problem-solving—cultures which emphasise the dependency of the organisation on people, and which give considerable attention to how these people are valued and encouraged to participate—the latter encourages a rational-systems culture which emphasises use of people as instruments to realise objectively measured outcomes and efficiencies.

MANAGERIALISM AS THE INTEREST OF A NEW ADMINISTRATIVE ELITE

If the managerialist agenda for administrative reform has come to prevail over the social and political agendas of administrative reform, this is not widely acknowledged in public bureaucratic circles. Guerin (1985a:384) offers some such acknowledgement when he declares: 'There are really two agendas. One is social and political, the other managerial. In most discussions they are thoroughly mixed, with managerial or organisational solutions being promoted for political problems, and vice versa.' He does not go on to ask whether they can be mixed in real terms, and he leaves as unproblematic their coexistence within documents such as the SA Review of Public Service Management ('Initial' and 'Final' Reports, March 1984 and February 1985, respectively). When the conflict between the two agendas is suppressed in this fashion, it is not difficult to see the mixing of democratic and equitable reforming rhetorics with the managerialist one as a way of selling the latter in the guise of the former. Certainly it raises the question of how empty and merely symbolic the democratic and equitable reforming rhetorics have become.

Conflict over these agendas is occurring *within* Australian public bureaucracies, but so far the interests concerned with democratic and equitable reforming directions have been disarmed to an alarming degree by the apparent rationality of the new managerialism. Within government policy and central agencies the democratic reforming direction seems to have lapsed although it is still taken seriously in the orientations of many of the regional managers and base-grade workers in departments concerned with direct service provision.

What is clear is that the managerialist agenda is in the interests of the central and controlling levels of public sector bureaucracies, and it is these who are controlling the pace and direction of reform. They can gather support from middle-management aspirants to top-level positions. The actual nature of what has been achieved in recent Australian public service reforms seems to bear out this interpretation. It is clear from the emphases of those leading the reforms

(Beale, 1985a; Guerin, 1985b; Cullen, 1986) and from what has actually occurred that it is the following 'package' of reforms which has been most important.

1 The devolution of operating powers to department heads (see Walsh, 1985, for the Commonwealth; and Guerin, 1985b, for South Australia) in order to make departmental heads more accountable, according to rationalised criteria, for what their departments do in pursuing objectives and for how those objectives sit with government policy and budgetary constraints.

2 The relative decrease of the old role of Public Service Boards in the direct and detailed overseeing of departmental performance and the tendency to relegate them to roles of monitoring and facilitating the management programs of departments and other agencies (see Hawkes, 1988; Kelleher, 1987; and Guerin, 1985a: 392 for a description of the roles of the newly established Government Management Board and Commissioner for Public Employment, which together replace the old Public Service Board in SA).

3 The creation of a senior executive service, a senior administrative elite, which is recruited by merit and has distinctive personnel arrangements. Beale's description of these arrangements for the Commonwealth Senior Executive Service has generic application, and includes SA, which has introduced an SES in all but name only:

—all positions which are not to be filled by transfer or rotation, are now advertised as open to outsiders for whom there are opportunities for fixed-term appointments with special superannuation options;
—in selecting staff more emphasis is placed on general management and policy performance rather than narrowly defined job experience;
—all promotions are made by the Public Service Board or its new equivalent on the recommendation of secretaries of departments. Rights of appeal against such promotions have been withdrawn [in SA this does not apply to entry into the Executive Officer range, i.e. to EO1 positions] and the Board or its equivalent is able to transfer staff between Departments. This has worked to enhance the power of the corporate executive levels of government and public bureaucracies. Laffin (1987) describes the strong role which a tightly disciplined Cabinet has assumed in the Cain Victorian State Government, and Kelleher (1988:9) points out that the federal Department of Prime Minister and Cabinet has 'significantly added to its own power and functions'.
—efforts in staff development have been intensified with new and revitalised management courses. (Beale, 1985:117)

All this may bring tensions of its own (for some anticipation of these, see Spann, 1977:82–84), but what is clear is that the thrust of these reforms concern the *leadership* levels of public bureaucracies, not the middle-management levels and certainly not the workers at the coalface. The reforms concern more effective and sophisticated centralised controls over public bureaucracies. These controls emphasise 'technique' and they are designed to offset and limit the influence of 'content', namely commitments and loyalties which are tied to particular departmental or agency portfolios and which acquire authority through the development of specialised experience and links to client groups.

When public service is defined as public management public servants are defined as (public) managers. In the 1980s, contrary to the emphases of some influential management literature (e.g. Peters and Waterman, 1982; Mintzberg, 1987) on the significance of values and of client-oriented service to the performance of an organisation, public management has been identified with the technical features of effective and financially accountable line command. This has tended to keep it insulated from the demands and complexity of its environment, and to ensure its responsiveness to the executive levels of that line command.

Thus, in the modernised Australian public services of the 1980s, management is viewed as context- and content-indifferent. A good manager can be a good manager anywhere, regardless of portfolio and the values, knowledge or experience of the manager. The belief that a manager is a manager wherever they are is especially entrenched in the Commonwealth Public Service (CPS). Senior personnel in the CPS are shifted from area to area without their having sufficient time to become familiarised with the area, or to establish effective working relationships with those whose roles and positions are tied in to the content of the area. State Government senior public servants have become well used to rapid turnover of the Commonwealth public servants with whom they are supposed to liaise and communicate.

This is necessarily a situation where people and their commitments and experience are not highly valued. It is certainly a situation which belies the management literatures which propose that it is 'people' and their relationships which make things happen and make high-quality outcomes possible. For those of us oriented to change, it is a situation which maintains the status quo precisely because it undermines the stability of networks and lateral connections between people on which any genuinely workable change is dependent.

The effects of the belief in context- and content-indifferent management are not conducive to good and creative public service.

These effects are many: first, the public servants themselves are placed under considerable pressure to appear to be in control of areas and issues with which they have little familiarity. It is not surprising if they are tempted to handle this pressure by overemphasising the technical aspects of program and policy management. This is also a situation which makes these public servants, however intellectually competent they are, relatively gullible in relation to the ideological features of new policy frameworks. They are more likely to be tempted in the direction of ideological prescription than to understand the context-dependent features of marrying principle with pragmatic requirements. This leads to great frustration on all sides when these public servants encounter context-bound public servants, service providers and consumers. As before it precludes effective development of lateral ties of communication across (Commonwealth, State, local) governments and across differently positioned players. It precludes also any bottom-up dynamic of program and policy development, and maintains the conservative hierarchical principle of vertical integration.

The centralising and elitist thrust of the managerialist reforms comes out clearly when we look at them more analytically.

1 Devolution of operating powers to departmental heads makes them more vulnerable with regard to whether their performance in setting and fulfilling objectives sits with ministerial and/or Cabinet objectives.

2 Creation of a service-wide corporate consciousness in a Senior Executive Service makes it a type of sophisticated managerial police for the service as a whole, the members of which have no interest in developing content-oriented commitments to particular sections or portfolios within the service. In this sense the SES represents the diffusion of a corporate (and central agency?) consciousness hitherto concentrated in Public Service Boards, not in departmental officers themselves.

3 Congruent with this corporate culture of public sector management designed to transcend and to bring into line sectoral/agency interests is the development of Public Service Boards (or their equivalents) into more sophisticated monitoring and facilitative instruments for a highly calculative, formal rational management style.

In short, administrative reform in Australian state bureaucracies in the 1980s has been structured by more sophisticated methods of centralised, top-level controls of these bureaucracies. These controls are intended to make public bureaucracies more answerable and accountable to the government of the day. Actually, their effect is to legitimise the existence of an administrative elite (see Thompson, 1985) and give it considerable power by endowing it with sophisticated techniques of control and a corporate identity. At the same time these controls work to withdraw from this elite any specific identity, honour or pride as a *public* administrative elite by making its membership and practices appear to be interchangeable with those of the privately oriented administrative elite of capitalist firms.

Administrative reform—notwithstanding certain marginal forms of rhetorical flourish—has little or nothing to do with actual improved services, or with increased autonomy for regional managers that would allow them the discretion and the resources for such discretion that responsive interaction between public servant and client requires (see Pomeroy, 1985:119–25). Such moves as have been made towards a more equitable and democratic administration are largely symbolic and/or devisory: for example, the Commonwealth keeps on increasing the charges for freedom of information (FOI) requests, and the SA Government has abandoned its intent to introduce such legislation; 96 per cent of the Commonwealth SES officers, as of 31 March 85 on data supplied by the Commonwealth PSB (cited by Thompson, 1985:22), are men and only 4 per cent women; and as any public department or agency can testify, they have been required to conform to equal opportunity requirements but have not been given the resources to do so. Pomeroy's (1985:123) regional manager perspective is eloquently expressed with regard to this last point:

... consultation in areas such as technological change, industrial democracy, equal opportunity and FOI take up more and more management time.

... many of us believe freedom of information, equal opportunity and industrial democracy are all long overdue; and their implementation has been all the more difficult because of a failure to make adequate practical provision for the demands they create.

The pattern is clear. Reforms towards a more equitable and democratic administration are delegated 'down the line' to those who have neither the authority nor the resources to put into practice the conception of these reforms let alone to implement them. This tendency indicates that these type of reforms are considered 'soft', and of little real consequence. Those down the line who take these reforming agendas seriously do so by converting the reforms into a new language of pastoral care, and risk their own frustration and credibility in being unable to deliver them in practice.

The creation of an administrative elite with a rationalised management education and culture represents the 'modernisation' of the Australian public bureaucratic elite. It would seem that in the past both Australia and New Zealand have lagged behind other western public bureaucratic cultures which have required their senior public servants to be highly educated (see Thompson, 1985; Sheriff, 1976:48–54). Historically, Australasian public bureaucratic cultures have been versions of the wider culture of a masculine egalitarianism, and in the past this placed a premium on seniority as a legitimate claim to promotion. With the current shift from 'administration' to 'management', and the increasing value placed on high degrees of proficiency in technical and interpretative skills, seniority has been displaced by merit as a legitimate claim to promotion (see Cullen, 1986:60). The dominant agenda of administrative reform means that merit is judged against managerialist criteria and that the preferred education of aspirants to the SES is a MBA. This will produce an educated administrative elite more comfortable with technique than with *telos* (see Konrad and Szelenyi, 1979), with microeconomics than with debates in social policy, perhaps because technical expertise is easier to reconcile with the older tradition of masculine egalitarianism. It is difficult not to be reminded of that aphorism with which Max Weber (1958:182) concluded his critique of the 'iron cage' of an all-pervasive administrative rationality: 'Specialists without spirit, sensualists without heart; this nullity imagines that it has attained a level of civilization never before achieved.'

There are a number of good and sensible aspects of the agendas of management improvement, and, from the value standpoint of a commitment to the values of equity and democratisation, there are some exciting aspects of the discourse of administrative reform and management improvement. To rescue these, however, we need to speak openly of conflicting agendas of administrative reform and conflicting interests. The complex and pervasive web of state administration is here to stay. The questions concern the structuring of this web: whether it is totalised as a technocratically managed system of control, or whether it is open to bids for 'participation' and to dialogue and contest over the values directing administrative decisions. The issues of participation and critical dialogue do not concern simply the relationship between public bureaucracies and public. Perhaps even more critically they concern relations between levels and interests within the public bureaucracies. Since the state has become so large and complex so too has its administrative staff. Struggles within this administrative staff are of consequence for the whole society, and it is towards a politics *within* the administration of the modern state that this chapter is intended as a contribution.

2 The concept of public management

In the 1980s there has been significant change in Australian public bureaucratic cultures. It is not too much to regard this change as a cultural revolution. In essence it is characterised by the adoption of the discourse of management as the frame of reference for how public servants should understand their tasks and identities. Historically the discourse of management has been developed and shaped by the requirements of management in private sector firms. It is a moot point how far the public sector can borrow and adapt the discourse of management without having its public service mission distorted and suborned by cultures and practices which developed to fit the administrative requirements of privately oriented, profit-maximising firms.

In discussing this change in Australian public bureaucratic culture in the 1980s, I want to address the following: 1. what is the nature of this change, and is it as significant as the term 'cultural revolution' implies? 2. what does the change imply for what we may expect of public administrative practices, and what benefits and costs might result from it? 3. why has this change occurred, and what broader contextual changes does it reflect which bear on conceptions of the role and place of the public sector in societies such as ours? 4. who within public service circles are the advocates of this change, and why are they so closely in tune with the style of leadership provided by Labor parties in government in the 1980s in South Australia, Victoria, New South Wales, Western Australia and the Commonwealth?

A CULTURAL REVOLUTION IN AUSTRALIAN PUBLIC BUREAUCRACIES?

There can be no doubt that changes have occurred. First, there has been a general change in nomenclature, where public service and administration have been relabelled 'public management'. This is evident, for example, in the Western Australian Government's June 1986 White Paper on changing and improving government administration in that state. The White Paper is titled *Managing Change in the Public Sector*, and it self-consciously offers definitions of the following: government; public sector; chief executive officer; senior officers; public sector managers; public sector employees. Some of this nomenclature indicates the reframing of the identity of public servants in terms of management discourse.

Second, this change in nomenclature is not merely formal but indicates a change in the identity of public administrators and what should guide their practice. A managerialist orientation is built into current expectations of administrative practice. For example, performance agreements entered into with the chief executive officers (CEOs) of particular departments and agencies facilitate the kind of autonomy any CEO might expect to allow him/her to get on with the job, but ensure also that what they are doing is constrained within the operational definitions of government policy and budget constraints agreed to by the government of the day. The model adopted is one based on the relationship between the CEO of a private profit-oriented firm and that firm's board of directors. In this model, 'management by objectives' refers to how the CEO translates government policy into operational goals; and 'let the managers manage' refers to governments letting the managers get on with the job by implementing these operational goals in relation to agreed resource constraints, and without further interference by government. The model also incorporates evaluation measures to scrutinise management performance: whether operational goals are being achieved economically, effectively, efficiently and on time; and whether the routine activities of their departments or agencies are ticking over smoothly. The Western Australian White Paper sums up the thrust of such evaluative measures (see Appendix A for details of the White Paper's construction of results-oriented public management in terms of 'Financial Accountability Mechanisms').

With these emphases on results-oriented management the purposes of public administration and public service tend to be reduced to the effective, efficient and economic management of human and financial resources. This is a technical approach to public administration and public service couched within a broader policy framework dominated by economic consideration. The latter is evident in the assumptions that government activities should be measured in terms of their effective resource management ('doing more with less') and that, where it is clear that for some reason such effective resource management is not possible (the service is too costly), the government should attempt to reduce this service or drop it altogether. The Western Australian White Paper (1986:1) illustrates these assumptions in its opening paragraph:

Since it came to office, the Government of Western Australia has taken a number of new initiatives designed to deal with an overriding problem which it believes is facing all Governments in the 1980's, namely that new or expanded services required by the community can no longer be provided by simply extending the tax base. Many Australians hold the view that the Government's share of the economy must not be allowed to increase further. This means that additional services must be funded both at the expense of other services and by improving efficiency in the delivery of other services, although new Government entrepreneurial activities will provide some additional reserve.

This is a 'rational' technical approach to public service and administration. Here, as in so many other instances, Weber's (1968:65) analysis of 'rationalisation' is apposite: '"Rational" technique is a choice of means which is consciously and systematically oriented to the experience and reflection of the actor, which consists, at the highest level of rationality, in scientific knowledge.'

Accordingly, a 'scientific management' approach was adopted by the Commonwealth Public Service Board in its 1987 Senior Executive Management Program (SEMP). The document which defines this program states that the program will provide learning opportunities for entrants to the Senior Executive Service in the areas of three 'core competencies'. These are: 1. 'personal and interpersonal competence'; 2. 'industrial relations'; 3. 'managing organisational change' (see Appendix B for the description of these three streams). The SES itself (the senior level of public servants lying immediately under the level of department or agency heads, or CEOs) is a conception of senior public servants produced by this scientific management approach. Their central task is defined not as a policy task but as an orientation to producing results through managing themselves and other people (see Appendix B, par. (a)).

To be sure, 'scientific management' has now in many quarters come to incorporate both a human relations and personal development component. Accordingly, skills in managing human resources (including oneself as a human resource) are stressed, with an emphasis being placed on adult learning mode for participants in the SES training program, and on their acquiring negotiation, communication, networking and stress-management skills. Also emphasised are 'skills in establishing processes for participative management practices'.

Third, as the management discourse has become adopted by public administrators, the discourse of administrative reform has fallen by the wayside. The point of management improvement is, as the SEMP 1987 Design Specification (see Appendix B) puts it, to require

15

managers to make government work as efficiently as possible for Australia by:
- doing more with less
- focussing on outcomes and results
- managing change better.

Equal opportunity in this context comes to be reframed in terms of what it can do to improve management, not of what it can do to develop the conditions of social justice and democratic citizenship in Australian society. Indeed the discourse of management sits uncomfortably with, and by its logic tends to preclude, reference to substantive public service obligations like maintaining the rule of law, upholding citizen right of access to fair and equitable government administration, and providing high-quality community services.

The reduction of administrative reform to management reform has signalled the adoption of 'scientific management' by Australian public bureaucracies. This has been a reform program directed by the Labor governments in the Commonwealth, South Australia, New South Wales, Victoria and Western Australia. Much of it may be rhetoric, but it does have consequences for the roles and practices of public servants, especially at the most senior levels but also at the middle levels. Moreover it is clear that these consequences represent a considerable change in the practical ethos of Australian public service. It is one which challenges the old dual-role public bureaucracy which was divided into a small stratum of policy-advisers (the peak of a very high and tapered pyramid) on the one hand, and a plethora of time-serving, rule-bound bureaucratic ritualists on the other. While the predictability and effective control over the latter's behaviour was best served by promotion through seniority, the former, especially in the Commonwealth Public Service, could be identified with qualities of creativity, intelligence and innovation which demanded a freedom of action and degree of influence not easily reconcilable with the place of the bureaucracy in the Westminster model of government.

The new bureaucratic ethos of scientific management withdraws legitimacy from both of these types of bureaucrat. The mandarin's brilliance is to be fenced in and about by performance agreements, and his/her vision for the good society, requiring as it does long-term strategic policy frameworks and planning, must be surrendered to the short-term considerations of results-oriented management and doing more with less. Genuine creators, entrepreneurs and visionaries will not accept confinement of what they do to the strictures of scientific management since these tend to reduce their substantive activities to technical types of activity:

As long as the action is purely 'technical' in the present sense, it is oriented only to the selection of the means which, with equal quality, certainty, and permanence of the result, are comparatively most 'economical' of effort in the attainment of a *given* end; comparatively, that is, insofar as these are at all directly comparable expenditures of means in different methods of achieving the end. The end itself is accepted as beyond question, and a purely technical consideration ignores other wants (Weber, 1968:68).

Mandarins will not allow the end itself to be accepted without question, not, that is, if they take their role seriously and orient themselves to it creatively.

Mandarins in the above sense of visionaries who are also strategic and pragmatic change agents are never thick on the ground in any context. If they attempt to practise within the ruling public management culture of the contemporary Australian state they face some peculiar difficulties, not simply those associated with the subordination of *telos* to technique. One of the most interesting features of this culture is the conjoining of rational-technical and line-command controls with highly normative and prescriptive directions for policies and progams. For example, policies and programs in the disability area currently evoke the values of independence and living-within-the-community for people with disabilities. These values are evoked in ways which make them akin to the core, orienting values of a party rally. They become ideological slogans rather than value orientations carefully reflected upon, where such reflection includes consideration of their relationship to other, possibly competing values, and to the practical complexities of daily living. When public values become public ideological prescriptions and/or slogans, they foster a situation where public servants and others think in terms of simple binary oppositions: in this case, *either* 'independence' *or* 'dependence'. This does not make for good, democratically oriented program and policy development. In this situation mandarins confront the likelihood of their being used as the producers of such ideological prescriptions and slogans. To the extent that this occurs their substantive strategic commitments and vision are effectively neutralised by being sequestered within the ideal and simplistic domain of ideology.

It is true that in Australian public services there has been very little of a bureaucratic mandarinate in evidence at any point of their development. If there has been one at all it has existed only in the senior levels of the Commonwealth public service, where indeed it has been identified more with certain departments than with others: Foreign Affairs, for example. In State public services in the past, top positions have gone either to time-servers who have come up from the ranks and whose loyalty has been thoroughly tried and tested, or to professionals or specialists, whose knowledge and skills are seen to equip them for the job. Thus, typically, engineers have been likely to head engineering and water supply departments, and doctors to head health departments.

In the spirit of the new scientific management, those who are recruited to the top and senior levels of the public service are not mandarins or time-servers or substantive specialists but what Gouldner (1979) referred to as the new 'technical intelligentsia'. The technical intelligentsia has higher-education credentials, but where a mandarinate values and acquires a 'liberal' and general education in, among other things, philosophical and ethical issues concerning the good society, the latter is oriented to the acquisition of university degrees both for the sake of credentialism and the acquisition of technical skills. All mandarin elite cultures depend on assumptions concerning 'aristocracies' of talent, and the elite itself is recruited in terms of a belief about where this aristocracy is to be found. These beliefs are always discriminatory in their nature and consequences. They make certain assumptions about what fits individuals to be cast in heroic roles. These assumptions exclude virtually all women as they do all those who do not exhibit an aristocratic conviction of their self-worth, vision and leadership capacities. The substitution of the technical intelligentsia for the mandarinate or for a top stratum recruited through seniority opens up the top and senior levels of the public service to a more democratic and less discriminatory construction of 'merit'. Those who have lacked either the social and cultural advantages which determine the aristocracy of talent or who have missed out on access to career positions and advancement (including women) are thus admitted to these levels.

When merit displaces aristocratic talent or seniority, technical knowledge and skills training become more valued and cultivated. Excellent technicians in the management of human and financial resources may be recruited and trained, but they are likely to be illiterate in the knowledge and skills required to comprehend and make judgments about the substantive purposes of public administration and service. Worse, they are likely to have acquired a trained diffidence to what they dismiss as 'philosophical', 'academic' or 'abstract' questions. Needless to say this technical intelligentsia is an easy mark for credentialled salesmen of economic pseudo-science (namely, dogmatic versions of neoclassical economics). In this environment even the potential mandarins must disguise their ethical and professional commitments or, where possible, give them a managerial gloss. This environment is not likely to encourage and produce great professional architects of public policy such as were represented in the past by H.C. (Nugget) Coombs, William Beveridge and John Maynard Keynes.

If the mandarinate has been remodelled in the form of a technocratically oriented senior elite of public servants, the old, 'traditional' type of rule-bound bureaucrat is being replaced by a new, up-to-date, more streamlined model in the middle ranks of the public service. This model draws the technical intelligentsia into the middle ranks of the bureaucracy. These are men and women with a degree and a highly rationalised and task-oriented conception of public administration work. They are not comfortable with unthinking acceptance of rules which are either imposed by the command of a bureaucratic superior or embedded in the customary practices of a particular government department or agency. They are open to improving the methods by which tasks get done, and to acquiring the learning and skills which enable them to do this. Accordingly they are both comfortable with and desire considerably more delegation of authority to them to get on with the task than was the case with the authoritarian personality of the older type of bureaucrat. The technical intelligentsia is also oriented to merit rather than to seniority as principles of recruitment and promotion in their ranks (see Gouldner, 1979:50).

This technical orientation to the task—and hence flexibility about how it gets done—sits with a flexible and tolerant attitude to others, a kind of generalised equal opportunity philosophy. Moreover, since the culture of the technical intelligentsia embraces the late-twentieth-century stress on the values of personal life, their bureaucratic culture dovetails with emphases on personal growth, change and awareness.

The spirit of the technical intelligentsia comes to pervade the public service, down to the base grades. The upper levels of the base-grade range also recruits those with credentials in higher education in most cases, and, accordingly, there is some degree of overlap in orientation between the base-grade and middle-level range of positions. However, the base grades, unlike the middle-level range, are not encouraged to view themselves as public managers.

The modernisation of public service culture, which is reflected in the technical intelligentsia's assumption of positions of leadership in the public service, represents a development in the modern principles of legitimation. There is a shift from a paternalistic and authoritarian administration of legal authority to a more flexible, participative and technically sophisticated management of the legally (or statutorily) defined brief of the public sector and of particular departments and agencies within it. Weber (1968:215) defines the rational-legal type of authority as 'resting on a belief in the legality of enacted rules and the right of those elevated to authority under such rules to issue commands'. It follows that, in a rational-legal type of order, there may be emphasis on the rule per se, with consequent inflexibilities and hidebound work practices, or there can be emphasis on a working within the legally provided frameworks in flexible and 'rational' ways.

Thus, for example, the central agency message about the new Government Management Employment Act in South Australia (July 1986) was that the new Act streamlined and rationalised conditions of public service employment, procedural frameworks and general requirements of public servants, especially of the top and senior levels, in such a way as to *facilitate* good management practices, not to *compel* them. Moreover, the process of drafting the Act was done in a consultative manner, involving substantial discussion and negotiations with the public service unions, existing permanent heads of departments (who were defined by the new Act as no longer permanent heads, but as CEOs on five-year contracts) and the management support group (a group of senior public servants from various government departments and central agencies). A large number of people were thus familiar with the changes signalled by the new Act before it was proclaimed. Once proclaimed, the Act was seen to have established a framework within which processes of management improvement and organisational change could occur.

The Act followed the Guerin Review of the public service, and it adopted a merit-based approach to recruitment and promotion with the consequence that all public servants lost their erstwhile lien on the positions they occupied. Simultaneously this allowed positions to be defined in a task-centred manner: accordingly if the task shifted or changed, the position would change, even disappear; public servants would be classified by level rather than by position occupied, and, within some limits, they could be shifted around between tasks (position-duties) defined as congruent with the level they are classified within.

There is then a shift to a new type of orientation to rational-legal authority. The shift is one away from a ritualistic adherence to legal rule to a conception of legal rules as useful framework settings which need to be changed if they prove to be anachronistic, inflexibly designed or inappropriately conceived. The flexibility allowed by this new orientation gives public servants more room to be technically creative and innovative in their work. Alvin Gouldner (1979:51, emphases original) brings out the implications of this shift for public bureaucratic cultures:

> Unlike the older bureaucrats, the new intelligentsia have extensive cultural capital which increases their mobility. The old bureaucrats' skills are often little more than being able to read, write, file, and are limited to their employing bureaucracies. The new intelli-

THE CONCEPT OF PUBLIC MANAGEMENT

gentsia's greater cultural capital is, indeed, *more productive of goods and services* and they are, therefore, less concerned to vaunt their personal superiority or to exact deference from those below them. As a result, the old bureaucrats and the new intelligentsia develop and reproduce different systems of social control. Bureaucrats employ a control apparatus based on 'ordering and forbidding', threatening and punishing the disobedient or resistant. The intelligentsia of the New Class, capable of increasing services and production, typically seek to control by *rewarding* persons for conformity to their expectations, by providing more material incentives and, also, by educational indoctrination. The intelligentsia of the New Class is a task-centred and work-centred elite having considerable confidence in its own worth and its future and, correspondingly, has less status anxiety that they irrationally impose on others. They are less overbearing and less punishment-prone.

The technical intelligentsia, then, comes into the public service and modernises it by subjecting it to its view of a rational-technical approach. This is indeed a cultural revolution in Australian public bureaucracies. Whether management is the only type of discourse which fits the cultural requirements of the technical intelligentsia is the next question to be asked and this is best done in the context of evaluating the costs and benefits of this cultural revolution.

THE COSTS AND BENEFITS OF THE BUREAUCRATIC CULTURAL REVOLUTION

As with so many things, the virtues of the technical intelligentsia as they inform the new public bureaucratic culture are, at the same time, its vices, as Table 1 shows.

Emphasis on outcomes; subjection of outcomes to performance indicators

First, there is an obvious benefit which comes from the task-centredness and performance-for-results orientation of the new bureaucratic culture. Bureaucratic rituals that cannot be justified on technical grounds are eliminated, especially those which were designed to maintain elaborate chains of deference and reporting procedures connecting layers of subordinates to their superiors. Moreover, focusing on the task and on results loosens up fixed ways of seeing and old time-encrusted practices.

It is entirely possible that a rational-technical orientation to the task in public service and administration may facilitate the development of a better theoretical understanding of the appropriate role of the state or public sector in our type of society. Sociological theorists of social differentiation would argue that, with the development of a

Table 1 Characteristics of the technical intelligentsia

VIRTUE	VICE
1 Orientation to tasks and results, bringing the benefit of an emphasis on outcomes rather than on bureaucratic process	1 Inappropriate subjection of substantive public service activities to performance indicators; fetishism of techniques
2 Democratisation of the 'line'	2 Management prerogatives and control
3 More autonomy for upper/middle ranks and more general tolerance for 'delegation' throughout	3 Reduction of substantive professional judgment and discretion to technical task controls
4 'Process' orientation and 'people' orientation	4 Rationalisation and enhanced sophistication of the techniques of social control in a mass-consumer, complex society
5 Inclusion of women and other 'minorities' within merit principle leading to a more 'representative' bureaucracy	5 Exclusion of the non-higher-educated from participation in authority structures
6 Capacity to take advice from, and desire of the good regard of professional knowledge-producers—thus some openness to value-oriented dialogue and debate	6 Bias toward technocratic types of knowledge-producers, and suppression of value issues
7 Technical flexibility, curiosity, openness	7 Philosophical indifference, and technological promiscuity, i.e. willingness to pursue any given end

modern rationalised division of labour in society, the distinct functions which maintain a modern society come to be undertaken in separate, though interdependent, specialised spheres of social interaction: the state, the economy, the family, the education system, and so on. From this perspective, developed by Durkheim, Parsons and Luhmann, the specialisation of particular social structures in distinct functions allows the functions themselves to become clarified and better understood, and facilitates the development of a science of each.

At the same time, a task-centredness and results orientation can lead to an overemphasis on the instrumental and technical features of public service and administration. When it is not possible to define a service in terms of a discrete task where results can be measured, the effect of a narrow and dogmatic task-cum-results orientation must be to make it appear as illegitimate and unnecessary. This can have grave consequences, as can be seen in the example of an Aboriginal community health service which is asked by the relevant central Commonwealth government agency to justify its activities (read, budget) in terms of 'performance-indicators'. The trust relations established between the service and the community it serves, the educational impact of the service, and much of its actual health work cannot be turned into activities measurable by performance indicators. In short, a fetishism of techniques, always a weakness of the technically oriented, can threaten to delegitimise and displace many of the requirements of good public service as community service.

Democratisation of line command; management prerogatives and control

The rational-technical orientation of the technical intelligentsia leads to 'democratisation' of line authority in public bureaucracies, where long and complex 'reporting' chains between superordinates and subordinates are flattened out and there is altogether much less of an authoritarian culture of command and deference. Instead there is something like a democracy of technical experts where it is expected that positions of authority and leadership are filled by those who know more and have more practical technically oriented experience than those who are placed as their subordinates. Furthermore, the exercise of authority is more or less legitimate depending on whether it can rationally account for itself, that is, be open to question and critical comment from those subject to it. This is the type of authority which results in dialogue with subordinates and which uses techniques of consensus like 'brainstorming', problem-solving, research and evaluation, and residential retreats for discussion and group learning. 'Building a participative environment', as the SEMP 1987 Design Specification puts it, indicates how this dialogical orientation to authority has 'participation' as a core value.

This democratic orientation, however, turns out to be an intra-class orientation, espoused by those with higher-education credentials for others like them. Management is democratised, but the adoption of management discourse as the leitmotiv for the modern, rational bureaucrat indicates that there is a central and basic distinction maintained between those who 'manage' and those who 'are managed'. Just where exactly, within public service ranks, this line should be drawn is somewhat ambiguous, as the Western Australian White Paper definitions indicate. There 'public sector managers' are defined as 'State public sector administrative staff *including but not confined to,* chief executive and senior officers' (my emphasis). Who else it includes is left unspecified. 'Public sector employees' are defined as 'All persons who work for State public sector organisations including not only public servants but also teachers, police officers, nurses, bus drivers, engine drivers, institutional officers, Ministerial appointees and the blue and white collar employees of various statutory organisations'. In this generic definition of public sector employees the line between the managers and the managed is blurred. The ambiguity about where precisely the line comes helps to maintain a democratic fiction. In practice, it appears that a line between the base-grade workers and those above them distinguishes the managed from the managers within public service ranks. It is clear, however, that the labelling of the intermediate strata as 'middle managers' draws them into the rational-technical discourse of management but does not necessarily confer on them the prerogatives of managers. In this sense the diffusion of the term 'manager' is a device which reconciles equality of status as members of the technical intelligentsia with the continuing hierarchy (however simplified) of authority within the management ranks. It indicates that, in principle, merit (including technical proficiency in networking and other 'low' political skills) rather than patronage or some other principle is the basis of promotion within the management hierarchy.

In general, adoption of the management culture indicates that members of the technical intelligentsia are quite clear that it is they who should manage, and that their technical knowledge and skills license them to exercise the prerogatives of management over the mass of workers, clients and consumers who come within the ambit of their authority. The technical intelligentsia has accepted that clients and consumers have a right to 'participate' in the policy and administrative decisions which affect their lives. They seem to accept consumer and client rights of participation much more readily than they do those of base-grade workers. Even with consumers and clients, it is not clear that this is a genuine acceptance and anything more than an enforced acknowledgement of the historical development of consumer demands for participation. Too often consumer and client rights are confined to token exercises of consultation and representation. They are expressed in ways which do not challenge or disturb the hierarchical principle of bureaucratic line command. In short, the technical intelligentsia believes in industrial democracy and consumer rights of participation for itself but it has no interest in any thoroughgoing democratisation of bureaucratic and professional authority. Such democratisation would involve the replacement of the hierarchical (vertical) principle of managerial/professional authority by the non-hierarchical (lateral) principle of reciprocal exchange between differently positioned and skilled participants and contributors.

Adoption of the culture of management allows the modernisation of the service to be reconciled with the continuing requirement of top-down, hierarchical control just as it ensures that the types of rationalisation undertaken will be primarily technical and will not engender substantive challenges to the nature of state activity and policy. It is not, therefore, a change which benefits all, but is one which gives a democratic gloss to the hierarchical relations of state domination.

Increased delegation; the subjection of professional judgment to management

The democratisation of the line of command, up to a certain point at least, means that the upper and middle ranks of the public service are given more autonomy in their jobs and that, throughout the public service, the spirit of 'delegation' becomes legitimate and practised. This is likely to use rather than to waste individual talent, and to encourage a spirit of innovation and enterprise. In a sense, this involves giving many more public servants than hitherto the status of 'professional', signifying that one has the authority and discretionary power to exercise considerable control about how to do what one does and to judge, within broad policy and procedural guidelines, precisely what should be done. This has to be counted a good thing from the point of view of public servants being made accountable for what they do and for the 'politics', or value-choices, inevitably embedded in what they do. It is impossible to ask for accountability from social actors unless they have first been delegated the authority to do whatever it is they have contracted to do.

However, the professionalisation of the upper and middle ranks of public servants is confined within the model of professional management. This is a technical or methodological professionalism. It vies with and even overrides the professionalism of substantive expertise. Thus professional engineers, doctors, social workers, lawyers and so on in the public sector may find that the discretionary authority they require to interpret their task and to respond to needs has been seriously circumscribed by the requirements placed on them by professional managers. The rise to power of professional managers in the public service is not only at the expense of the erstwhile authority of substantive professional positions in the public service. It leads also to a deskilling of the latter by reducing, as far as possible, the type of work involved to technical input and output measures. Accordingly, for example, the discretionary and 'craft'-like activity of case-work intervention and treatment is de-emphasised for social workers in a Department of Community Welfare. What is emphasised instead is the number of cases they process, assess, and refer on to other agencies.

People-and-process emphasis; enhanced techniques of social control

The new rational-management ethos of the public service is one which has developed at a point when scientific management is a relatively mature body of knowledge. The original scientific-management revolution, the one associated with Taylor, was led by engineers (see Meiskins, 1984). The mechanistic emphases of that school have been corrected by the human relations school; and, since then, the rational-systems orientation of financial and budgetary approaches to organisational performance has been checked and balanced by the recognition that 'people' are the key to an organisation and its performance (see Peters and Waterman, 1984). This latter-day emphasis on human agency and the needs of human agents as central to organisational behaviours and health is influenced by, and coincides with, the much more highly individualised expectations that those with higher-education credentials have of themselves and others. These expectations express themselves in such things as greater self-awareness; commitment to individual maturation understood as a process of growth and self-development; commitment to resolving and eschewing self-destructive behaviours, which indicate a negative self-concept which also projects onto others and devalues them; and, taking responsibility for determining and communicating what one wants and needs. The so-called 'growth movement therapies' and the contemporary women's movement have each contributed to developing this culture of self-awareness, personal growth and individual autonomy, and have been responsible for the diffusion of this culture across not simply what Gouldner (1979) describes as the higher-educated 'new' class but many politically motivated groups and individuals as well.

There can be no doubt that this culture of personal life represents another cultural revolution which intersects with the one at issue here. It is not just the up-to-date scientific management manuals which lead to a stress on 'process' and 'people' in the current public service management discourse. Woven in with the adoption of this is the promotion of general and feminist growth-movement ideas and values by individual advocates of these ideas and values within public service leadership circles. These ideas and values lead to emphases on effective communication with staff, respect for their individuality, cultivation of their autonomy, and contracted work agreements with them concerning goal achievement. The effect of all this is to humanise public service employment structures and work conditions in the public service.

However, it has become clear that the 'people' and 'process' emphases run a poor second within the general culture of public service management to emphasis on economy, efficiency and effectiveness. People-and-process advocates try to argue that efficiency and effectiveness are served best by their approach, but they cannot come up to the hard-nosed financial accountability controls which now dominate the management of Australian public services. Doing more with less is the name of this game, and it is not congruent with a people-and-process emphasis.

It is fair to say that the people-and-process emphasis has not entered the general culture of public service management as a set of practices, even if it has entered some of the rhetoric. This emphasis has entered the training program for the Commonwealth Senior Executive Service, and this is likely to be symptomatic of the kind of 'Personal and Interpersonal Competence' (see Appendix B) expected of this elite level in most public services. However, the personal and interpersonal competence skills aim to make members of the SES better managers, and are limited by this goal. In this context, a process-and-people emphasis does not question the 'workaholic' professional culture and expectations to which members of the SES must adapt if they are to be successful. Nor does it bring into question the elitism of the SES itself which encourages a 'status' orientation rather than a strictly functional orientation to the differences between senior and base-grade levels of the public service. Thus, for example, SEMP is aimed at the SES levels, and it would be heretical to suggest that such programs should be aimed at base-grade staff or at groups mixing top, middle and base-grade levels together.

Finally, it is clear that there is a gender dimension of the process-and-people emphasis (see Bryson, 1987:32–35). Many, though not all, committed advocates of this emphasis are women in the public service. Of these most would be self-conscious holders of feminist values. The current emphasis on financial accountability management is one which disarms all who advocate, and may benefit from, the process-and-people style. The former, which is thoroughly masculine in cultural style and orientation, may succeed even in removing most of the resources on which equal opportunity and industrial democracy units at present depend. This is one area where different sections of the technical intelligentsia may have different interests, and which may therefore provide grounds for conflict. However, as long as the people-and-process advocates remain contained within a *technically* oriented culture, they can be disarmed always by top management who will accommodate them only as far as it is convenient to do so. Without doubt, the people-and-process orientation is progressive, but it must remain a very fragile service priority and a largely personally elected management style unless it is connected up to a substantive grounding and development of the values behind it.

Inclusion of 'minorities' on merit; exclusion of the non-higher-educated

It is clear that the modernised management culture of the new intelligentsia puts a premium on 'merit'. Merit is a principle which emphasises competitive performance, either potential or actual. As Martin (1987:436) points out, there 'are three standard ways of assessing merit: examinations, credentials and work experience and performance'. Merit is a principle of selective distribution of rewards which maintains hierarchies of control and access to resources (see also Martin, 1987). However, because it places emphasis on functional criteria of being able to do a particular job, it is a principle which promises always to redistribute access to power and resources away from those who have achieved positions of advantage through political networking or dominant group status to those who can demonstrate that they are effective performers.

While debate over what should count as the criteria of performance constitutes what may be called the 'politics' of merit (see Martin, 1987; Burton, 1987), historically the merit principle has been a vehicle of extending opportunity and access in privileged occupational positions to those who have been excluded from them. Equal opportunity, indeed, is the ideology of the meritocracy. When the merit principle is expressed as equal opportunity, affirmative action, and access and equity programs, it has the benefit and value of making the public service more representative of the society it serves. It also introduces social and cultural diversity into public service ranks.

The merit principle can be another point of tension within the culture of professional management since functional criteria of effective cooperation and communication may frequently cut across the status criteria that maintain hierarchy. At the same time the merit principle establishes a new elite and its culture within the public service: those with higher-education credentials who can speak and manipulate the rationalised discourse of this new class (see Young, 1961). Gouldner (1979:28) characterises this discourse as the 'culture of critical discourse' which he defines as 'an historically evolved set of rules, a grammar of discourse, which (1) is concerned to *justify* its assertions, but (2) whose *mode* of justification does not proceed by invoking authorities, and (3) prefers to elicit the *voluntary* consent of those addressed solely on the basis of the arguments adduced'. This elite and its characteristic culture of domination depends thus on the former exploiting its cultural capital, and establishing a position of competitive advantage in relation to those who do not possess cultural capital.

Openness to expert-led value debate; subordination of value issues to technique

Because the technical intelligentsia values and is oriented by a rational approach to its tasks within the public service, it values and seeks out all relevant knowledge and knowledge-producers. In this respect it is remarkably open to new ideas. To a certain extent this encourages an overlap of identity and interests with those of humanistic intellectuals (Gouldner's term), especially when the latter concern themselves with issues of relevance to public bureaucracies, the state and the public sector at large. On some occasions, therefore, there can be, depending on the participants and the flexibility of the agenda, participation of the professional public managers in value-oriented dialogue and debate about issues in public administration and public policy.

Many public servants who are direct service deliverers or who are responsible for the policies informing direct service delivery *are* interested in value-oriented debates concerning what should be policy objectives and the processes of their implementation; that is, they have what we might term substantive commitments. They are not at all indifferent to theoretical and analytical debates concerning strategies of redistribution and social justice, and the so-called crisis of the welfare state. Many of these public servants are clearly committed to a conception of a public interest, which is not reducible to a sum of private preferences, but which refers to the life and needs of a community. Policy, in short, for these public servants represents collective responses to collective needs. They demonstrate also willingness to debate and evaluate policies, both through effective consultation with those members of the community involved and affected, and through analysis shared often with academics of the logical coherence and empirical basis of proposed or current policies.

These public servants conceive their work in terms of specific content-oriented commitments which cannot be reduced to technical performance-for-results criteria. For example, they may be committed to publicly provided childcare services on the basis of a belief that a citizenry ought to support and help to subsidise those who are parenting on behalf of their society. To an extent, the content-oriented public servants can deploy the performance-for-results orientation precisely in order to ensure that policies are rationally scrutinised and subjected to some kind of rigorous policy evaluation. However, they are inevitably on the defensive in relation to the dominant cultural force within public bureaucracies: the ethos of professional management. This is particularly true at the present time when the combined force of financial-accountability emphases and neoconservative public-choice theory not only threaten the resource base of community services but their philosophical underpinning as well.

It is important to recognise that 'new-class' public servants, who are oriented to the substance of public policies and public values, can develop a combined technical and substantive orientation to their work. While this integration is poorly developed in both the training and practices of public administration, it is something which the more innovative and adaptive public administration practitioners and academics can see as necessary (see Radin and Benton, 1985).

Such integrated orientations cannot dispel the tension between technical and substantive aspects of public service. For example, there will be tension always between the record-keeping and auditing requirements of public service and the pursuit of substantive public ends. However, when public servants develop a combined technical and substantive orientation to their work they can allow this tension to become a focus for awareness and critical scrutiny. This will almost certainly permit the exploration of different record-keeping and auditing methods to fit the requirements of different types of public service activity. Where there is an open acknowledgement of the inevitable tension between technical and substantive aspects of public service, there is more likely to be debate and criticism when either aspect subordinates the other too completely.

This tension between technical and substantive aspects of professional identity is one that is imported into the public service as a result of its new-classing. It is a cultural conflict between what Gouldner (1979:5) calls humanistic intellectuals (who have a primarily substantive orientation) and the technical intelligentsia. It is a tension which exists between different sections of public servants (for instance, social workers *vis-à-vis* finance officers) and it exists also *within* the consciousness of many middle-upper-level public servants.

It is true that public servants cannot be humanistic intellectuals, at least in the classical, autonomous university-based or self-employed sense, because they lack that degree of cultural autonomy, and are required to accept the authority of professional managers in the public service. This, however, is no longer a simple point of contrast between public servants and, for example, academics. Just as a secular, rationalised culture of critical reflection has seeped into the public service in the wakes of the ethos of scientific management and the new-classing of the public service, there is also increasing pressure on academics to become, in part at least, a technical intelligentsia servicing the research requirements of industry and the state. In short, a basis for integration between humanistic intellectuals and the technical intelligentsia is developing, which promises a much more advanced and sophisticated dialogue between technical and substantive aspects of all social activities, including those which belong to public policy and administration.

If at the moment the tension between technical and substantive aspects of a rationalised public service is poorly articulated, and is pushed to the wings by the dominance of a technocratic orientation, this will not always be the case. An interesting and dynamic politics of contest between humanistic-intellectual and technical-intelligentsia orientations may develop. Even the most technocratic of professional managers may be forced to become more literate in substantive public service requirements. How this politics develops depends on the willingness of public servants and academics, who are genuinely committed to the values of the public sector and to a community-based idea of the public interest, to take a lead. For academics this means they will have to address the new issues posed by the professionalisation of discipline-based knowledge. This process of professionalisation has proceeded to a point where each discipline is relatively self-sufficient, with its own technical concepts and methods, and does not respond readily to the 'cross-disciplinary' substantive social issues which are involved in the business of public administration.

In the public service, concern for substantive issues depends on the extent to which public servants accord the public interest and the public sector an identity which distinguishes them from private interests and the private sector. When, from certain points of view, especially that of professional management, this distinction loses salience and relevance and the two sectors/sets of interests can be regarded as the same, the substantive aspects of public service culture recede and the technical aspects come to occupy centre stage. Accordingly, it is very important how the government of the day, and the wider community, understands the differences and the relationships between these two spheres, for it is these which will determine the legitimacy of substantive as distinct from technical considerations within the public service.

Technical flexibility; teleological promiscuity

The technical flexibility, curiosity and openness of the professional public managers are extraordinary. This virtue encourages the hope that it might be placed at the service of our welfare as a community. The problem is that the technical orientation of public managers can be used for any set of value-commitments. In this respect the professional managers are relatively indifferent to which ends their technical services are given. They are teleologically promiscuous.

As for public managers, whose brief allows and encourages them to be simply technocrats and to have virtually no concern for substantive social and political issues, they are likely to be more comfortable with value-commitments and ends which are disguised in the form of objective necessity, especially of the allegedly economic kind, than they are with openly declared value-oriented issues and debate. Many of this type of public servant are also likely to accept the appearance of 'the' economic order as a natural order, that is, one which must take the forms it does because they reflect the nature of things. This means that they accept as natural givens the private orientation of our (capitalist) type of economic order. From there it is a small and easy step to take for granted that the tasks of the public sector and public service must be framed not only to accommodate but to foster privately oriented economic activity as the only type of genuine economic activity. If, on the other hand, economic activity is discerned as the social action it is, it can be approached in terms of questions about the kind of mix of public and private economic activity the state should encourage in order to maintain and foster both a democratic polity (supported by social or public capital) and private individual initiative (see Stretton, 1987: especially chs 1 and 2).

Technocratic public servants, who can be trapped within this naive construction of economic activity, are vulnerable to neoclassical economic theories of public choice. These theories operate on the premise of a natural individualism which makes all social conventions and institutions appear to derive from private individual choices coming together in various contractual or aggregate modes. In this approach there is no public interest, except as it is reducible to procedures and institutions which aggregate private preferences. When this approach permeates the technical cultures of public servants, it is clear that there appears no basis to distinguish public service and private sector management, and that both types of activity can be embraced by the single metaphor: management.

REASONS FOR THE DOMINANCE OF MANAGEMENT DISCOURSE IN AUSTRALIAN PUBLIC SERVICES IN THE 1980S

With the development of a complex and interventionist state in the twentieth century, the fates of the 'new class' and the state have become bound up together. This is because the increasing complexity of the state has demanded from its administrators and policy-makers a more extended knowledge base. At the same time the peculiar kind of arrogance which distinguishes the new class means that its members believe that their knowledge equips and entitles them to determine the public ends which the state as the agent of sovereign power seeks to realise on behalf of all those who belong within its jurisdiction. Thus the modern twentieth-century state requires the skills and knowledge of the new class just as the new class seeks to extend its power by staffing the upper reaches of the state and thereby borrowing its power (for some elaboration of this thesis, see Konrad and Szelenyi, 1979). This has been no less true of the development of a complex, interventionist state in Australia than elsewhere, and these trends have been especially evident since the early 1970s in Australia, although they have been in train since the adoption by the Commonwealth Government of a Keynesian model of public economic policy in the mid to late 1930s and of a modern system of social security in the Post-War Reconstruction period (see Watts, 1987; Coombs, 1981: Part I). The Whitlam Government in the early 1970s sponsored an expansion of the interventionist state which created a new range of opportunities for employment of young people with university degrees. They could be attracted not only because their own (environmentalist, anti-Vietnam war, feminist, social justice) enthusiasms matched the Government's but also because the range of public service jobs on offer involved expanded policy tasks which could draw on the backgrounds and interests of these university graduates. By the mid-1970s, this interventionist state was firmly in place, and it received continued support from the culture of expectations it had established in the new class.

The vehicle of bringing the public service and public sector into line with the new governmental ethos of neoconservative 'economic' management in the 1980s has been the Labor Party. Labor has been in power in the Commonwealth since 1983, South Australia since 1982, New South Wales 1976–March 1988, Victoria since 1982 and Western Australia since 1983. Labor, historically, has been the party and political movement symbolically associated with the state and the public sector. The revival of economic liberalism in the late 1970s and 1980s, with the ideology of small government it has brought in its wake, seems to have cast Labor, in the Australian context, in the role of renegotiating the relationship between the public and private sectors, and ensuring the freedom of the latter from what is regarded now as undue government regulation and 'interference'.

If Labor could present itself for this role it was because the party itself had radically changed in the social composition of its leadership and much of the rank and file over the course of the last two decades. Its leadership, much of the branch membership, and, from the mid-1970s onward, most of the ACTU leadership, the researchers employed now by individual unions and the leadership of the increasingly prominent white-collar unions are drawn from the new class (see Ward, 1986; Ward, 1987; Looseley, 1987; Schacht, 1987). All of this was presaged by the Whitlam Government (Whitlam himself and key members of his ministry) and indeed by the assumption of leadership of the ACTU by R.J. Hawke in 1969 (see d'Alpuget, 1984: especially 168–71).

The 'new-classing' of the public service and of the Labor Party means that there is a high degree of convergence in outlook, philosophies and cultural style between the two. Thus, when the administrative reform rhetoric of the Labor governments gave way in the mid-1980s to a distinctive Laborite form of neoconservative emphasis on public management, financial accountability and commercialisation of public services, the public services involved did not appear to flinch at the prospect of what promises to be a long campaign of cutbacks in public services, and corresponding reduction in the employment base of public servants.

Laborite neoconservatism takes the form of defending the public sector by making it appear as well managed as the private sector. This has been the reason for the spirit of scientific management permeating the public services in the 1980s. This has fitted and even flattered the professional self-conceptions of the members of the new class who populate the middle and upper reaches of the relevant public services. While the Laborite version of neoconservatism is strongly oriented to maintaining the health and vigour of the private sector (private capital), it does so from the point of view of professional management. This advocacy of the private sector and its freedoms curiously enough does not threaten professional public servants, again because of their cultural kinship with the spirit and orientation of scientific management. This probably would not have been the case if the same types of policy outcomes in general terms had emanated not from this new-class type of government (and ministerially selected policy advisers) but from the 'old' middle class of businessmen, farmers and self-employed professionals like doctors, accountants and lawyers, who espouse an older version of free-enterprise doctrine, unadorned with the trappings of scientific management.

Management has become the ruling paradigm in Australian public bureaucracies in the 1980s. This reflects the new-classing of the upper and middle ranks of these bureaucracies, especially under Labor governments.

There are several tensions which arise as a consequence of this cultural orientation of public bureaucracies to scientific management. The first is a tension within management discourse itself, where a people-and-process orientation sits uncomfortably with an instrumental orientation to people as human resources and a tendency to reduce the organisational entities involved to calculable and ultimately financial inputs and outputs. The second is between the open, merit-oriented and functional requirements of scientific management and the necessity to maintain state domination over the political process by placing public servants within pyramidally arranged ranks, which are accorded different degrees of status and authority. The third tension concerns the sophisticated requirement of the modern interventionist state (in its welfare state and other guises) that public servants possess substantively rational as well as technically rational skills. This leads to a breakdown in the structural segregation of the technical intelligentisa and the humanistic intellectuals, and introduces into the state itself the tension between the cultures of these two components of the new class. The orientation of public services to scientific management appears to favour the agenda of the technical rationalists over those of the substantive rationalists.

This issue can, following the work of Claus Offe, be stated differently. Offe (1984) accords the capitalist state two central tasks: legitimation and accumulation. If the requirements of accumulation can be assimilated to the style of scientific management, this is not true of the requirements of legitimation. These require a substantive orientation to community service, to 'serving the public', which cannot be contained within the constraints of scientific management.

Finally, the scientific managers within the state espouse the fiction that precepts of good management hold true in public and private sectors, and that therefore the wisdom and experience of one (usually the private sector) can be transferred to the other. This is true, of course, of rational techniques of management as such; and the tautological quality of this proposition will be evident. It is not true when techniques are married—as in real life they are—with the quite different purposes of the two sectors to become distinct operational administrative practices. The public sector and public service missions require that their managements become involved with issues and values to which private sector management can remain justifiably indifferent (for some discussion of this point, see Pollitt, 1986). Paradoxically, while the notion that good management is sector-indifferent is clearly unrealistic, it serves to maintain some insulation of the new class as scientific managers from the pressures of private capital. Good management and profit are two quite different principles which often coincide but often do not (see Meiskins, 1984; Konrad and Szelenyi, 1979).

It is this paradox which characterises the Labor Government's adoption of scientific management for the public service and the public sector in the 1980s. On the one hand, this orientation makes their political agendas extraordinarily sensitive to the interests of capital accumulation as these are represented by the spokespeople of private capital. On the other hand, it authorises a strong, rationalised set of state bureaucratic practices on behalf of accumulation which, in a curious way, maintains and modernises the 'mixed' economy.

3 Democratisation and the administrative state

> ... the principal problem of organizational life is not rationalism or behaviouralism; it is domination, whether bureaucratic, political or psychological.... The moral force opposed to domination is the principle of multilateral dialogue and discourse (Lane, 1986:131).

As many have remarked, the development of a modern interventionist state which reaches into virtually every aspect of our lives has created difficulties for principles and institutions of democracy that were created in a context where this administrative state was barely developed. It has become evident that a great deal of decision-making goes on within the administration of policies and programs that is undertaken by the staff at all levels of the administrative state. Yet these decision-makers are not afforded any legitimacy within the models of democracy that we have inherited.

There are three broad responses to this situation. The first, which has been championed by neoconservatives and the New Right, is to disestablish as much as possible the interventionist state, and to bring the state back to something like the role classical liberal theorists such as Locke conceived for it. This is the role of 'umpire', where the state, as the embodiment of the principles of public justice and law, ensures that groups and interests within civil society stay within the law, arbitrates disputes between them, and punishes wrongdoers. To this neoconservatives add a restricted welfare state role: the use of the state's taxing and subsidy powers to provide assistance directed to those most in need (see Hendrie and Porter, 1987:20–30).

This response overlooks the fundamental reality: that the modern administrative state reflects principles of complex social organisation that are here to stay. It is not possible for the scope of the state's activity to contract, for it reflects the entanglement of the state with all other branches of a complex social division of labour. Accordingly, neoconservatives propose initiatives which seem to promise contraction of state administrative and regulative activity, but these very proposals require an intensification of state bureaucratisation. For example, the policy of 'effective targeting' of welfare assistance requires for its implementation more complex eligibility criteria, more administrative resources (including staff) to administer these more complex criteria, and more administrative effort to police cheating and other forms of fraud with regard to various state-provided benefits.

The record of governments influenced by neoconservative political agendas seems to indicate there is no escape from the principle that modern organisational complexity demands that the steering, regulating and directive powers of the state enter into how the relationships between all parts of society are articulated. Neither the Thatcher nor Reagan governments have managed to bring about significant decreases in the scope of state activity or in the number of state employees, although there have been significant changes in the distribution of state activity and in which types of employees have been (dis-)favoured by this. For example, Fry (1988:4) points out that 'towards the end of the second Thatcher term in office, taxation and public expenditure were higher in real terms than in 1979', and goes on to say:

> When compared with the scale of change that has taken place in the private sector during the Thatcher years, and in parts of the public sector too, such as British steel where the number of employees fell by 56 per cent between 1979 and 1982/3 ... the career Civil Service might be said to have got off lightly. The number of non-industrial civil servants was cut by 14 per cent between 1979 and 1986. At 1 April 1986 the number of such civil servants, recorded as 487,895 ... was only just below the total employed in 1945 [i.e. in a fully mobilised and state-directed war economy]. ... The cuts in numbers since 1979 have been very largely achieved by natural wastage.

The second response to the difficulty of reconciling the administrative state with democratic government is to reassert central controls by the government of the day over the bureaucracy. This is done in a number of ways, all of which have been evidenced in Australia, especially in the Hawke Labor Commonwealth Government and in the Cain Labor Victorian State Government (for the latter see Cullen, 1987; Laffin, 1987). These include: 1. the enhancement of Cabinet control over government policy-making by developing the corporate solidarity and discipline of members of the Cabinet; 2. the enhancement of individual ministerial control over their departments by locating ministers in the role of a chief executive officer who requires of the senior manager of the department a performance contract, where the objectives of the department for a stipulated period of time are clearly named in relation to both ministerially interpreted policy and departmental resources; 3. the development of ministerial advisers to extend the minister's information and knowledge base so that he or she is not snowed or captured by his or her bureaucratic advisers; 4. the development of centralised and corporately oriented financial controls over departmental budgets, and claims that have budget implications; 5. the creation of a Senior Executive Service within the bureaucracy which permits more effective controls by the government of the day and individual ministers over this level of staff by detaching the career advancement of members of the SES from a particular departmental location and relocating it within the corporate identity of a bureaucratic elite (see pp. 8–10).

This response necessarily increases centralised decision-making and emphasises control more than it does service-delivery approaches. Control approaches are those which enhance and legitimise the power of the executive levels of the state over front-line state workers (those who work with consumer advocates, service providers or who themselves provide services to members of the public), direct providers of publicly funded services, and members of the public for whom these services are intended. Service-delivery approaches are those which enhance and legitimise the capacity of those front-line workers, direct service providers and members of the public to influence the range, extent and types of publicly funded services. When control approaches are uppermost, senior-level public servants are required to act as the instruments of executive control, and to filter, restrain, and keep off policy agendas the demands from front-line workers, service providers and members of the public for better and more extended services. When service-delivery approaches are accorded legitimacy, senior-level public servants are asked to assume a role of facilitating these demands so that they may inform efforts to improve public services. The most effective control mechanisms are financial, where there is both tight control of how resources are used, and cutting back of the resources available in the service-delivery areas of state activity.

Control approaches thus boost the power of the executive levels of government. This permits a 'democratic' control of the administrative state only if by democratic we mean the broad mandate to govern which is given to a democratically elected government. It is certainly not democratic on other criteria, such as accountability of the executive to the legislative branch of government, this branch representing more adequately than the executive branch the elective choices of the citizenry, or the participation of the citizenry in the policy-making activities of government and the delivery of services.

If the first response to issues of reconciling the administrative state with democratic values seeks to reduce the problem of reconciliation by reducing the state, and the second seeks to control the problem by controlling the bureaucracy, the third response accepts the problem and develops a new conception of what it means to live in a democratic and complex society by moves to democratise the administrative state. This it does in a number of ways: 1. democratising the administrative staff by changing recruitment and promotion practices so that it becomes more representative of the population it is servicing; 2. acknowledging the participation of administrative staff in policy-making by requiring their decisions to be open to citizen scrutiny (e.g. freedom of information legislation) and to appeal; 3. appointing citizen advocates (e.g. ombudsmen) to troubleshoot and attempt to resolve citizen grievances in relation to particular state administrative agencies; 4. acknowledging the impossibility of effective executive control over the implementation of policies especially at the point of service delivery, and building in accountability to citizen groups by consulting with them or including them as participants in the planning, design and delivery of services.

This third response is the only one of the three to be driven by democratic values. This is indicated in its realist's acceptance of the challenges of democratising a complex and interventionist administrative state. In this acceptance it is the only one of these responses which is able to accord to the administrative staff of the state a legitimate role in the business of democratic governance. This allows this role to be understood as an important and creative one. Instead of controlling or reducing the administrative staff, this is a response which inquires how public administrators should understand and express their duties as citizens within their work in public administration (see Cooper, 1984). It is a response which is able to articulate differentiated roles for the government of the day, public administrators and the citizenry within the business of democratic governance, and to locate these roles within a partnership of democratic governance.

Before I elaborate these points, it is necessary to emphasise that the administrative state is here to stay, and that the challenges it poses for democratisation are ones we must accept. Then it will be necessary to clarify a confusion which is commonly shared within the management strata of both public and private complex organisations. This confusion arises out of a belief that organisational complexity is such that democratic modes of management should be adopted because they work better than non-democratic ones.

THE DEVELOPMENT OF THE MODERN ADMINISTRATIVE STATE

Over the course of this century the business of government has become extraordinarily complex and its scope has grown. Three particular historical developments accelerated this development of the modern interventionist state. First, the Great Depression of the

1930s, and the response to it in the form of public economic policies, both fiscal and monetary, entailed more direct and systematic management and steering of the economy by government (for Australia, see Watts, 1987:ch. 1). Second, the Second World War consolidated and extended the regulatory reach, controls and surveillance of the state by bringing all citizens and activities within consideration of their relationship to the war effort and, in many instances, subjecting them to direct controls and planning efforts (for Australia, see Watts, 1987:ch. 2; and Coombs, 1981:ch. 1). The state-led 'war economy' developed and consolidated the infrastructure of a *national* state administration. Third, postwar reconstruction and the development of the modern welfare state, which brought into being the modern social security system, expanded the reach of the state further, and developed the highly bureaucratised and professionalised sector of state-sponsored human services (health, education, welfare).

It is arguable that with the recent increased efforts to control public expenditure, to decrease the level of public debt, and to stimulate a more competitive, export-oriented national economy, governments in the 1970s and 1980s have developed the state into, as Winkler (1981) puts it, increasingly directive as distinct from supportive relationships to the economy. In this context it is important to understand that strategies of deregulation and privatisation do not represent the diminution of the administrative state's power, but changes in how it operates (see Harrison, 1984:1, 2). Effectively, as Winkler argues, these are strategies which delegate public policies to private organisations in ways which presuppose ongoing coordination of activities within various forms of government-led corporatism.

Indeed, in a global economy of 'restructuring', there is likely to be a tendency for the administrative state at national and provincial levels to free up as much activity as possible to permit flexibility of response and to encourage a general ethos of 'management for change'. This tendency encourages a dismantling of rule-bound, administrative structures encrusted by all sorts of custom and practice.

In this context it is likely that the excesses of the older type of administrative state which declared themselves in red-tapeism, bureaucratic officiousness, and inflexibility are likely to be transmuted into different sorts of excess: selective economic rewards for those sufficiently flexible, mobile and multiskilled to catch themselves up within the trajectories of successful economic restructuring, and benign neglect of those who cannot do this. This occurs within a corporate ethos of discretionary executive state authority. In this, as Winkler again points out, there is an overall increase in the sphere of discretionary power of the state. There is a general shift from legislative and legalistic controls on administrative activity in the direction of increased state discretion at, it is important to add, the executive levels of the state, namely the executive of the government of the day together with the most powerful, senior layer of the state bureaucracy and powerful peak-body leaders. He argues:

> The general principle has been hammered home again and again in microcosm by organisation theorists.... Those who seek positive action (direction) in a changing or 'turbulent' environment will incline to 'organic' (flexible, discretionary) rather than 'mechanistic' (rule-bound) forms of government and administration. The point applies at the level of the State as well as the Corporation (1981, 92).

This flexibility is permitted by the state 'using economic power rather than law as its control mechanism' (Winkler, 1981:99). A good case study of this shift in the Australian state is in the area of higher education 1987–88. The state has disestablished the Commonwealth Tertiary Education Commission (see Marshall, 1988), brought publicly funded higher, technical and further education under the new Commonwealth Public Service mega-Department of Employment, Education and Training, and has established a new system of devolved controls for the management of individual educational institutions. The latter will now be governed by a mix of enabling administrative guidelines (see Winkler, 1981:94), negotiated performance contracts (the 'educational profiles' of the institutions) and selective reward for performance which the discretion of the state judges to fit best current 'national priorities'. This mix involves also what Winkler (1981:99) calls 'the delegation of enforcement':

> The general principle here is that when the state does reach agreement with private organisations, by financial pressure or any other means, it may then oblige them to implement the bargains themselves. It is effectively delegating the enforcement of public policy, and the state may ensure that this delegation is efficiently carried through by the prompt and flexible manipulation of its company-specific financial controls should the private partner stray from its agreed obligations. The relevance for administrative discretion is that the state may, if it chooses, thereby avoid the procedural requirements, minimum standards and public law remedies that would apply if the same policy were implemented by government agencies.

An excellent example of this 'delegation of enforcement' is the increasing tendency in human service areas for the state to adopt different forms of contracting out of these services. For example, an agency which has been concerned with the needs of intellectually disabled people and their families changes its principal role from that of direct service provision to that of contractor of services. This means that the agency contracts out to a mix of public and private service providers the services required for its target population. The results of this are twofold. First, the policy and program conceptions of the agency can become increasingly divorced from the practical, on-the-ground requirements of service delivery, and this encourages policies and programs increasingly to assume the features of prescriptive ideals which sound persuasive, but which tend to be conceived in ways that are unalloyed by the pragmatic requirements of trade-offs between competing values, and of adaptation to complex environments. Second, the service providers to whom the agency contracts out its mission are multiple in character, and, to an extent, placed in competition with each other. The effect is to fragment the service. This makes it difficult for consistent practice standards for the service to be maintained, and it enhances the capacity of the service providers to fulfill their contract with considerable discretion. In this situation, the providers tend to be divisive rather than cooperative in relation to one another. This weakens their professional culture, at least the professional culture at the point of delivery, and makes it difficult for them to articulate and research shared problems and issues. The fragmentation of the practice-based professional culture is likely to enhance the power of government agencies, professional associations and the relevant training institutions: they all become relatively unconstrained by the demands of practice where issues of different types of professionals and workers coordinating their services in relation to real clients are the pressing ones.

These newly elaborated strategies of state control may keep in check the types of bureaucratisation that were associated with the development of the older type of bureaucratic welfare state apparatus. Increased delegation of direct service delivery to 'community care', i.e. to the formal and informal voluntary sectors, and moves in the direction of more localised structures of service delivery, may even de-bureaucratise in certain ways the formal organisations of the public sector. However, it is important to emphasise that this will not diminish the scope or extent of state control, although it is likely to make those aspects of it which concern the privatisation of care unaccountable.

Modes of state administrative organisation may change, but the likelihood is that these changes will be in the direction of increasing complexity. A good deal of current devolution/delegation effort will lead to new types of differentiation of state organisational activity. In part the degree of this differentiation will be possible because of the new opportunities for centralised brainpower afforded by the new information technologies.

This does no less than parallel what has been happening with private organisations. The principle of formal organisation is further developed and differentiated. This is because, as Marshall Meyer (1987:215–16) argues, we use organisations to 'order and make sense of complicated environments'. Marshall (1987:216) proposes that 'under uncertainty, continuous organizing is understood as reasonable and rational conduct in modern societies'. There is nothing arbitrary about this: continuous organising permits the development of intelligent selective concentration of effort in strategic relationship to a changing environment, and the concomitant reframing of collective effort in complex contexts of interaction.

Contrary to Marshall, however, I would propose that the principle of organisation can lead in relatively de-bureaucratised as well as in bureaucratised directions. This point is neatly encapsulated in the stress on 'loose' as well as 'tight' organisational properties in the recently adopted bible for both private and public sector managers: Peters and Waterman's *In Search of Excellence* (1984).

The systems theory that modern cybernetics has influenced points to similar conclusions. In this theory organisational complexity concerns principles of differentiation which distinguish a system of effort (an organisation) from its environment. As Luhmann (1982:191–92), one of the most important sociological systems theorists, argues:

> Recent developments in systems theory ... focus on the environment of a system, attempting to understand systems as dependent upon and communicating with their environment. These developments, while differing among themselves, can be summarized as a whole in the fundamental idea that systems are reductions of the complexity of the world. They must therefore constantly sustain problematic relationships to an environment that is not itself similarly reduced. Systems acquire an identity through their characteristic means of reducing complexity.

DEMOCRATISATION AND ORGANISATIONAL COMPLEXITY

Those who advocate democratisation have to understand what this might mean in the complex organisational environment that our world has become. This can be a confusing task because many contemporary organisational theorists seem to propose that democratisation is an inbuilt tendency within a successful organisational activity.

It is clear that, as new forms of flexible interpenetration of public and private organisations develop, the classical bourgeois concept of 'the public domain' by itself is not adequate to the task of maintaining an open, dialogical and information-sharing interactional environment. The idea of the public domain presupposed the possibility of grouping within the one central social space the various key decision-making activities that affected the whole society. When these activities were relatively simple and confined to the few key institutions of a parliament, a newspaper which reported parliamentary debates and foreign policy, and several noteworthy publications which offered commentaries by leaders of public opinion on social and political events, it made sense to think of a bounded and centralised public domain, and to define struggles of democratisation in terms of extending the privileges of who had rights to participate in that public domain (through property ownership and the correlative rights of the suffrage, standing for parliament, serving on juries, and so on).

If executive modes of discretionary decision-making have come to the fore in the complex and interpenetrating organisational environments that we now inhabit, it would seem to augur badly for the democratic values of open and public debate, participation in such debate, and widely distributed information-sharing. However, the development of such executive modes of discretionary decision-making is only part of the picture.

Complex organisations and the systemic webs of inter-communication and relationships that they involve demand an extensive staffing base. Within the modern state-societies that have shared in the historical culture of liberal democracy it is now the case that the vast majority of employed persons are located within complex public or private organisations. Executive modes of decision-making presuppose the administrative collaboration and cooperation of these employees. This produces some important constraints on the degree of secrecy that can attend executive modes of decision-making.

The constraints go further than this. Effective organisational capacity demands highly intelligent, flexible, and multiskilled decision-making capacities of the administrative staff of complex organisations. Decision-making at executive levels can effectively only establish frameworks for the more specific kinds of decision-making that the administrative staff have to engage in in order to adapt executive decisions to complex environments. In other words, the effective implementation of executive decisions is whatever interprets broad executive directions or frameworks into programs or products which make for a successful adaptation of the organisation to the environment. This means that the staff who do the implementing have to keep the boundaries of the organisation highly permeable to information from that environment, specifically from people or organisations within that environment who are actual or potential users of the organisation's skills, programs, or products.

This sensitivity to the environment is produced in several ways, two of which are obvious, namely the consumer's option to turn to competing organisations where they exist, and the citizen's right to complain about poor service delivery within the open channels of the liberal democratic public domain (either to their local parliamentary representative, or within letters to the editor). The less obvious route is manifest in a good deal of the recent debate about public sector size and priorities, where much of the substance of the debate concerns how this system ties in with private organisations within their shared environment. It is impossible for complex organisations, whether they are single government agencies, firms or provincial governments, to stay insulated from each other. They exchange too many services or commodities, and thus interpenetrate with too many other organisations for one of them to be allowed to atrophy or die without, at least, a careful strategically planned intervention to redefine and resituate those interdependencies so that the organisation can die.

Accordingly, there are interorganisational networks of intelligence which monitor single organisational performance and adaptiveness and thereby provide feedback to organisations. Some of these networks are accorded authoritative 'central agency' types of monitoring and sanctioning roles. These permit a brake, not always heeded, on the ways in which specific organisations can become narcissistically focused on their internal processes rather than effectively atune with and responsive to their changing environments. These roles also allow, if required, direct intervention into the organisation. The United Nations, the World Bank, the network of central stock exchanges, as well as governments in relation to their own 'nationals', are all instances of such networks.

Executive levels of organisations depend on the staff of those organisations, and effective decision-making of both the executive and the staff of the organisation depend on highly evolved feedback loops of information relating to people and systems in the organisation's environment. These dependencies provide significant checks to authoritarian, secretive and tyrannical modes of executive decision-making.

It is appreciation of these dependencies that leads many management theorists to propose that democratic organisational cultures of decision-making are likely to be more functional in most contexts than what they view as old-fashioned top-down directive organisational cultures. Of course, systems theory of this kind indicates only why some norms may be more functional than others, not why they are in principle preferable to others. It is obvious that these norms would become less functional if modern democratic values concerning respect for persons were forced into some kind of retreat. But then so too would complex organisations be forced into retreat, for their very complexity depends on according many thousands of people within and outside their boundaries respect for their opinions, and room for their autonomous judgment, and on providing them with as much information as they can absorb.

Several implications follow from modern organisational and inter-organisational complexity. First, organisational effectiveness does not appear incongruent but congruent with the principles of democratisation that emphasise information-sharing, participation and dialogue. This is in marked distinction with classical theories of democracy which were generally understood to be at functional odds with the organisational requirements of effective decision-making. Democracy, by introducing popular views and values, was understood as complicating and slowing down informed and thereby efficient decision-making: hence the various attempts to reconcile democratic norms and elite rule (see Pateman, 1970:ch. 1). Of course, it is noteworthy that complex organisations demand and produce people who are educated to cope with high information loads, who have reasonably sophisticated principles of selection in respect of such information, and who are literate in the various information languages.

Second, modern organisational complexity changes how 'power' is understood. In a simpler world there were fewer decisions and much could be left to take care of itself, within the custom and practice of local contexts faithfully adhered to by people who mostly stayed within those contexts. In this context, 'decisions' not only appeared within a sacred aura of standing above or beyond the traditional, natural way of doing things, but inevitably they were the privilege of those who were identified as possessed of special qualities which permitted them to rise above the daily forms of custom and practice. These privileged decision-makers told the rest what to do. Hence power was understood as the capacity of A to tell or to influence B to do what A wanted. Necessarily efficacious management in this context was understood as precluding democratic participation. As Luhmann (1982:150–51) argues, systems theory demands a different conception of power from that expressed in the simpler command model of power:

> The classical theory is based ... on a supposedly causal form of communication. That is, it tries to conceive of power as a cause that brings about specific effects, or generally as the ability to make others act in a way they would not have chosen of their own volition.... This leads to a transitive, hierarchical conception of power, excluding the possibility of circular and reciprocal power relations. Furthermore, it understands power as a kind of possession that can be gained or lost and that remains constant within the system: every loss of power means a corresponding gain of power for an opponent and vice versa.

Complex systems, on the other hand, demand the development of 'circular and reciprocal power relations' within bounded organisational systems or subsystems which set this area of activity off from other activities, and thus make it possible for the participants to share the same purposive system. Luhmann (1982:151–52) proposes that this allows these decision-makers to enter into clearly distinguishable exchanges with what becomes the environment for their shared purposive system of activities. They understand their dependence on such exchanges, and, accordingly, they interact with both their own staff and with agents outside the organisation in ways that maximise the information value of such exchanges.

Power then in complex systems requires two-way flows of communication and information, and a sharing of influence. The consequences of this are: less distance of power-holders from those who they manage; procedural norms rather than substantive decisions become the reference points for organisational predictability and stability; and, rather than being highly precise statements of organisational objectives, decisions or laws take on enabling features which allow operating goals to be reinterpreted in relation to changing contexts.

Third, modern organisational complexity decentralises and disperses information and its analysis, but interorganisational complexity demands the development of central arenas of information-pooling, information-sharing, dialogue and debate. These central arenas which are developed in increasingly global ways are quite different from the sharply demarcated and centralised space of the classical bourgeois public domain. They are developed by a multiplicity of differentiated but often connected global networks of communication and debate which precludes any idea of a single public constituted by rational consensus on particular norms and values.

Fourth, there is nothing in the functional requirements of intra- and inter-organisational complexity which demands attention to or respect for those who are defined as marginal to the field of this complexity. It may not make good systems-theory sense for an organisation or government to define key players in its environment according to class, gender, ethnic and racial discriminatory values, but here we hit the limits of systems theory and the kinds of technical functionalist logic it entails. What systems theory tells us is that organisations and governments have to selectively constitute what are for them the salient features of their environments, otherwise they collapse under the overwhelming complexity of these environments. This selective constitution is inevitably in accord with dominant cultural definitions of the situation. Thus, key players and environments tend to be constituted in ways that maintain and reproduce relationships of class, gender, ethnic and racial domination. These relationships are not uncontested, but the legitimacy and efficacy of the contest depends on an exogenous cultural variable from the point of view of systems theory: a value orientation and commitment to democracy and justice.

Accordingly, organisational complexity may explain some of the limiting and permissive conditions for developing contemporary democratic modes of governance, but it cannot by itself produce the democratisation of modern organisations, not least of them being the modern administrative state. This is an effort of value commitment which takes us beyond the functional, instrumental discourse of management.

THE DEMOCRATISATION OF THE MODERN ADMINISTRATIVE STATE

The democratisation of the internal processes of state administration depends on a complex of value-commitments on the part of the citizenry and elected governments which includes open government, due process, natural justice, client-oriented public services, the participation of relevant publics in the development and delivery of services, equitable access to public services and to public employment, and honest and efficient management of public resources. It is these value-commitments, and the struggles of citizens to maintain and develop them, that are responsible for the executive levels of government introducing policies which are intended to democratise public administration. It is these same values that lead to the contesting of executive-led modes of corporatist decision-making which make private deals with peak bodies, and close out the citizenry from knowing about or participating in these deals. In the end, then, it is the vitality of these value-commitments and a widely based culture of sharing in them that is the important factor.

In the past, democratic theorists have been the custodians of democratic value-commitments as they relate to the business of modern government. However, while contemporary literature on public administration accepts and works on the challenges of democratising the modern administrative state, it has been largely ignored by democratic theorists. As Gruber (1987:29) observes:

> ... democratic theorists ... rarely deal with the problem of bureaucracy at all. It is generally ignored, assumed away by defining the role of administration as neutrally implementing legislative policy, or taken note of but dismissed. Direct application of theoretical orientations is often impossible, since the theories have been formulated without reference to the problems posed by bureaucracy. Dahl, for example, both maintains that one of the eight conditions for polyarchal democracy is that the 'orders of elected officials are executed' and realizes that this condition 'is the source of serious difficulties,' but then drops consideration of the

issue entirely, saying that 'the extent to which this condition is achieved is perhaps the most puzzling of all to measure objectively.'

The relevant (English-language) literature in public administration is largely led by United States contributions. These include Emmette Redford's *Democracy in the Administrative State* (1969), Frederick Mosher's *Democracy and the Public Service* (second edition, 1982), H. Kranz's *The Participatory Bureaucracy: Women and Minorities in a More Representative Public Service* (1976), J.L. Fleishman et al. *Public Duties: the Moral Obligations of Government Officials* (1981), and Judith Gruber's *Controlling Bureaucracies: Dilemmas in Democratic Governance* (1987). There are also significant Australian contributions, notably Peter Wilenski's *Public Power and Public Administration* (1987), and Geoffrey Hawker's *Who's Master, Who's Servant: Reforming Bureaucracy* (1981).

It is no accident that this literature has been produced in the last twenty years and that it has been part of the development of the 'new public administration', a movement in public administration circles which denied that 'policy' and 'administration' could be kept separate (for an account of this movement, see Kelly and Wettenhall, 1975). Peter Wilenski (1988:2–3) gives the context of these developments:

> It is by now commonplace that the modern public service performs tasks very different to those for which its original organisation and structure were designed. The public service was established when the role of government was extremely limited, the service was small and political control relatively easy. As time went on the demands of a democratic electorate and the needs of national development greatly expanded the role of the public sector. Where the tasks of public servants were once largely mechanical such as the expenditure of relatively small sums of money in accordance with strict and detailed regulations, the tasks now became complex and demanding, ranging from the administration of large social security systems to the making of major capital investment decisions. This led to the crisis in values in the public service which became a subject of so much debate in the 1970's and was marked by the rise of the movement then termed 'the new public administration'.

'The new public administration' was a movement driven by the influences within its wider environment of the 'new social movements' such as the women's movement, the civil rights movement, the gay rights movement, the various consumer movements which sought to challenge professional dominance in the definition of consumer needs, and environmentalist movements. All these movements have represented a renaissance of citizenship claims and democratic values. They have made state administrative practices problematic in the following ways. First, they have extended the claims for political, economic and social citizenship on behalf of 'minority groups', namely groups excluded from mainstream structures of political, economic and social citizenship. In particular, since the administrative state has become a significant employment base, its recruitment and employment practices were called into question by these claims. Second, by focusing on how structures of exclusion of minority groups operate, these citizenship claims brought to light the structures of dominance implicit in the organisational cultures of mainstream institutions ranging from the nuclear family to the local housing authority to the doctor's office. This kind of political challenge meant that issues of government concern a good deal more than the formal institutions of representative democracy, and that if domination was to be contested then the sphere of democratic governance would have to be extended to cover local service delivery, relationships within families, client–professional relations and the ways in which public servants implemented government policies.

These challenges laid bare the microstructures of power and decision-making and made the participation of public servants in policy-making much more obvious. If this was the general social context of the new public administration, many of the participants of the new social movements came into public administration in the 1970s and were able to develop their citizenship claims from within the state (see Radin and Cooper, 1988). There they became the architects of the new types of policies which fostered the democratisation of state administration such as equal opportunity in public employment.

The broad thrust of the new public administration has been to develop a new model of democratic government under the conditions of the interventionist administrative state in a complex social environment. This model is a new variant of the old conception of the separation of powers as a necessary condition of effective checks on tendencies to concentration of power.

The elected government of the day, the bureaucracy and the citizenry are constituted as three partners occupying distinctive roles within the business of government. The elected government through its executive, and in relation to public debate within the legislature and the media, establishes the broad frameworks of policy and policy priorities within which the other two partners are to operate. The bureaucracy puts these frameworks and priorities to work by turning them into programs, whose implementation in turn refines the idea behind the program and tests its relevance to its users and clients. Thus, all levels of the bureaucracy from the senior executive of an agency which establishes its objectives and priorities, through the middle-level managers who are concerned with issues of developing and coordinating the implementation of these objectives and priorities, to the administrative staff at the counter who are undertaking the delicate task of fitting agency programs to client needs, are all involved in the creative responsibilities of interpreting and implementing government programs. Finally, the citizenry is a crucial partner in this picture. The citizenry in aggregate elects the government of the day, and the parliament, and it accepts this principle of representation as justification of its obligation to pay taxes. At this level of relationship to the executive and legislature of government, the citizenry participates in the various channels of public debate which influence how the government of the day determines those broad policy frameworks and priorities. The citizenry also has a significant relationship to these policies once they have assumed the specific features of programs implemented in relation to specific citizens either as groups or as individuals. At this disaggregated level, which is often that of local communities, citizens become crucial to the effective implementation of programs. Not only is their cooperation required—a passive sense of citizen participation—but as citizens demand more of government services, these services become dependent on the active participation of citizens in order to have their demands reflected in the service.

This new model is still under-theorised. Hawker (1981), who comes closest to it, shares the predominant tendency in the literature of conceiving the business of democratising state administration as requiring the control by the politicians, parliament, ministers on the one hand, and by the community on the other hand, of the bureaucracy and public service. Thus, in two figures, he amends the old Westminster model, which has the electors controlling the parliament and politicians who in turn control the bureaucracy and public service, in order to introduce another direction of control, from the community to the public service (1981:26):

Figure 1

Community/Electors → Parliament/Politicians/Ministers → Bureaucracy/Public Service → Community/Electors

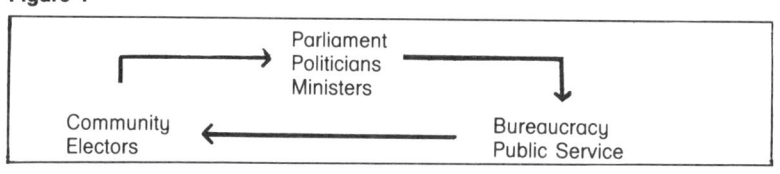

Figure 2

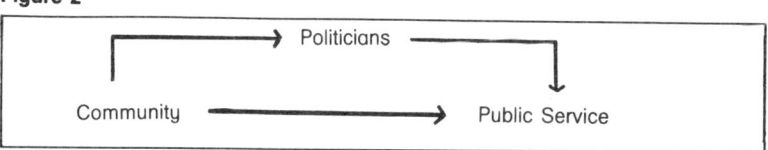

Community → Politicians → Public Service; Community → Public Service

Hawker's arrows run one way. The model of democratic governance outlined above would have them run both ways. In particular, the public service and bureaucracy is accorded positive and creative agency in making broad government policies into operational programs and in responding effectively and sensitively to citizen demands and participation.

This model expresses the conception of power that is appropriate for complex systems, namely one of two-way influence and reciprocal feedback flows of information. It converts this model of power into a normative model of 'multilateral dialogue and discourse'.

In order to work, this model demands that a positive professional identity for public servants be elaborated which encourages and values their creative contributions to the strategic development of operational policy objectives, to the design and implementation of programs, and to effective delivery of services. For this professional identity to be assumed, public servants need to be educated in its requirements. These include education in the professional ethics congruent with this identity. There are a number of attempts to specify these professional ethics, and most would agree with Warwick's (1981:115–24) specification of 'five ethical principles':

1 *public orientation*: an orientation to the public interest should take precedence over the pursuit of personal or professional interests and over that of agency interests;

2 *reflective choice*: this 'implies, as a minimum, that public officials be clear about the values to be promoted or protected, rather than embrace them without examination; be reasonably sure that the information used is adequate and reliable; and be consciously persuaded that assertions linking facts to values are soundly based' (Warwick, 1981:118).

3 *veracity*: there are three implications, the first being 'the obligation to avoid lying', the second being the 'obligation to be truthful in presenting information to superiors and to the public', and the third being 'the obligation to respect the ability of others to gather and present true information relevant to public policy' (Warwick, 1981:119–21).

4 *procedural respect*: 'established procedures should be observed unless there are compelling reasons for deviations' (Warwick, 1981:121–22), in which case the official(s) would have the obligation to report these reasons and, if necessary, to seek to change procedures.

5 *restraint on means*: 'This standard requires the official to hold back from using means that violate the law or the civil liberties of

individuals, entail unfairness in the application of laws or administrative regulations, produce unjustifiable physical, mental, or social harm, or undermine citizen trust in government' (Warwick, 1981:123).

In suggesting that the public administrator has a professional obligation to be oriented to the public interest, there is no implication that this is a simple or unproblematic concept. It would be valuable if the education of public administrators introduced them to the changing history of the concept of the public interest, to the conceptual debates on this idea, and impressed on them the value of conflict and debate about what constitutes the public interest. In broad terms the public interest concerns the interests of the citizenry and the maintenance of the democratic political community that the citizenry comprises (see Cooper, 1984:143), but this leaves plenty of scope for difference on the interpretations of this.

As Hawker also suggests, this three-way partnership model of democratic governance introduces into the picture of public administration a conflict model of bureaucratic decision-making. It is obvious that public servants may be caught in conflicting pulls with regard to the government of the day and the citizenry. If they are to be accepted as creative agents and professional public administrators, their relationship to conflicting values, including those of professional public administrators, needs to be acknowledged. This means legitimising and welcoming intra-bureaucratic debate over value issues, as well as encouraging public servants to participate openly in value debates between the government of the day and the citizenry.

It is noteworthy that this partnership model of democratic governance enjoys no support from neoconservative and New Right quarters. These political movements accept citizenship only insofar as it concerns the negative freedoms (the rights of citizens to enjoy life, liberty and property free from undue state interference), and tend to attempt to discredit positive claims on the state in the interests of citizenship by making them appear the attempt of particular interest groups to capture the state. Nor do these political movements endow public servants with a professional role and identity that is accorded social value and respect. Instead they tend to project onto public servants the motives of the marketplace—namely motives of self-interested material acquisition—and to make their public service appear self-interested careerism. Inevitably these orientations to both citizens and public servants encourage a strong control model of the administrative state, wherein the government of the day strictly rations citizen claims on the state, thereby keeps the growth of the state in check, and maintains the fiction of public servants as technical instruments for implementing government decisions.

It is parties of a social democratic hue that are most likely to move to democratise the administrative state in accord with the directions suggested by this partnership model of democratic governance. It is these parties that are philosophically disposed to upholding public values and to maintaining a public sector which is the institutional site of these values. Because of this it is these parties which are more susceptible to the claims on citizenship of the new social movements.

These parties may be seen to have had an interest in accepting the challenges to the public sector from the neoconservatives and New Right, challenges often posed in terms of whether the public sector could claim to be as effectively and efficiently managed as successful private firms. Where they have come to power, social democratic parties have worked to bring about management improvement in public sectors, to bring them to a point where it was evident that public administrators were doing more with less (i.e. had improved their productivity), and were using scarce public resources effectively and efficiently. In so doing, these parties have contributed considerably to maintaining the legitimacy of the public sector in a context of renewed economic liberalism. This has been even more the case where these parties in government have been able to link improved public sector performance to visible successes in attracting new capital investment and economic restructuring within their jurisdictions.

Of considerable interest for the development of a partnership model of democratic governance is the appearance after a major wave of such sponsored improvement in public sector management of renewed attention to the principles of service delivery. This is evident in the Labor-governed jurisdiction of South Australia, as these excerpts from a recent speech of Bruce Guerin (1988, 5), the director of the Department of Premier and Cabinet and the chairman of the Government Management Board, indicate:

> In the State public sector we are talking up the subject of customer service but it is clear that it is going to take us a long time to get its importance really well understood and to have good service delivered consistently.
> The culture of our public service is still product oriented. However, many of our important products are intangible and include, for example, advice, care and counselling. The people who generate these products often call them 'services'—almost the same word as 'service'.
> It is only recently that we have discovered that although we have been talking about service for some time, many people assumed that we were talking about services (or products). Having made that discovery we are hopeful of seeing some real progress made in the improvement of service in the next few years.

In Australian public administration, usually under the leadership of various Labor governments over the course of the 1970s and

1980s, there seem to have been three steps in the direction of democratising the administrative state and developing this partnership model of democratic governance. The first step comprised a wave of 'administrative reform', which introduced into various public services principles of equal opportunity, and which developed such checks on unaccountable bureaucratic discretion as the institution of ombudsman and administrative appeals tribunals (see Wilenski, 1987:ch. 9). This wave began to peter out in the mid-1980s, or rather to be swallowed up within the second step, a wave of management-improvement initiatives. The mediation of administrative reform within these initiatives was expressed in the adoption of the term 'Access and Equity Plans' for Commonwealth Government departments 1987–88, where these plans co-joined corporate planning with access and equity criteria. The third step, which seems to be emerging in South Australia 1988–89 and perhaps elsewhere, concerns a renewed sense of overall public sector mission in a new emphasis on providing services in ways that are responsive to the needs and values of clients.

This is not the only national state administrative context where this is occurring. There is some indication that the Local Government Training Board in the United Kingdom is adopting this emphasis on service delivery, in a 'public service orientation' which speaks of service *for* as distinct from service *to* the public (see Stewart and Clarke, 1987:161–77). Consider the opening paragraphs of Stewart and Clarke's (1987) explication of what they mean by 'public service orientation':

> Local authorities search for a sense of purpose that can drive forward management and motivate their staff. The answer may lie in words so familiar that their meaning has been lost: public service.
> The activities of a local authority are not carried out for their own sake, but to provide service for the public. Under the pressures of resource constraint, the essential rationale of public service can be overlooked.
> The public service orientation recognises that:
> —a local authority's activities exist to provide services for the public
> —a local authority will be judged by the quality of service provided within the resources available
> —the service provided is only of real value if it is of value to those for whom it is provided
> —those for whom services are provided are customers demanding high quality service
> —quality of service demands closeness to the customer.

What is fascinating about this 'public service orientation' is the way in which the private sector management values of enhanced productivity, outcome orientations, and 'closeness to the customer' are harnessed to renew the sense of purpose of public sector administration (see Corkindale, 1988). This is indicated also in a Swedish public administrator's report on the 'renewal of the public sector in Sweden' (Gustafsson, 1987:179–91). Gustafsson's description of the 'problems' that the newly elected Social Democratic Government in 1982 sought to solve by setting up a new government department of which he is Secretary of Planning, the Ministry of Public Administration, represents an acknowledgment of the necessity of democratising the administrative state:

—Economic resources were scantier than before. New problems could no longer be solved by committing additional resources. Reappraisals and streamlining measures were called for.
—The gap between public agencies and the individual had widened, due to public organization having become excessively complicated and unduly preoccupied with technical considerations. Public activities had been divided into various sectors which did not in themselves 'mirror' the way in which people formulated their demands on the community.
—Public activities had excessively supplanted the active involvement of the citizen in solving individual or collective problems.
—The public took an increasingly serious view of shortcomings in the service-mindedness of the authorities and in their capacity for dealing with the general public. These shortcomings included the way in which public authorities responded to private persons, and the difficulties involved in adapting the repertoire of public services to the needs and preferences of the individual citizen.

Gustafsson declares that: 'In contrast to the changes undergone by the public sector in many other countries, the Swedish Government in principle rejects privatization as a method of solving the problems of the sector' because it was viewed as leading to 'distributive injustices, especially in the fields of care, health and education'. Instead, the Swedish government has embarked on a public sector renewal program which is guided by four principles: greater freedom of choice, greater democracy, more service and less red tape, and improved efficiency. Of particular interest to the partnership model of democratic governance is the association of increased client influence with increased delegation of government authority to the direct service deliverers. This is expressed in the concept of 'conditional delegation' (Gustafsson, 1987:180), which works on the principle that 'developed client influence' presupposes that staff, who have direct contact with clients, have sufficient power and responsibility to be responsive to that influence. Delegation of decision-making powers is made to employees at the local government point of delivering services on three conditions: 1. they must consult the clients before making a decision, and where there is disagreement, the matter is referred to a higher authority; 2. these decisions must fall within the law and the municipality's objectives and guidelines; 3. these decisions must not 'involve irresponsible use of the economic resources allocated'.

It is worth noting this principle of conditional delegation is quite different from the practice of contracting out of services, discussed earlier. The former principle maintains a public field of accountability and dialogue, while the latter disperses accountability and effectively takes services out of a coherent public field of debate and dialogue between governments, policy-makers, service deliverers and clients about what services should be provided and how. Necessarily, if the principle of conditional delegation were to be meaningful, it would not only require commitment to the partnership model of democratic governance. It would require also the willingness of citizens and private firms to pay taxes at levels which effectively resourced a democratic and just public system of service provision. This willingness has been a good deal more forthcoming with Swedish Social Democracy than with Labor forms of corporatism in Australia of the 1980s. Indeed Labor corporatism has done much to foster various forms of deregulation and the supplanting of public cultures and systems of services by privatised services.

FINAL REMARKS

The development of strategies to democratise the administrative state will depend on vigorous advocacy of democratic values, and on the social movements in whose interest it is to uphold these values. The model of a partnership in democratic governance of the administrative state which involves, along with the elected government of the day, the positive participation in the business of this governance of both the citizenry and public servants is a model we need to develop.

One of the problems about advocating this model is that it is all too likely that it will require a thorough overhaul in the context of emerging challenges for established governmental jurisdictions that are posed by their situation within a global society. It is becoming clear that issues of redistribution and citizenship cannot be considered independently of global claims for redistribution and citizenship. It will be increasingly difficult to insulate domestically oriented discourses of service delivery and democracy from challenges concerning the ways in which democratic jurisdictional boundaries are maintained to conserve existing global distributions of privilege. For example, issues of how far 'aliens', and even those who are legal residents but are non-citizens, within a particular national jurisdiction are entitled to receive the services provided by the state are likely to develop. There is indication of this already in the recent Australian (FitzGerald, 1988) report on immigration, where it is argued that 'Access to the Australian public purse for non-citizens must be reviewed', and 'user pays must be applied to immigration services'.

Democratic models of governance are currently under sustained attack. This is because democracy depends on commitments to public values, a public domain, and publicly funded services which foster equal citizenship of those who fall within the democratic jurisdiction concerned. The erosion of these commitments by the revival of the ideology of the free market, and by the increased global capacities of capitalist firms to shift from one jurisdiction to another, threatens the very foundations of a democratic polity.

It is difficult to be optimistic about the fate of democratic values in the short term. They have been weakened by all the ways in which an over-bureaucratised and not particularly democratic welfare state have seemed to deserve the neoconservative critiques of the interventionist state. Democratic values will not be served by neoconservative advocacy of user pays, deregulation and small-government principles. To keep democratic values alive it is critical to keep on making democratic models of governance relevant to the demands of the present. This is an ongoing challenge, to which this chapter is offered as a contribution. In the meantime it is important that we maintain and renew democratic models of governance so that we can effectively contest those who would turn the administrative state in non-democratic directions.

PART II
Femocrats and the Australian State

4 Are femocrats a class of their own?

In the various discussions of Australian femocracy it is common to find some acknowledgement that the privileged access of femocrats to well-paid and high-profile employment positions creates a significant difference between them and the majority of Australian women. Implicit in this acknowledgement is a questioning of how far the position of femocrats takes them out of a shared gender-class location with the majority of women.

This kind of questioning can apply not just to femocrats but to all women who have been fortunate enough to establish access to well-paid, full-time professional and managerial positions. Does this access which permits these women sufficient earnings and assets to be economically independent thereby enable them escape out of their gender-class-determined position of economic dependency on men, either as individuals or in their corporate expression as the patriarchal state?

Of course, gender-class position is a matter of relative advantage and disadvantage, the essential issue being whether women as a class are disadvantaged relative to men as a class. Accordingly, if femocrats, and other women professionals and managers, are materially disadvantaged relative to their male peers, namely men in similar positions, they may legitimately claim identification with the interests of women as a gender class.

In the case of femocrats this identification is a requirement of their job: they are paid advocates of the interests of women as a gender class. This distinguishes them from other women professionals and managers, who otherwise share similar conditions of employment and career advantage. This difference represents the existence of a political feature of the femocrat labour market. It is a labour market which depends on the persisting legitimacy of the ideology of feminism. It is the political force of feminism which leads governments to create these advocacy positions and which demands of their female occupants a commitment to feminist ideology. In this sense femocratic positions demand a convergence between the material interest of women professionals or managers and the ideal interest of feminism.

This chapter raises a number of questions about how femocrats and class analysis may be brought together. It does so with two principal aims. The first is to pursue the rarely asked question: where do femocrats fit into the class structure? The second is to propose that, if the critical tradition of class analysis is to maintain vitality and relevance, it must move beyond its patriarchal origins to accommodate this most significant and historically unprecedented feature of late-twentieth-century occupational systems: the capacity of a significant minority of women to establish themselves as economically independent through their own labour market activity.

CHALLENGES FOR LATE-TWENTIETH-CENTURY CLASS ANALYSIS

Of late there has been much more willingness among the (male) academic custodians of class analysis to move beyond the classical marxist two-class model of bourgeoisie (the capitalist class) and proletariat (the working class). This has been driven by an acknowledgment that the classical model has no purchase over a central dynamic of twentieth-century social structure, namely processes of professionalisation which have brought into being a class or stratum which is neither capitalist nor working-class and quite distinct from the petit bourgeoisie as conceived by Marx. The petit bourgeoisie connotes a stratum of small business proprietors and self-employed artisans, professionals or other kinds of service delivers/producers, a stratum always vulnerable in the face of downturns in the business cycle, with such vulnerability often pushing the members of this stratum down into the proletariat. Professionalisation has combined with the dynamic of credentialism, namely an increasingly inflated requirement of an education credential in order to obtain access to privileged labour market positions which have chances of promotion ('career structures') attached to them. Both these dynamics are evident in the occupation of nursing, which now has a career structure tied to a base-line entry requirement of a college degree in nursing, and where promotion is likely to depend increasingly on gaining further (post-basic) education credentials. Professionalisation and credentialism have combined with the development of complex organisations, mass education and other community services to create a steady demand for professionals of various types and to give them safe, often salaried and tenured employment, as well as a middling ('middle-class') level of income (see Gouldner, 1979; Bledstein, 1976; Ashenden, 1988). Modern professionals constitute a stratum that live off their socially certified (credentialled) claims to knowledge of a technical and/or substantive kind. They are the modern intelligentsia (see Konrad and Szelenyi, 1979; Szelenyi and Martin, n.d.).

There has been also an acknowledgment that classical class analysis does not accommodate the development of modern complex organisational structures, with long chains of command, elaborate communications systems, and mass clienteles. Such complex structures have brought into being a species often grouped together with the modern professional, namely the modern manager. If the former sells and exploits his/her professional (human or cultural) capital, the latter exploits what Wright and Martin (1987) call his/her 'organisational assets'.

Class analysts like Goldthorpe (1982) group together professional, administrative and managerial employees within the same 'service class'. It is not often acknowledged that the social structural claims of professional capital and organisational assets respectively work in different ways, and constitute the identities and rewards of professionals and managers differently. Organisational loyalty is demanded of the latter and thus sanctioned positively or negatively, so that 'trust' relations and 'networking' are crucial organisational assets for a manager. While performance is important, all other things being equal, performance criteria are subordinated to organisational demands. For professionals, the reverse tends to be the case: organisational demands are subordinated to performance criteria. Their access to organisational assets may be important to their getting things done within complex organisational environments, and individuals who start off as professionals within an organisation may end up with a management role in that organisation, as occurs for example when academics are recruited into the vice-chancellorial management group of a university. Professional identities and assets depend on the effective exploitation of skills and knowledge in ways that are in principle open to open debate, independent evaluation and impersonal assessment by professional peers (those who possess the same knowledge and skills). In short, the effective exploitation of professional assets depends on an impersonal, low-trust environment of critical debate and evaluation. To be sure networks of influence and contacts are crucial supports in the promotion of visible professional performance, and without such visibility professional performance cannot be translated into success.

If managers and professionals need to be accorded an independent class location because they cannot be satisfactorily subsumed under either the bourgeoisie or proletariat, and because, unlike the petit bourgeoisie, they are a healthy and even growing species, their introduction into class analysis is of especial interest in relation to femocrats. On the face of it, femocrats appear to be women who have established access to the class positions of managers and professionals. Does this mean that they are upwardly mobile in relation to their gender-class location? Or does their gender-class location compromise and contradict their privileged access to the class positions of managers and professionals? Or are both these propositions true?

At the very least it is worth playing around with the categories of class analysis, ancient and modern, to see what can be done with femocrats. In part, this is to point up how extraordinarily uncurious the masculine custodians of these traditions of class analysis are. They seem completely indifferent to the ramifications of the revolution in the labour force status of women in this century, and to some of the most important aspects of this revolution. As I have proposed already, it has involved the development of strata of women in the labour force—professionals and managers—who earn enough to choose to be economically independent of the patriarchal structures of income support, namely marriage and state-provided welfare dependency. This has involved an extraordinary qualitative change in the position of the women concerned relative to their *mothers*: a particular kind of upward mobility, which also goes unremarked in the class literature.

This indifference on the part of class analysts to the radical changes in the social structural location of women extends also to an almost total neglect of the gender segmentation of the intelligentsia, and of the possibility of an ensuing line of fracture and ideological conflict within the intelligentsia. There is a tradition of sociological inquiry into the class interest of the intelligentsia which begins with the critique of Mannheim's (1936) idea of the free-floating intellectual by Gouldner (1979), and Konrad and Szelenyi (1979). There has been no inquiry into what it may mean for the class interest of the intelligentsia for it to be internally divided into masculine and feminine segments, the former occupying the most highly paid, the most powerful and the most prestigious types of professional employment. While there is a significant tradition of debate within marxist thought on the relationship of the intelligentsia to the development of revolutionary ideologies and movements for social change, there has been virtually complete neglect of 'feminism' as the ideology of the feminine segment of the intelligentsia, and of its relationship to movements for revolutionary and social change.

WHO ARE FEMOCRATS FOR THE PURPOSES OF CLASS ANALYSIS?

The term femocrat appears to have been an Australian neologism invented to refer to a feminist bureaucrat. The neologism is possibly an Australasian one since it is a term used also in New Zealand, though there is some evidence that it is coming into North American usage (see Weir, 1987:98), and Scandinavian feminists have developed the term 'state feminism' to refer to their own version of femocracy (see Dahlerup in Showstack-Sassoon, 1987:28). The term originated to refer to official or state feminists, namely women who are employed within state bureaucratic positions to work on advancing the position of women in the wider society through the development of equal opportunity and anti-discrimination strategies of change. This professionalisation of feminism and its incorporation into the state have been significant points of tension with feminists still identified with a grassroots women's movement, who were able to consider their ideological commitment to be uncompromised by either motives of career advancement or by incorporation into agendas of a state which is still under the control of men. As Anne Summers (1986:60) put it, 'What evokes suspicion about the women (and some men) who work in women's units is the lack of accountability to the women's movement that a bureaucratic appointment entails'. Femocrats are viewed as owing their positions to movement pressure but as giving their ultimate loyalties to the employing government body.

Originally, the term femocrat referred to the women bureaucrats who staff specific agencies identified with promotion of the interests of women. These have been in Australia agencies or units such as the Commonwealth Government Office of the Status of Women (a unit located within the central agency of Prime Minister's and Cabinet) (see Dowse, 1988; Ryan, forthcoming), the South Australian Government Women's Adviser to the Premier (a unit located similarly within the Department of Premier and Cabinet), and the various equal opportunity units within government agencies, or the various equal opportunity or anti-discrimination commissions charged with ensuring conformity to the laws that have given them their mandate. Most equal opportunity units or agencies are now charged with ensuring the provision of equal opportunity for all the groups identified as 'disadvantaged groups', but most originated as responses to feminist struggles for equal opportunity for women, and have been staffed mostly by (professional) feminists.

Femocrats are distinguished from women career public servants in non-femocrat positions because the former occupy career positions which feminism has legitimised. More specifically, as Eisenstein (1987:6) puts it, a femocrat is 'a feminist in an official capacity, that is, someone for whom their feminism is considered a qualification for which they are selected to do the job they are performing'.

Sociologically speaking, Eisenstein's definition is an especially promising one because it draws attention away from the origins of femocrat positions and in the direction of a social structural identification of a femocrat position. The first characteristic of a femocrat position, then, is any occupational position for which a central qualification is a commitment to feminism. In this context, a commitment to feminism may be taken to mean the promotion of women's rights to enjoy equal rights of citizenship with men, and to have access to whatever supports and services are needed to enable the exercise of those rights.

Second, it is clear when femocrat positions are referred to that they are full-time, professional or career-level positions. This places them within what are called primary as distinct from secondary labour markets. That is, they enjoy privileges of permanent tenure, access to career ladders, relatively high salaries with annual increments until the next promotional bar is reached, and important occupational welfare privileges like annual paid leave, sick leave, and, in many cases, superannuation.

This primary labour market characteristic is the most important feature of femocrat occupational positions which distinguishes them from the vast bulk of women's labour market positions. The latter are in secondary labour markets, especially in part-time and casual labour markets, where their earnings and attachment are much lower than women in primary labour markets. This distinction between the two kinds of labour market has been made in recent years, and Barron and Norris (1976:47) join it conceptually with a gender segmentation of the labour market.

With regard to most women's participation in secondary labour markets, there is a reciprocal relationship between demand and supply, where their labour market availability is compromised by their substantial domestic and family commitments, and where their relatively low earnings works to give them less leverage than male family members in determining who does the lion's share of domestic familial work. Women's domestic and familial commitments arise out of the modern patriarchal gender division of labour, a relationship where the class of men exploits the domestic labour of the class of women, which has the consequence of freeing men from domestic labour. Men's participation in the dominant, mainstream structures and cultures of labour markets and occupations in the public domain is predicated on freedom from substantial domestic commitments. Accordingly, there has been very little development of social provision of supports which make it easier for people with domestic responsibilities to participate in the public worlds of work, professional life and politics, and, the telling factor, there has been no redesign of mainstream occupational structures and cultures so as to permit their participants responsible domestic attachments.

Accordingly, the third characteristic of femocrat occupational positions is that they are predicated on the relative freedom of their holders from domestic labour. This means that femocrats have to be so placed in the intersection of their domestic and work lives that they can give most of their energies to the latter.

This they may achieve in a number of ways, all of which are unconventional by the standards of the modern, patriarchal gender division of labour. For example, they may minimise their domestic commitments by not having children, or by not living with a sexual partner. Or they may work out an equal domestic division of labour with their partner, where this is predicated on mutual support for each following their career. Whichever way they go here, as women they will always be entangled in a web of cultural (externalised and internalised) expectations about their domestic capacities and commitments. Accordingly, even if they minimise these, they may still be answerable to the claims of close kin and friends. It is then usually a partial freedom, and moreover one which may have taken considerable time and resources to arrange. Femocrat career or professional commitment is then something women struggle to achieve against many internal and external barriers. The tension that arises from arranging their lives to be free for a professional life is a fundamental and ongoing one for femocrats.

The fourth characteristic of femocrat positions is that because they are career or professional positions, predicated on a relative freedom from domestic labour, they confer on their holders the privilege of establishing their own class location. That is, femocrats (and other female occupants of full-time career or professional positions) are not subsumed under the class location of their fathers or husbands. They have a class position of their *own*. We will examine the significance of this further in the next section.

The four defining characteristics of femocrat positions in the occupational structure are then: 1. performance in these positions demands a commitment to feminism; 2. these positions are located in full-time, primary labour markets; 3. they are predicated on a relative freedom from domestic labour; and 4. they confer on their women occupants the privilege of establishing their own position in the class structure.

If these are the characteristics of femocrat positions, who then qualifies as femocrats? It turns out that those who qualify are not only the femocrats staffing the women's adviser and equal opportunity units in public bureaucracies. They are also the women who staff women's community health centres, rape crisis centres, and women's refuges, where positions in these agencies turn out to be either professional positions in their own right or effective stepping stones to career public service positions. And they are also the women academics who are identified with the academic pursuit of feminism in universities and colleges, especially those who are employed to teach 'Women's Studies', and other feminist academics who were employed with the understanding that they would contribute and develop feminist perspectives within their discipline. Within such publicly funded institutions, the Commonwealth Government's requirement of affirmative action policies and coordinator roles has intensified the development of equal employment opportunity positions, which have often recruited feminist academics who have not been able to gain a tenured position.

This point is important given the degree of tension that there has been between feminist practitioners and academics (see Eisenstein, 1987:7–8), the latter often arrogating to themselves the freedom of critique that the women's movement like any social movement represents. While this freedom is a value intrinsic to the culture of modern intellectual life, feminist academics have expressed it often in ways that seem to indicate that they are free from the bonds of cooption and privilege in a way that practitioner femocrats are not. Sociologically speaking this is nonsense since there is nothing to distinguish the class position of feminist academics from feminist practitioners. It may be objected that the latter are located within the structures of state control while the latter are not. However, this is an increasingly moot point given the close relationship which has developed between the modern interventionist state and higher education. Moreover, it would be virtually impossible to distinguish the ideological commitments and political strategies of bureaucratic and academic femocrats in terms of how they pursue equal opportunity objectives within their own institutional environments.

Of course, as suggested above, it is the case that the kinds of tension which arise from the differences in how organisational as distinct from intellectual assets are exploited must create inevitable points of friction and disharmony between academic and practitioner femocrats. It is not the case that academic femocrats are better feminists than their practitioner peers, but they often like to think they are. The globe-trotting, international networks and conferencing of the academics and their relative freedom from bureaucratic line command can encourage the usual sort of academic snobbery towards those who work in local organisational environments, and whose ideals and values are embedded in practice.

Academic analyses of state power in the 1980s have become more complicated than those permitted by the mid-1970s marxist analysis, which identified state power with the political dictatorship of the ruling class. The elaboration of the neomarxist idea of the relative autonomy of the state has allowed the development of a conception of the state as a site of struggle between different interests, classes and social movements. In this context feminist-academic commentary on bureaucratic femocrats has become more appreciative of their struggles (see Franzway, 1986), but it is still the case that academic femocrats have not applied the same types of political-sociological analyses to themselves.

This is an interesting phenomenon, given the degree of exchange between feminist academic and femocrat practitioner ranks. For example, the first Commonwealth Government Adviser in Women's Affairs, Elizabeth Reid, had been employed as a tutor in philosophy at the Australian National University (ANU) when she was recruited in 1973 to become the first femocrat; when Sara Dowse resigned from the position as head of the Commonwealth Government Women's Affairs Section she became a tutor in the newly established women's studies program at ANU; Hester Eisenstein, who served in the New South Wales central EEO unit, and who then led the EEO unit in the NSW Department of Education, had been an important academic leader in US women's studies, and has returned to academia in the United States; Deborah McCulloch, the first women's adviser to the Premier in South Australia, was recruited from a lecturing position in one of the then still unamalgamated South Australian colleges of advanced education; and there have been a number of important practitioner femocrats with academic doctorates (e.g. Anne Summers, Meredith Edwards).

Speaking more broadly, one would expect there to be considerable exchange between academic and practitioner branches of an intelligentsia oriented to social change. Many academics are likely to want the chance to put their ideas into practice, and many practitioners need to reflect on their practice by drawing on feminist scholarship's elaboration and exploration of feminism as an ideology. Moreover, for the latter, academic credentials and publications are often very useful in helping them establish not only credibility, but leverage across networks within public bureaucracies that are increasingly dominated by the higher-educated members of the new class.

The examination of femocrats in terms of class analysis raises questions such as the following: 1. to what extent do femocrats and non-femocrat women in well-paid career jobs share the same class interest? 2. to what extent do femocrats and women in lesser kinds of jobs share the same class interest? 3. to what extent are femocrats themselves united in sharing a class interest since they include both those who exploit their organisational assets ('managers') and those who exploit their skill and cultural assets ('intellectuals')? 4. what is feminism when it functions as femocrat ideology and how does it express the class interest of femocrats? In what follows I attempt some reflection on these questions with the hope that it may stimulate further and more systematic work.

FEMOCRATS AND CLASS ANALYSIS

Class analysis as a tradition goes back to Marx, and to his emphasis on class exploitation and class struggle. Class exploitation is a way of conceiving the structured patterns of inequality in the distribution of the social surplus so that the focus is placed squarely on an exploiter class deriving its position of material advantage from its control over the labour and life chances of the exploited class. Marx's emphasis on class struggle indicates his insistence on placing these class relations within an action framework, where there is a dynamic arising out of the exploited class(es) resisting the dominance and exploitation of the ruling class. Marx, in short, firmly ties class analysis to the classical issues of distributive justice, and to a normative commitment to social equality.

A strict marxist class analysis maintains the primacy of the two-class model of a capitalist society, and locates the agency of social change with the proletariat. However, as already indicated, this strict model has become anachronistic, especially in a post-industrial capitalist society where the proletariat is declining along with the relative decline of the manufacturing sector. This is why Wright and Martin (1987) reformulate the categories of class analysis. They maintain the productivist orientation of marxist class analysis, but extend the number of types of assets or capital which can be exploited: 'In the new concept, exploitation is defined in terms of social relations built around the ownership or control of different elements of the forces of production: labor power, capital, organization, and skills or knowledge. Exploitation exists when the control over these assets gives people effective claims on the social surplus' (1987:23).

Wright and Martin argue that 'The expansion of managerial class locations represents not simply the effects of postindustrial forces of production on the class structures of capitalism; it also represents the strengthening within capitalism itself of postcapitalist class relations' (1987:24). However, they argue that this does not mean that 'the incumbents of such postcapitalist class locations are necessarily or even tendentially anticapitalist in their political and ideological orientations'. Their insistence on mixing the development of new (post-marxist) social classes into the old (marxist) model clouds the significance of the former, and makes it appear that the dynamics of social change still reside in anti-capitalist struggles on the part of the proletariat.

In my view, we need to be altogether more agnostic and heterodox in our relationship to class analysis if we are to remain committed to its dual emphasis on social inequality and social struggle for redistribution. I prefer to admit a plurality of effective claims on the social surplus which arise from a plurality of exploitative class relationships. These include those which Wright and Martin have usefully identified, and they involve both capitalist and non-capitalist types of class relationship. They can be listed as: 1. effective claims on the social surplus through the exploitation of *capital* assets, i.e. of productive and finance capital (the capitalist class relationship of exploitation between bourgeoisie and proletariat); 2. effective claims on the social surplus through the exploitation of *organisational* assets (the class relationship between managers and the managed); 3. effective claims on the social surplus through the exploitation of cultural and human capital (see Martin and Szelenyi, n.d.), namely skill and knowledge assets (the class relationship between the knowledge/ information-rich and the knowledge/information-poor); 4. effective claims on the social surplus through the exploitation of primary labour market assets (the class relationship between those who effectively establish access to primary labour markets and those who do not). These four relationships may be crudely termed 'economic' class relationships, because they are based in the distribution of different types of productive and marketable assets.

How individuals are located in relation to access to these various economic class assets is strongly influenced by a fifth relationship: gender assets or capital (the gender-class relationship between men and women). The relationship structures the relationship of the market and the occupational structure to the domestic/familial domain. It is thus more than an economic class relationship, and it is the ability of the gender-class relationship to translate from one sphere of operation to another that makes it so powerful.

A sixth class relationship concerns the effective claims on the social surplus which are made through the exploitation of racial and/or ethnic assets (the class relationship between the ethnically/racially advantaged and the ethnically/racially disadvantaged). This relationship has also the ability to translate from one sphere of operation to another.

In a global context it is important to add a seventh class relationship: access to imperial/metropolitan assets (the colonial class relationship between national societies which exploit and appropriate the labour and resources of other national societies). Status as a metropolitan mediates all the other types of class relations, so that, for example, black people in the USA are positioned in relation to the distribution of the global surplus differently from black people in Ethiopia.

Clearly how these relationships work together is a complex matter. What is important to understand is that they do work together, and that they mediate each other. Thus, the class position of an Indochinese-Australian woman outworker is irreducibly different from that of a white, English-speaking Australian woman cafeteria worker. This does not mean there cannot be bases of alliance between these two workers.

My proposal is that the dynamics of social change and struggles for social redistribution arise from the struggles of those who are negatively positioned in relation to these different asset bases against the privileges of those who are positively positioned. How these struggles work, what kinds of trade-offs the members of a particular negatively positioned class are willing to settle for, and what kinds of alliance may develop, are important questions.

Certain observations can be made. The vast majority of men are positively located in terms of their capacity to exploit their gender assets, but many of these will be negatively positioned in terms of access to capital, skills, organisational and ethnic/race assets. Second, all women are negatively positioned in terms of their access to gender assets, and the vast majority of them are negatively positioned in relation to capital, skills and organisational assets as well. The exceptions here are the minority of women who are located as managers and professionals in primary labour markets. Third, even this minority of women are disadvantaged by their gender class in terms of their relationship to primary labour markets. It turns out that the latter are themselves segmented by gender (for discussions of the gender segmentation of professional labour markets see Roach, 1986; Epstein, 1970; Patterson & Engelberg, 1978; Grimm, 1978). Fourth, a negative relationship to a particular category of assets does not in itself guarantee struggle against this particular class of inequality. It is arguable that a negatively positioned class may need to share identity with a positively positioned class before it is willing to struggle against its negative positioning. The struggle comes out of its perception of relative disadvantage. Thus, early English working-class men's struggles were informed by struggle against the perceived loss of the status of a male independent householder who was in control of a productive household and of the labour of those within it (see Seccombe, 1986). Later, when male working-class organisations won a 'family wage', this seeming reinstatement of their status as independent household head blocked the possibility of any perception developing that male workers shared in the same negative relationship to capital as female workers. Indeed it ensured that male working-class organisations colluded with middle-class reformers and feminists in the development of protective legislation, which when combined with the institution of the male family wage, had the effect of segregating men's and women's work (see Boxer, 1986).

Historically, gender, race and ethnic assets have all worked to keep working-class men who belong to the dominant racial and ethnic groups relatively identified with their capitalist exploiters. This is not simply a situation where gender, race and ethnicity are used by those who are most dominant to divide and rule. No such conspiracy is necessary. White, Anglo working-class men actually benefit from their gender, race and ethnic class assets, and they act to maintain these assets relative to those who lack them.

ARE FEMOCRATS A CLASS OF THEIR OWN?

This type of analysis of how contradictory class locations may operate can be applied to femocrats. They are the disadvantaged class in terms of gender assets. Like all women, they are responsible for domestic labour, and this means their relationship to primary professional and management labour markets is less established and privileged than that of men in the same labour markets. However, they enjoy the possession of skill/knowledge and/or organisational assets, and these class advantages distinguish them from the vast majority of women. Indeed, it is clear that femocrats as professionals or managers exploit the labour of women who are placed under them in clerical positions. Femocrats, moreover, are overwhelmingly women who enjoy ethnic and race assets. The effect of this on the ideology of feminism, and its capacity to embrace the interests of all women, is still under-examined.

Here I want to address the contradictory class location of femocrats that arises out of their possession of economic class assets as professionals or managers while at the same time they lack gender-class assets. In principle, femocrats could work to 'resolve' the contradiction by attempting to be upwardly mobile with respect to their gender class. This they could attempt to do by buying their freedom from the privatised world of domestic labour. They could exploit other women as their domestic servants, where these other women become the former's surrogates as housewives (housekeepers, maids) or mothers (nannies) (see Ostrander, 1987). If, in principle, they could do this, it is important to note that such upward gender-class mobility that they could thereby achieve is partial. It does not carry over into personal relations with members of the dominant gender class (men), although avoidance tactics may be used here to sustain the illusion of upward gender-class mobility. Moreover, it does not carry over into impersonal relations with members of the dominant gender class, since these women's professional and management opportunities are still structured by their subordination to the dominant gender class within the public worlds of work and politics. Positions of power and authority within complex organisations and professional institutions continue to be identified with men. To be sure, vicarious identification with men in such positions of power and authority, achieved in the orthodox manner by becoming sexually involved with them, may sustain an illusion of upward gender mobility for women with professional and/or organisational assets.

However, what distinguishes femocrats from non-femocrat women professionals and managers is that the former unlike the latter do not possess, even in principle, these opportunities for partial or illusory upward gender-class mobility. The femocrat is deprived of these opportunities because her position is predicated on her professing a commitment to feminism. This means that her career interest is identified with the promotion of the interests of all women. Accordingly, it becomes very difficult for the femocrat if it should turn out that she has exploited the personal services of another woman in order to delegate her privatised responsibilities for her domestic life.

However, there is nothing against her striving to reduce these responsibilities by her seeking change in the *distribution* of responsibilities for domestic life. This she can do in several ways, and these can be treated as complementary rather than alternative options. First, she can seek to restructure how the gender division of labour works in her privatised domestic life by persuading the man to whom she relates to become an equal partner in the domestic work. Second, she can buy goods and services which help diminish her domestic labour. Third, she can work with other feminists to develop the public provision of services, the most important of which is childcare, so that responsibilities for domestic life are valued enough to be supported socially. This option works to redistribute domestic labour from private to public domains, and thereby calls into question the gendered public/private division of labour.

The femocrat is positioned to contest rather than to collude with the gender-class dominance of men. This is because her professional and/or organisational assets work only as they express the material and ideal interests of feminism. Feminism legitimises femocratic striving for career promotion even as it links their objectives and policies to the improvement of the life chances of all members of their gender class.

If feminism intersects with the class interest of femocrats to distinguish them from non-femocrat women professionals and managers, it distinguishes them also from the majority of women workers who are situated in secondary labour markets. Indeed it distinguishes them from non-feminist women in general. For it is not just that femocrat women are materially positioned by salary and occupational welfare benefits to set up their own households independently of private and public forms of patriarchal income support, but that their feminist ideology ensures that they strive to do this. In this sense they are committed to establishing a class position of their *own*, independently of the class positions of the men who may be their fathers or husbands. This is why the symbolic markers of this independence—using the title *Ms* or retaining one's *own* (patrilineally, matrilineally conferred, or chosen) surname—are so crucial.

This commitment among femocrats to establishing their own class position, independently of the men to whom they relate, does indeed distinguish them from most women in the labour market even as it links them to their not yet successful or less successful sisters committed to the same ideal, and willing to practise it even if it means relative poverty. For most married women, it is clear that their conjugal status does affect their labour force participation. Indeed, O'Loughlin and Cass (1984:3) show that, contrary to claims that women's increased participation in the labour force has increased class inequalities by resulting in a more unequal distribution of family income, it seems to have the opposite effect: 'Where husbands have earned income, highest labour force participation rates are recorded for wives of men earning less than $10,000; a second peak occurs for wives of men earning $25,000–$29,999; lowest participation rates are recorded for wives whose husbands earn between $10,000 and $24,000, and also where husbands earn $30,000 or more.'[1]

This commitment to the establishment of their own class position is what distinguishes femocrats from their mothers. In this sense they aspire to be upwardly mobile in contrast to their mothers most of whom, lacking the ideal interest of feminism and the material professional and organisational assets of femocrats, subsumed their class position under that of their fathers or husbands.

The mutual dependence of the material class interest of femocrats and their ideal interest in feminism is not understood by students of the class mobility of women like Goldthorpe and Payne (1986), Goldthorpe being an eminent British sociologist of class mobility. Goldthorpe and Payne argue there can be three approaches to the mobility of women. First, on the assumption that their class position is conferred by that of their husband, one may examine whether this involves mobility in respect of their class of origin, as measured by the class position of their *father*. On this 'conventional approach', they remark, analysis does not establish that 'either mobility opportunities or mobility risks for women via marriage are at a generally higher level than are those for men via employment' (1986:548). Second, one may allow them to establish their own class position through their labour market position (the 'individual' approach), where it turns out of course that here 'women more often than men display downward mobility from their class origins', again as determined by their father's class position (Goldthorpe and Payne, 1986:548). Third, the 'dominance' approach can be adopted, where class position is derived from whichever family member's labour market position is dominant (see Goldthorpe and Payne, 1986:544). On this approach, 'what is chiefly gained', Goldthorpe and Payne unsurprisingly remark, 'is systematic information on the mobility experience of women who are unattached or themselves family heads'.

Goldthorpe's and Payne's argument is polemically framed by their seeking to determine whether feminist critiques of the neglect of women by mobility research are justified. They argue that the empirical evidence tends to 'confirm the idea of the family rather than the individual as being, still, the basic unit of class structure'. Most married women not only perceive their class position as derived from their husband's employment, but their style of life depends on the class position of the family, and on joint earnings. They conclude their argument by saying that 'the validity of the individual approach to the class location of women remains to be demonstrated'.

This is an intelligent attempt to refute the feminist critique of class analysis for its continuing to use the family rather than the individual as the unit of class structure. Goldthorpe and Payne are correct to point out that (most) wives subsume their own class status under that of their husbands. It follows that for women like these, who derive their class position vicariously from that of their husbands, the salient issue concerning mobility is whether their husband's class position is upwardly or downwardly mobile or immobile as against their father's class position.

Gender class works to position (most) women in this way, and it is why the results of marital breakdown are so devastating economically for most wives. They have not established their own (individual) claims on class assets, and when their condition of conjugal-class dependence breaks down, they are assetless except by the grace of their ex-husband, who may make over to them the marital home, or a share in it. We can be sure that if (most) women were not positioned by gender-class identification to assume their husbands' (fathers') economic class position, they would have organised effectively long before now to establish their own direct claims on the range of economic class assets, namely capital, skill/knowledge, organisational, and primary labour market assets.

Goldthorpe and Payne do not point out the vulnerability which (most) women incur by deriving their economic class position from that of their husbands (fathers), and the ways in which this structures their relationships to labour markets so that they tend to be positioned in the secondary (including part-time, part-year) professional and non-professional labour markets. They adopt an appallingly complacent relationship to this patriarchally determined position of most women in the face of the increasing numbers of female sole supporting parents who are living with their children in poverty (see Burns, 1987; Judy Raymond, 1987).

The only remedy to this situation is to make women's relationship to their economic class position an individual one, and while this depends on the gender-class consciousness of women themselves, it depends also on public policies. Public policies can help more or less to diminish the dependence of women on their husbands' economic class position. They are favourable when they operate to develop equal opportunity in primary labour markets, and when they make public provision of income supports and childcare to help sole supporting parents. Here the conclusions of Goldberg and Kremen (1987:10) are relevant. They surveyed five capitalist and two socialist industrialised societies to determine what variables seem to determine higher or lower rates of the feminisation of poverty:

> Despite the conventional wisdom that government transfers supplement or replace earned income, we found that the capitalist countries with relatively small male-female wage differentials were also the ones that provided the most generous benefits to women. The five capitalist countries ranked similarly on these two factors, Sweden being the highest, and Japan and the United States, the lowest [the other two were Canada and France].
>
> Demographic factors ... need not be directly related to poverty or its feminization. When a country pursues policies to increase women's economic equality, treats them more equitably in the work force, and provides transfers to compensate for the economic and social burdens of single parenthood, then family structure is not necessarily associated with poverty. This is true in Sweden, where high rates of divorce and single parenthood do not result in the feminization of poverty, and it appears to be true in the two socialist countries [Poland, Soviet Union] where rates of divorce are also high (sufficient poverty data are lacking). Countries with low divorce rates are not fully safeguarded against feminization of poverty. In Japan and Canada, where divorce rates are relatively low but rising, female poverty is likely to increase, unless there are changes in overall social and labor market policies.

Goldthorpe and Payne offer an apologia on behalf of the patriarchal structures of economic class. In so doing, they suppress the existence of women whose ideal interest (feminism) and material class location permits them to establish their own, individual economic class position. This suppression works to occlude the significance of these women in the challenge they represent for the patriarchal determinations of the class structure. The more of these women there are the more effective will be their mobilisation as feminists demanding that labour markets become desegregated and that the state develop public policies which ensure that women can establish their own economic independence.

FEMINISM AS THE IDEAL INTEREST AND IDEOLOGY OF FEMOCRATS

The preceding analysis has demonstrated that femocrats *are* a class of their own in a twofold sense. First, they are women who are committed through their adherence to the ideology of feminism to establishing their own, individualised economic class position. Feminism becomes located as the ideal interest which legitimises these strivings.

77

Second, they are a peculiar class: they neither share the gender-class privileges of men and their superior life chances in the various economic assets markets, nor do they share the gender-class position of most women which hooks them symbiotically into dependence on patriarchal (public or private) types of economic support.

The existence of a femocrat culture depends on the existence of a feminist social movement. Certainly, the resources and strength of this culture are affected by the numbers and occupational placement of femocrats themselves. In Australia, this turns largely on which party and set of ideological commitments are in control of the state, for it is state commitments which underwrite the *raison d'être* and salaries of femocrats. Academic femocrats enjoy some degree of independence of state agendas, but, if there were to be a serious disestablishment of state commitments to equal opportunity for women, there can be no doubt that this would affect the legitimacy of academic feminism.

Femocracy represents the professionalisation of the ideology of a social movement. This professionalisation has occurred within the negatively positioned class for whom this ideology is designed. Historically, this is the first time the intellectuals who formulate and elaborate the ideology of (gender) class liberation are drawn from the oppressed and exploited class (for marxism as a point of contrast, see Gouldner, 1979).[2] This places these women intellectuals and professional revolutionaries in the paradoxical position where their organisational and intellectual assets distance them from the gender-class position of most women, and where the continuation of the effective exploitation of these assets depends on their ideological commitment to improving the position of all women.

This commitment has expressed itself in a core three-prong mission: 1. the removal of barriers and hindrances within labour markets to women's participation on terms equal to men's; 2. the facilitation of women's effective labour market participation by the public provision of quality childcare; 3. the redesign of the nature of work so that it can be combined with domestic commitments, especially parenting, and so that it takes on androgynous (masculine and feminine) features as far as work culture, skills valued and style of management go. Again it is clear that this mission as ideology coincides with the material interests of femocrats themselves, and thus becomes their ideal interest.

The salience of this ideal interest is likely to last as long as there are women who have the access to professional and organisational assets but who are still exploited and oppressed by gender class in both their private and public existences. The numbers of these women are increasing, although so too are the numbers of women in part-time professional labour markets. Femocrats are women professionals or managers who have identified their own individual identity and interest with the ideology of feminism. If this ideology should subside so too will its contribution to framing the ideal interest which gives femocrats their distinctive class identity and mission.

NOTES

1 They conclude: 'These analyses of both the 1978–79 Income Survey data and of the 1981 Census would appear to provide little support for the hypothesis that married women's labour force participation has a regressive effect on family income distribution. Rather, it would appear that married women are more likely to be employed, and to be employed full-time, when their husbands are relatively low income earners, and that this relationship is strengthened when there is a young child in the family. It might be inferred from these findings that married women's labour force participation has a progressive effect on family income distribution' (1984:8).

2 Why this should be so is a complex question deserving separate treatment. Historically women have had an important degree of access to the development of a modern intelligentsia, even while this access sequestered them within women's pursuits such as writing novels, for example. With the developments of compulsory schooling, of a professionalised hospital system, and of professionalised approaches to charity, several very important professional avenues of claims on human and cultural capital opened up for women: schoolteaching (first at the elementary levels), nursing, and social work. While there is a considerable literature on women and the professionalisation of areas like these, there is no theorising concerning women's relationship to the modern intelligentsia, and feminism as the ideology of women intellectuals.

5 Dilemmas for femocracy

> Marxism is the false consciousness of cultural bourgeoisie who have been radicalized. 'When the [First] International was formed', wrote Marx, 'we expressly formulated the battle cry: The emancipation of the working class must be conquered by the working classes themselves.' But who was the 'we' who formulated that battle cry? Commitment to the *self*-emancipation of the proletariat is an act of theory made by a theoretical elite and therefore embodies a profound false consciousness. (Gouldner, 1979:75–76)

In chapter 4 I argued that feminism as the ideal interest and ideology of femocrats places them in a very different situation from that of marxist intellectuals. Feminism directly corresponds to the class interest of femocrats which is to successfully establish their own individual economic class location so that they are economically independent of the patriarchal structures of the welfare state and marriage. Such successful establishment requires access to full-time, primary labour markets. Typically Australian femocratic labour markets are those provided by the development of femocrat positions within the middle-management levels of the state and within the middle, tenured lecturing ranks of academia.

If, unlike marxist intellectuals, the practical and theoretical developments of feminist ideology undertaken by femocrat practitioners and academics correspond to the 'true' class interests of femocrats, we may ask whether this is invariably the case. After all, they are positioned in organisations which are structured by the gender-class dominance of men, and it is in the interests of this gender class to maintain the modern patriarchal gender division of labour. It is worth inquiring whether certain value-quandaries or dilemmas arise for femocrats when their own feminist agendas become subordinated to patriarchal agendas.

If this may be one area of value-quandaries for femocrats, the other area concerns their feminist commitments. Put to work as practical policies and programs, these commitments make most sense for women who have established access to full-time, primary labour markets. These women are already positioned to make equal employment opportunity, newly achieved access to occupational welfare benefits such as superannuation, and affirmative action, work for them. Their condition and aspirations fit the dominant employment cultures and practices that inevitably colour how commitments to equal opportunity and the merit principle get realised. However these are a small minority of women in the workforce.

Accordingly, a dilemma appears for femocrats when it is appreciated that their feminism, when set to work in practical policies, usually turns out to be an effective ideology and class consciousness for them, but not for the vast majority of women. Should femocrats allow their feminism to be bounded by the dominant masculinist employment frameworks, or should they do battle with these and thereby call into question both the segmentation of the labour market on gender lines and the tie-up this segmentation has with a class division between workers in the primary and secondary labour markets? Their privileges, as workers with the assets of the primary labour market, would therefore be challenged, and their class allegiance put to the test: would they be willing to subordinate this privileged class identity to the gender-class identity they share with other women?

Femocrats, then, confront two dilemmas: 1. their attempts to develop feminist objectives within organisational and political settings that are subordinated to the patriarchal class interest of men; 2. their efforts to speak on behalf of all women when their practical ideological commitments often best express the interests of women who like themselves are positioned within full-time primary labour markets. Given these dilemmas, and notwithstanding rhetoric which proclaims the contrary, there is an inevitable tendency in the development of policies and programs to reproduce the dualism that inheres in the modern gender division of labour: a commitment to *feminism* gets expressed in policies like EEO and affirmative action, which benefit those in the privileged sections of the labour market, but women less privileged, outside the primary labour market, get something less like self-determination and much more like the old patriarchal ideologies of protection for themselves and their children.

This inevitable tendency in femocrat practice indicates the intractability of the modern gender division of labour. However, without awareness of these distinctively femocratic dilemmas, we are not in a position to debate how we may struggle to resolve them in feminist directions, where our goal is the emancipation of all women from their shared condition of gender-class exploitation.

Femocratic leadership in and contributions toward the emancipation of women *is* in the interests of femocrats as members of the gender class of women. It might be argued that it is not in their interests as a privileged stratum of women for the division between primary and secondary labour markets to break down. However, what is likely to offset any tendency to preserve stratum privilege of this kind is the persistence of a shared condition of oppression and exploitation with other women. Femocrats, like all other women workers, suffer the 'double burden' of combining paid work and domestic responsibilities, and like all other women workers, they confront the structures of patriarchal dominance within their own work worlds. Thus, if femocrats benefit from the newly adopted rhetoric of equal opportunity and anti-discrimination within their own work environments, they are situated also within professional and management labour markets segmented by gender. A femocratic politics which appreciates the complexity of this picture, and which connects up feminist struggles for equal pay with struggles against gender discrimination within employment practices, seems at present to be emerging (see Burton, 1987; and the National Pay Equity Coalition Submission to the 1988 National Wage Case).

THE PATRIARCHAL STRUCTURING OF THE AUSTRALIAN STATE

The modern gender division of labour positions women as a gender class which is responsible for the privatised social relations of parenting and of personal and familial ties, and for the management and provision of such labour as is needed to maintain individuals in their daily requirements for food, clothing, leisure and a healthy, clean environment. These relations and this type of labour are classed together because they are identified with the domestic life of households. Men are the gender class which commands the labour power of women so that women tend to the domestic requirements of men, thereby freeing men from domestic demands. If men become involved in maintaining domestic relations and in domestic labour, their freedom is sustained by this involvement being a matter of their choice. Women's lack of freedom is underlined by their lack of choice about domestic involvements: they may minimise these involvements, but they can never get free of them.

The relationship between gender classes is like all other class relationships, one of exploitation by the dominant class of the energies and agency of the subordinate class. Like the capitalist class relationship it is kept relatively insulated from modern distributive ideas of justice and equality by the private character of the world within which women's work occurs. Struggles against the exploitation of women by men are necessarily struggles over the extent to which women's work should be left to private choices and obligations which are unaccountable to social standards of justice and lack social supports.

Resistance to such exploitation is what drives femocratic ideologies and commitments. Like all contemporary feminists, femocrats seek to deprivatise this relationship of exploitation, and to make it subject to contemporary criteria of justice. Strategies of deprivatisation lead to a close dependence of feminist politics on the cultures and practices of the public domain, and on the structuring of these cultures and practices by the modern state. Inevitably this means that feminist politics tends to be caught within the dominant framing agendas of the state, which maintain the gender division of labour. To be sure, feminists may contest state policies and practices from the vantage point of a feminist exposition of public values, but this is a difficult contest to maintain if feminists themselves become incorporated into state policies and practices. Femocrats are caught therefore in a double bind.

This is not least because the activities of the state itself are structured and conceived in ways that fit the broad culture of the modern patriarchal gender division of labour. There are 'hard' and 'soft' areas of the state. The former include the areas of economic and financial policies, foreign affairs, immigration, trade, defence, policing, labour and industrial relations. The latter include the areas of human and community services, namely childcare, health services, social security and social welfare, and education. Where a 'hard' area takes on a 'soft' aspect, as in the settlement programs attached to the immigration brief, which have a number of welfare and community service features, there is a feminisaton of this aspect in contrast to the dominant culture of the agency in which it is located. Where a 'soft' area takes on hard aspects, as when the education brief is tied to labour market programs and economic restructuring, there is a relative masculinisation of the area. Indeed in this case, with the establishment of the new mega-Department of Employment, Education and Training (DEET) in 1987, Commonwealth education policies and programs have been effectively wrested from 'human services' orientations and cultures and relocated within the orientations and cultures of economic restructuring, labour and industry.

This gender segmentation of state activity is bound into a more general patriarchal culture of power and authority that underwrites the cultures of hierarchy which structure the workings of government agencies. There is a general tendency for central agency and policy activities to be more highly valued than agencies and activities which are program- or service-oriented and which are close to the field and/or clients.

This tendency emerges clearly in Michael Pusey's study of the Commonwealth Government Senior Executive Service (SES) officers, on which he has published a preliminary report (1988a and 1988b). Pusey (1988a:109) classified the 215 SES personnel that he interviewed into three different groups of departments: 1. central agency officers from the Department of Prime Minister and Cabinet, Treasury and Finance; 2. officers from the market-oriented departments of Trade, Primary Industry, Resources and Energy; and 3. officers from the program and service departments of Health, (pre-DEET) Education and Youth Affairs, Aboriginal Affairs, Social Security, Community Services and Veterans' Affairs.

Two of his preliminary findings are relevant here. First, the central agency SES personnel were the most conservative of the three groups in terms of their economic rationalism: 'On four closely associated items that were used as one measure of "economic rationality": namely assessments of (a) deregulation of dollar, of (b) capital and financial markets, (c) of labour, and (d) of distribution of GNP in Australia today; it is the central agencies that rank highest, with the market-oriented departments next and, predictably, the program and service departments lowest' (Pusey, 1988:119). Second, it is clear that central agency personnel disdain and distance themselves from the activities of their SES colleagues in the program and service departments:

> ... program and service departments have to administer and manage programs and services (!), and ... this is not highly valued in the formal and informal pecking orders that are premised on what looks very much like a fetishisation of 'policy' and 'policy-making'. For example, even the most senior of the Commonwealth government's officers in the states, say a Regional Director of Social Security in one of the larger states, may be directly responsible for the management of some 70 or so branch offices and some 5,000 staff(!) and yet although these people may be at level three or four in the SES (i.e. about halfway up the tree) in the informal order of prestige they are among the lowest of the low and have far less status than the 35-year-old level one and level two officers in the central agencies. Typically these central agency people say that program managers and their departments 'get too involved, that they are less able', and, again, that they are 'captives of their clients' and that they 'just do administrative work' and, 'don't really do policy work'; a judgment that is applied to them equally by their peers in the market-oriented departments—[and] 'policy work' ... is in the process of being defined in such a way that only economic policy work counts. (Pusey, 1988a:115, emphases in the original)

It is unfortunate that Pusey did not deem it relevant to indicate the gender patternings of these hierarchies, and he provides no breakdown of how men and women were distributed between the three areas of the SES. However, from another source we know that in December 1986, women constituted only 7 per cent of the SES, the same proportion as they did in December 1985 (Office of the Status of Women, 1987:238). Pusey (1988b:22) himself states in passing that at the time of the survey, there were no women in Treasury, and we can surmise that there are very few women if any in Finance. Those in the know characterise this department as full of young, brash, male economists with next to no professional experience of the complexity of populations outside the very middle-class/upper-middle-class town of Canberra and of the complexity of government experience in substantive areas including productive investment and enterprise.

Set against this is the clear gender-linked dual labour market within Federal and State public services. The vast majority of clerical staff in these services are women—99 per cent of the Commonwealth government keyboard groups are women (Office of the Status of Women, 1987:238)—and there is an effective 'bar' on the likelihood of promotion out of these ranks into the ranks that are identified with management, and within which promotion is identified with career service (see Deacon, 1982; 1983; Bryson, 1987). The higher one goes up within public service hierarchies the more the personnel tend to be male and the more masculine the style and culture of work (see Bryson, 1987:especially 265–69).

Of course there are many very talented and creative male public servants who are committed to good program and service delivery within the regional arms of the Commonwealth Government, as of course there are many such within State Government public services. Within the latter, there are likely to be found executive-level male public servants who enjoy considerable prestige and respect within their own public service, and who are profoundly committed to principles of good, responsive and democratic service delivery.

The point is that, in the general world of the Australian state, these men are identified with the more feminine types of state activity relative to those which partake of the most powerful levels of the state or are identified as the most powerful activities of the state. 'Power' is a masculine quality in societies which are structured by a patriarchal gender division of labour, and it is structured so as to maintain a strict hierarchical ordering of the general division of labour in society. As Rosaldo (1974:26–27) saw so clearly various types of distancing mechanisms 'provide interactional support for male claims to authority':

> Distance permits men to manipulate their social environment, to stand apart from intimate interaction, and, accordingly, to control it as they wish. Because men can be separate, they can be 'sacred'; and by avoiding certain sorts of intimacy and unmediated involvement, they can develop an image and mantle of integrity and worth. Women, by contrast, would have considerable difficulty in maintaining distance from the people they interact with. They

must care for children, feed and clean them, and perform the messy chores.

Hence the *hauteur* with which Canberra central-agency SES officers regard those who are positioned much closer to ordinary citizens and clients. Hence also in an egalitarian and liberal democratic state-society like Australia, where military rank and power are not acceptable expressions of masculine authority, the likelihood of something like the technocratic culture of a quantitatively oriented orthodox economics becoming the medium of the assertions of masculine power and authority. Hence also the very strong functional logic which requires femocrats to be associated with things, spaces and relationships within the state's sphere of activity that are regarded as 'feminine', for whatever these femocrats do, it must not upset or undermine too far the basic patriarchal hierarchy which structures the state.

Thus femocrats are identified either with the feminine areas of state programs and services like childcare or with an advocacy role on behalf of 'disadvantaged groups', who include women. While this advocacy role may place them in central agencies, in the way that the Office of Status of Women is placed within the Canberra-based Department of Prime Minister and Cabinet, or in the way in which there is an equal opportunity unit in most State Government central agencies, it is a relatively weak role.

This claim is best illustrated by how the semiotics of equal opportunity work. As Cate Poynton has shown, in a preliminary (and unpublished) analysis of one of the significant Commonwealth Government 'restructuring' policy documents—*Skills For Australia*—if we examine the characters who play roles in the story told by this policy document, the categories of agency are reserved for the character of 'the Government'. This is the character in the story which 'does' and 'says' things. As Poynton says, doing and saying are two particularly powerful roles, and they constitute also actions which are understood as impinging on the natural world. However, when we come to the section in *Skills in Australia* (1987:15–17) which is titled 'Employment and Training for Disadvantaged Groups', we enter a world of characters who do not say or do things, but who are objects of government policy. This section begins with this paragraph:

> The Government will maintain its commitment to improving education, training and employment opportunities for the long-term unemployed and other groups identified as disadvantaged in the labour market. These include Aboriginal people, migrants from non-English speaking backgrounds, disabled people, sole parents and women seeking to enter or re-enter the labour force, and those

without marketable skills who are displaced from employment through structural and technological change.
In this section other things are also evident. 'The Government' is an actor whose *noblesse oblige* in relation to 'the disadvantaged groups' establishes an appropriate degree of aristocratic distance between it and these groups. Where in other sections there are references to 'our' ('our major trading partners and tourist markets', p. 8, 'our tertiary institutions', p. 9, 'our human resources', p. 13, etc.) and to 'we' (e.g. 'We ... need to examine new ways to impart the less measurable skills on which future prosperity depends', p. 9), there are no references to 'we' and 'our' in the section on 'disadvantaged groups'. 2. Again it is clear that 'disadvantaged groups' are created both as 'disadvantaged', *and* as grouped together, entirely independently of the actions of the individuals who are characterised as belonging to these groups. When the document declares 'Still more needs to be done', it is the Government's assessment of what needs to be done, not that of these individuals, and this declaration comes towards the end of a paragraph which begins with 'Much has already been achieved in these areas' (p. 15). The section also shows that the objectification of individuals who are classed within these disadvantaged groups is thoroughgoing and consistent, as is evident in this statement: 'A society which does not respond to the needs of its disadvantaged groups will incur the heavy socio-economic costs of under-developed and under-utilised human resources' (p. 16).

Two evaluative comments are necessary. While, in this policy document, the Commonwealth Government expresses a 'concern' about 'the persistence of an excessive degree of occupational segregation by gender in the Australian labour market' (p. 16), the logic of the Government's approach to 'the disadvantaged groups' is to constitute, as it is to reproduce, a division between primary and secondary labour markets.

The same kind of piety is found also in *Australia Reconstructed* (1987:128) under the heading 'Labour Market Segmentation':

> The degree of labour market segmentation in Australia is totally indefensible on efficiency and equity grounds. If we are to build on our international competitiveness, structural barriers preventing the full participation of women in the market must be removed. This will require measures to encourage women to participate in non-traditional occupations. More generally, workers with family responsibilities will require assistance if they are to participate fully in the labour market. Again, the Government has introduced legislation and program initiatives that go some way to addressing these problems. This effort includes the Sex Discrimination Act, the Affirmative Action Agency, and increased child care places, but much more needs to be done. Programs like the Women's Research

and Employment Initiative Program (WREIP) have been limited in their effectiveness by minuscule budgets.

What is noticeable about this statement is that the problem is constructed so that it has no relationship to the agency implied in 'we'. That is, the problem is objectified, so that it is 'structural' barriers which 'must be removed' (by whom?), not barriers toward which the organised actions of the male-dominated and masculinist trade union movement contribute to constitute. Here it would seem that the Government is established as the character who will rescue women if anyone will (see Curthoys, 1988:137).

This brings me to my second evaluative comment. It is clear that femocrats are set up, by the logic of how the Government constitutes its relationship to 'disadvantaged groups', to be the advocates for these disadvantaged groups. This ensures a double distancing of the Government from the disadvantaged groups. It is not the efforts of the most powerful actors in government but the efforts of some of the least powerful who are to advocate on behalf of disadvantaged groups. Indeed femocrats are assimilated to something like the gender order of patriarchal domestic government, where they are permitted to speak up on behalf of the least powerful members of the household: its children and, when they still existed, its servants. Like the good wife they share the patriarch's culture of consumption and are accordingly located in career rungs of the public service. In return for the expectation that they will represent claims for patriarchal concessions to the needs—again, as 'objectively' assessed, i.e. by the advocate or patriarch not the children themselves—of the children, they are expected to obey loyally the patriarch's decisions.

I have undoubtedly exaggerated the structure of the situation in which femocrats find themselves, and I have done so with the intent of indicating that it is my belief that this structure is highly intractable, and that the first point of resistance to it is to become fully conscious of this. In the next section I want to indicate how it seems to have governed some recent femocrat efforts.

AUSTRALIAN SOCIAL DEMOCRACY AND FEMOCRATS

Sara Dowse (1988:206), in a brilliant essay, 'The Women's Movement Fandango with the State: the Movement's Role in Public Policy since 1972', begins by identifying the problem of 'the ideological separation of the social and the economic', and the consequent tendency for 'the mounting political pressure from women' to be 'siphoned into a narrow range of "social policy" issues'. This essay was written and published first in 1982, the year before the election of the Hawke Labor Government to run the federal level of the

Australian state. In looking back on a decade of femocratic involvement in public policy, Dowse makes these prescient comments:

> The resurgence of feminism coincided with the Labor Party coming to office for the first time in 23 years. The 1972 election and the resulting Labor government had a profound effect on the development of the women's movement in Australia. The convergence of the rise of 'new wave' feminism and the election of a social democratic government after so long a period of conservative rule is perhaps unique in contemporary western democracies. It put a stamp on the nature of the involvement of feminists with and in government and indeed determined the parameters of the women's movement itself. (1988:207-8)

The significance of the party in power for the development and tenor of femocracy cannot be underestimated. It is unlikely that Australian femocracy would have developed to the extent it has without the crucial coincidence of a reforming federal Labor Government and a dynamic women's movement in the period 1972-75, and without the renewal of this connection with the election of the Hawke Labor Government in 1983.

The hiatus 1975-83 at the Federal level was not as great as it may seem for two reasons. First, from 1975 to 1977, at the federal level, initiatives were sustained and developed until the Office of Women's Affairs was transferred from the central agency of Prime Minister's and Cabinet, and relegated to a minor and new Department of Home Affairs (for the account of this, see Dowse, 1981). Second, there were two important reforming Labor administrations at the State ('second-tier') level of government during the period of Labor not being in power at the federal level, 1975-83. In South Australia the Dunstan Labor Government was in power 1970-77, and continued a legislative reforming record which its precursor Government (the one led by Walsh, then by Dunstan) in 1965-68 had initiated (see Parkin and Patience, 1981). The commitments of this Government to using the law to promote anti-discrimination and equal opportunity in the areas of race, ethnicity and gender contributed to the base it established for a South Australian femocracy with the appointment of the first women's advisory unit within the Premier's Department in 1976 and the establishment of an equal opportunity unit within the State public service in 1977 (see Mills, 1981; Bradley and McCulloch, 1985). In New South Wales the Wran Labor Government was elected in 1976, and this was also a Labor government which enjoyed a long period of office, losing office only in March 1988 (although Wran himself resigned in 1986). With its own style, and a commitment to 'representative bureaucracy' stimulated by Peter Wilenski's review of the State government administration, the Wran

Government also established an important base for Australian femocracy and femocratic policy initiatives (see Eisenstein, 1985). In these ways the policy commitments, experience, networks and culture of Australian femocracy could go on growing and developing in the period 1975-83.

The consequence of this has been an extensive involvement of the Australian contemporary women's movement with the state. Dowse (1984:139) comments on this: 'What has intrigued me ... throughout my life as a feminist activist is the fact that, despite my scepticism about the so-called democratic process of government and my philosophical abhorrence of the modern capitalist state, when I want something done I look to just that arena. My expectations are low, but my directions are clear. I look to the public sector. And despite all claims to the contrary so do most of my feminist sisters, even the most radical among them.' Specifically, femocrats have been oriented to a positive and cooperative relationship with the government. In turn, under Labor administrations, they have been integrated as an arm of government, and they have played a crucial role in legitimising Labor's revision and modernisation of its mission in the 1970s and 1980s.

This role has had two particular features. First, the identification of femocrats with the policy areas of equal employment opportunity, anti-discrimination and representative bureaucracy has placed femocrats as the brokers and mediators of the claims of the new social movements on the state in these areas. At least this is true for the social movements for whom issues of inclusion and exclusion in respect of mainstream structures are salient: gay rights movements, ethnic movements and organisations, Aboriginal movements.

Second, femocrats, especially under the Hawke Labor Government, have been used to rationalise and modernise the Australian residualist system of social security. A residualist system of social security is one built around the notion that publicly provided 'welfare' is to be provided only for those who cannot get adequate access to the private avenues of income support: the market and the family (see Wilensky and Lebeaux, 1965:11). Femocrats have been used in this way at a time when an ethos of small government has intensified this residualism, and biased policy-makers against universal entitlements and services (see Castles, 1988: especially ch. 7). The Social Security Review, a substantial exercise which began in June 1986, and which has not yet been completed, has been led by Bettina Cass. Cass is a feminist sociologist, whose research includes excellent work on the history of women's relationship to the welfare state, specifically the history of child endowment and family allowance policies (see e.g. Cass 1988a; 1988b).

The fate of Cass's declared commitments in relation to the Hawke

Government's selective implementation of the Social Security Review is instructive. Cass has been the most sustained and well-researched contemporary advocate on behalf of horizontal redistribution to women and children. This is undoubtedly one reason why she was selected to head the Social Security Review in a context of increased formation of sole-parent families, where the vast majority of these sole parents were women, and were dependent on public income support (see Cass 1986:15, Raymond, 1987:4). Cass's commitment to horizontal redistribution in the interests of gender and life-cycle equity did not avail her in the face of the Hawke Government's insistence on 'targeting', i.e. directing income support and services to the poorest families (see Cass's acknowledgment and handling of the debate concerning income-tested and universal benefits, 1986:79–89, 103–113). The word 'targeting' encapsulates the idea of the disadvantaged as being *objects* not agents. Moreover, for the Government to use a feminist social scientist to target policies and programs to sole supporting parents is a clear instance of its using advantaged women to police, while they speak for women without such advantages.

Cass presided over the Social Security Review at the time (May 1987) when this Government abolished the universal Family Allowance, first introduced in 1976. The Government replaced the universal family allowance with an income-tested family allowance, and introduced a family allowance supplement in December 1987 for the poorest families. Cass (Baldock and Cass, 1988:84–88) comments on this history. First she sets the scene:

> The objective of maintaining horizontal equity, which recognises the increased costs incurred by all parents caring for children and legitimates a universal program of family allowances paid to all mothers regardless of their own or their spouse's income, was said to be in conflict with the objective of vertical equity, which places priority on redistribution to low income families.

As Cass indicates, there was public criticism of this shift in policy coming from both the women's movement and the welfare lobby. The reasons for this criticism were various, and included: 1. 'the erosion of the concept of universality in family support'; 2. Income-tested family allowances presuppose that women have access to family income, a presumption which has been shown to be false in many instances (see Edwards, 1985); 3. the abolition of *universal* family allowances meant there was 'no longer a mechanism in the tax/transfer system to recognize the increased costs incurred by all families with children'.

Cass points out that, by prioritising the objective of vertical equity over that of horizontal equity, the Government was choosing to express its redistributive concerns in a way that favoured the poor, not women. In this context, Cass remarks, class rather than gender seemed to prevail. However, since the Government left the dependent spouse rebate intact and sought neither to have it income-tested or debated, and since men comprise 96 per cent of recipients of this tax rebate (comprising in cost to revenue $1.10 billion in 1985/88), Cass's final comment is apposite: 'it could be said that gender interests prevailed after all'.

This particular history of a femocrat's engagement with the Australian state under a Labor administration indicates what femocrats are up against and how limited is their power. At the same time that the Social Security Review has been occurring, and with its support, there has been a concerted policy effort to reduce the number of sole supporting parents who are dependent on government-provided income support. This effort has been one of shifting sole supporting parents from public to private forms of income support, where the latter are to involve both income derived from their own labour market participation, and child maintenance support from the non-custodial parent. Femocrats have been prominent in this policy effort to privatise income support for sole supporting parents. Meredith Edwards, at present first assistant secretary of the Social Policy Division in the Department of Social Security, and who is also a feminist economist who did pathbreaking work on gender inequalities in the distribution of income within households (see Edwards, 1985), was given a major role in writing the policy proposal on child maintenance (*Child Support: A Discussion Paper on Child Maintenance* 1986). The Cabinet Sub-committee on Maintenance which recommended the proposal comprised: Brian Howe, as Minister for Social Security; Lionel Bowen, as Attorney-General; Don Grimes, as Minister for Community Services; Paul Keating, as Treasurer; Peter Walsh, as Minister for Finance; and Susan Ryan, Minister Assisting the Prime Minister on the Status of Women. Among other things, the argument of this proposal is structured by the deeply regressive principle that 'all children have a basic right to share in their parents' income'.

This proposal, which is now government policy and has taken effect, deducts maintenance payments from the wages of non-custodial parents through the Australian Taxation Office. Maintenance payments from non-custodial parents apply to all non-custodial parents who separate after 1 June 1988, or, where they have not cohabitated, parents whose child is born after that date. The scheme is compulsory for all sole-parent pensioners, and it applies not only to new pensioners but to parents who were already receiving a sole-parent pension on 1 June 1988. In other cases the custodial parent can opt out by advising the Child Support Agency (Harrison,

1988:37). It is significant that sole-parent pensioners are brought compulsorily under the new maintenance scheme, and that they are not accorded the usual principle of not applying legislation retrospectively. This betrays the Government's intent: the effort to reduce public income support to sole parents by privatising the responsibility for maintenance. Where pensioners receive maintenance, this allows the amount of the Sole Supporting Parent Benefit to be reduced accordingly.

This looks like welfare rationing and it is welfare rationing. It is predicated on a principle of privatisation which pushes responsibility for income support of children and also young people as far as possible back onto their parents (for how this is affecting young people, see Yeatman, 1988d). Philosophically the maintenance proposal erodes the notion of a collective responsibility for contributing through publicly provided benefits and services towards the costs of rearing the children who will be the next generation of this society's citizens. Thus the policy proposal *Child Support* (1986, 14) begins with the following propositions:

> The Government sees a need to strike a fairer balance between public and private forms of support to alleviate the poverty of sole parent families and to achieve some constraint on government outlays on sole parent payments. Specifically, the Government believes that all parents have an obligation to support their children financially ...

Femocrat support for the maintenance proposal was turned into a brief to ensure that the proposal went forward. The Office of the Status of Women, under the leadership of Suzanne Brooks, undertook to ensure that the reform would go forward. It is clear that femocrat support for this reform was forthcoming because it was interpreted as a sanction against the apparent neglect by non-custodial parents (mostly men) of their parenting responsibilities. Only about a quarter of eligible sole-parent beneficiaries received maintenance payments, and the amount received was fairly low, with two-thirds of those receiving it getting less than $31 per week (Cass, 1986:75).

The discussion paper *Child Support* provided no data on the capacity of non-custodial parents to pay maintenance or how much maintenance, although it did offer these remarks: 'Some non-custodial parents would not have the capacity to pay much, if any, maintenance. Others give financial priority to children of a second marriage' (1986:12). It also made some acknowledgment that many parents have settled their affairs by making, instead of maintenance, a settlement in kind (e.g. the marital home). The implementation of the proposal has taken this into account and where non-custodial parents make over a lump sum in a property settlement, amendments to the Social Security Act require this to be quantified for the income test on pensions and benefits (Harrison, 1988:39).

The discussion paper makes the point that 'In the average case where the woman was a sole parent and the man was living alone, the man was $175 per week better off than the woman, after payment of tax and after the payment of maintenance' (1986:13). The significance of this data needs to be assessed in relation to what proportion of these male non-custodial parents are living alone and have not incurred new family responsibilities.

The way in which the contrast between the non-custodial and the custodial parent's situation is represented in the above quotation from the discussion paper makes the relative penury of the latter appear a function of the private choices of the former. This obscures how the modern gender division of labour structures the choices and access to income of both parties. When the male non-custodial parent's labour force participation patterns are compared against those of the female custodial parent's it is clear that he is likely to have much more money that she does. The rate of female sole parents' participation in the workforce is relatively low (40.8 per cent compared to 50.5 per cent of married women with children, Cass, 1986:18) although the Government is also trying to provide labour market programs for sole parents through its JET (Jobs, Education and Training) program introduced in March 1989. How effective such programs can be remains to be seen given the relatively marginal relationship of women to labour markets, a situation that does not appear to be improving as O'Donnell and Hall (1988:30–31) bring out:

> For women, marginal employment is the norm, in that over half the female workforce is part-time and/or casual ... Women are four-fifths of all part-time workers and 38 per cent of women workers are part-time, compared to 7 per cent of employed men and 19 per cent of all employees. Part-time employment is increasing faster than full-time, and the increase in part-time work for women was the most important contribution to total net employment growth in the period 1973–83.

The point I am raising is whether, in relation to feminist analyses of the social structures of the modern gender division of labour, it is logically coherent to regard the individual non-custodial male parent as privately responsible for the condition in which his erstwhile partner in parenting–if only in the act of conception–finds herself as a sole supporting parent. If it makes sense to assign him some of this responsibility, it cannot be regarded as his alone. As a single individual, he may contribute to but he is not privately responsible for the social practices and institutions which maintain and reproduce modern patriarchy. The objection may be made that why should he be able to privately renege on his responsibilities when other non-custodial parents pay maintenance and when his ex-partner is privately lumbered with the main business of child-rearing with all that it entails. My point is that feminist analysis has moved generally in the business of deprivatising the arrangements our society has made for the parenting of children, so that responsibility for these arrangements become issues of social justice and public policy. This means that it is legitimate to require men to assume full co-responsibility for parenting, but if they do this as private individuals class differences between men will make some more 'responsible' than others. Redistribution of responsibility for parenting requires a social transformation of the class relationship between men and women as it does of the class relationships based on unequal access to private property.

Equity in relation to transfers from those who are free from parenting responsibilities to those who have these responsibilities is best served if the former are taxed so as to provide appropriate public income support and services for the latter. Philosophically this proposition depends not only on viewing parenting in terms of a social division of labour but on viewing it as an activity carried out on behalf of us all as the society we comprise.

This position does not rule out and indeed should not rule out the importance of people making an informed choice about taking on the parental role and about the ongoing commitment to the child that this role entails. It does follow from the assumption that people choose to have children that they thereby incur most of the material and non-material costs that attend that choice. It does not follow that they should go it alone, or be deprived of substantial social support.

It is a moot point whether current gender roles permit this condition of informed choice. Certainly there is nothing in traditional assumptions concerning masculine financial responsibility for such children as he has wittingly or unwittingly fathered which indicate that this situation involves a male's choice to parent children. It is questionable whether his being forced to assume maintenance responsibilities will encourage him in the direction of choosing to assume parental responsibilities, for of course these are not the same thing.

The child-support proposal tends to suborn feminist discourse and to subjugate it to the non-feminist discourse of masculine possessive individualism (masculine private property). It reinstates a situation where women and children are to be regarded as economic dependents of men as private individuals, and thereby reinstates the modern patriarchal conception of men as possessors of the private property on whom the former depend. In this picture there is no social responsibility for parenthood which requires the whole society to make appropriate support to those who have children. The logic of privatisation which inheres in the child-support policy comes out clearly in Hendrie's and Porter's support for such a policy:

> ... it must be acknowledged that at present *tax payers* are meeting much of the cost of caring for *other people's* children. *Public* provision of income transfers ultimately has the effect of reducing *individual responsibility* for maintaining *family* income. With less than 30 per cent of custodial parents receiving regular maintenance payments ... it would seem important that family law changes are effected to ensure that non-custodial parents share more fully in the cost of supporting their *own* children in accordance with their ability to pay. (1987:27, emphases added)

As this statement makes clear, the child-support policy reinstates the family as the unit of the class system, and makes the 'individual'—namely the individual with effective market capacity—responsible for his own family. If he is financially capable of supporting his children he should do so, and the taxpayers' support should be invoked only if this capability does not exist.

It should not surprise us that femocrats should have supported a policy which reproduces in the appropriately gender-neutral language of the 1980s—'non-custodial' and 'custodial' parents, indeed the term 'parent' itself—the good old gender division of labour we know so well. There has always been a traditionalist component within feminism threatening to turn feminist radicals into conservative 'god's police' who help upright and proper patriarchs bring their errant brethren back into the patriarchal-nuclear-family fold. It is a fairly easy matter to mobilise feminists' feminine resentment at the ways in which men, individually or collectively, have classically reneged on their responsibilities to their dependants.

Nonetheless by giving their support to a proposal which moves in the direction of privatising responsibility for children, femocrats are colluding with the more general efforts to roll back the welfare state by privatising it either in the direction of market provision or family provision. The proposal does not redistribute income from men to women, but permits a reduction of government-provided support to women, in a context where the masculinist trade union movement is demanding tax cuts, and there are concerted efforts by masculinist neoconservatives and other apostles of deregulation and privatisation to roll back the state. The quandary in this case concerns not only femocratic conformity with patriarchal Labor Government policy but, in addition, the relative lack of analytical and critical scrutiny of the proposal by academic femocrats, free from the bureaucratic femocrat pressures of pragmatic adaptation to government policy. Up to now, there has been no analysis of the child-support proposal in *Australian Feminist Studies* and I have not been aware of anything other than apparently justified bureaucratic femocrat assumptions that other feminists would find the proposal's virtues to be self-evident (although see Earle and Graycar, 1987).

The symbiosis between Australian feminism and a Labor-led state over the last decade and a half has proved to be a complex and difficult business for both bureaucratic and academic femocrats. Franzway (1986:45) is correct in seeing this symbiosis as having entailed a special relationship between Australian feminism and the welfare state. In particular, it has profoundly implicated femocrats in the various and distinctively Labor corporatist strategies of rolling back the welfare state in the 1980s (see chapter 7, and Yeatman, 1988d).

The Labor governments have proved to be adept in harnessing femocrat energies to patriarchal strategies of 'protection' of women and children. These strategies maintain the hierarchical principle of paternalism and have nothing in common with strategies of redistribution. In looking to the state as an arena for getting some things done feminists need to be careful. At present the dominant culture of the state is one which favours privatised rather than public-collectivist principles of distribution of goods and services. In this context it is unlikely that femocrats will be able to espouse and implement policies and programs which are redistributive in class or gender terms.

This is to remind feminists of how important it is to maintain a significant degree of independence from the state. This reminder has tended to get lost amidst both the hopes which Labor governments have aroused and the particularly intimate types of cooption they have offered to feminists.

PART III
Restructuring and the Crisis of the Welfare State

6 Restructuring and Australian public policy

There is general agreement that the Australian national economy, like other industrialised, 'developed' economies, faces significant challenges. There is also wide agreement that these challenges demand that the Australian national economy be 'restructured' in the directions of developing its manufacturing base, developing a high-tech capacity, and investing in the training, education and skills formation that are needed for this process of restructuring to occur. There is much less agreement about how this should be done, and in particular what the role of public policy in this process should be.

Present challenges of restructuring are variously interpreted. Leaving aside the 'politics' of restructuring where different ideological commitments structure a debate about trade policy, for example, the interpretations of these challenges vary depending on what is taken as the unit of intervention. This may be the whole national economy, or the management practices of particular firms (for an excellent discussion of the scope and variations of the American industrial policy debate, see Thompson, 1987). However, the overwhelming tenor of debates about public policy response to the challenges of restructuring is economistic. Non-economic aspects of response are hinted in debates about how to promote not simply the quantity but the quality of productive investment (Thompson, 1987:44), and about what kinds of investment should be made in human capital in order to promote increased economic growth and productivity. Both of these areas begin to introduce the critical cultural variable of *motivation*, to be economically active, creative, entrepreneurial and productive. This not only introduces basic questions like what rewards are needed to elicit this motivation, but also questions of how this motivation may be harnessed to ecologically sound economic activity in a post-colonial, socially complex global economy.

The cultural dimensions of restructuring have been largely glossed over in the public policy debates. In this respect the moral components of economic activity have been neglected. It is true that the unique geo-economic and historical position of a national economy within the global economy colours its public policy responses to the challenges of restructuring. Thus, for example, Australia's location within the thriving economic relationships of the Pacific Basin national economies has caused the Hawke Government to emphasise Asian Studies and Asian languages within the development of higher-education curricula and the degree structures of students. While economistic in character, this is a type of public policy response which tacitly concedes the argument of anthropologists (Mauss, 1967; Sahlins, 1972) that economic exchange relationships are established on the basis of ritual exchange relationships, namely moral bonds which link the exchanging parties over time.

This chapter raises some of the issues involved in the cultural dimensions of restructuring of the Australian economy. Issues like the following: Who in Australia is most likely to understand and develop the moral bonds which are needed to inform successful economic links between the Australian and other national economies within the Pacific Basin? What kind of ethos of economic motivation is needed at this point of historical time in order to release new energies of Australians as economically creative and powerful actors? Who does this ethos need to include as economically active citizens? Which needs, public and private, does this ethos need to express? Issues like these pose fundamental questions about how current public policies construct the challenges and the tasks of restructuring.

While the discourse of restructuring has been the plaything of dominant masculine forces in Australian society, including the trade union movement, there is no need for this to go unchallenged. It is true that such discourse licenses an unrestrained economism which operates to delegitimise social, cultural and moral claims. When the discourse is situated within this kind of facile economism, it is clear that those who belong to the gender category non-productive and non-economic—namely women—are refused admission to the central decision-making forums on restructuring. Since restructuring is accorded metapolicy status, i.e. viewed as the policy framework within which all other specific policy challenges are to be located, this means the effective exclusion of women from the central decision-making forms per se.

As suggested already, the contemporary discourse of restructuring in Australia is not confined within economism. Economism in the current historical context refers to the metapolicy claims of neoclassical economics, which has come to assume a dominant position in the Anglo-American economics profession, and its offshore enterprises in Australian universities. The characteristics of this economism combine the generic feature of all economistic types of discourse, namely a tendency to reduce all salient phenomena to economic ones, and certain assumptions which associate economic vitality with unregulated market activity and with a correlative decrease of government involvement in the economy (see Whitwell, 1986, chs 9, 10).

Other significant contributions to the public policy debates about restructuring have been led by the Hawke Labor Government in the areas of skills formation, higher education and labour market programs. These are: The (Kirby) *Report of the Committee of Inquiry into the Labour Market Programs*, January 1985; *Skills for Australia*, a policy document circulated by the Minister for Employment, Education and Training and for Employment Services and Youth Affairs in 1987 and *Higher Education: A Policy Statement*, 1988. These have indicated the relevance of human capital development and investment, an area which arguably has more to do with sociology than with economics. This Labor Government has also commissioned substantial policy reports on immigration: the Fitzgerald Report, *Immigration: a Commitment to Australia*, 1988 and *Towards a National Agenda for a Multicultural Australia*, 1988. Both these reports accord the agenda of economic restructuring a central place in their recommendations, so that both a specific immigration policy and multiculturalism are strategically aligned with an effective national economic response to the challenges of restructuring. The mixing of the discourse of economic restructuring with the discourses of a strategic immigration policy on the one hand and of multiculturalism on the other is especially interesting for its introduction of a cultural dimension into the business of restructuring.

To be sure, this cultural dimension is weakened by the lack of coherence in current government thinking on the relationship between immigration and multicultural policies. However, it is clear that these policies are widely understood as reflecting crucial issues for Australian restructuring. These issues relate to the geocultural task Australian society faces in adapting its identity as a satellite of the white Anglo-American cultural, economic and military empires within the emergent regional cultures of the Pacific and Asian Basins.

The cultural dimension of the Australian discourse of restructuring suggests also that restructuring might have something to do with issues of citizenship, not only in the restrictive sense of who gets to be chosen from those seeking to immigrate to Australia, but also in the expansive sense of how cultural and linguistic diversity may contribute to a creative restructuring response. This contribution presupposes membership in a citizen community.

This is a particularly rich and promising context for developing an entrepreneurial, creative and democratic discourse of restructuring, where the challenge of the Australian context is accepted as an opportunity for a more general process of national development. In making this judgment, I am proceeding on the basis of one of the organising premises of this essay: namely, that vital and successful economic activity depends, as the great sociologist Max Weber argued almost a century ago, on an ethos or ethic which provokes, drives and motivates individual actors to be creative, and productive in economically relevant ways. Today, this is not likely to mean the 'protestant ethic' as Weber (1958) conceived it, because that ethic demanded a self-abnegation which is incongruent with contemporary values of personal life and selfhood (see Levine, 1985; and the commentary on Levine by Yeatman, 1986). If Australia is to meet its current restructuring challenges, an economically oriented entrepreneurial ethic needs to be developed in ways which both build on, and fundamentally change, the practical, democratic and egalitarian traditions of this society. It must be for the first time in European Australian history an inclusive ethic, one that genuinely and with no qualifiers confers on all Australians a potentially productive relationship to a national economy which is structured by their shared citizenship claims. Among other things this must involve a preparedness to look in unorthodox directions—unorthodox at least for (neoclassical) economists—for economically productive activity, and to do what is necessary to nurture its economic potential. For example, a good deal of innovation is contained within government departments or instrumentalities where often the skills, knowledge and creativity involved are intrinsically bound up with public purposes and public service. These activities can be commercialised, but the ways in which this commercialisation occurs have to be congruent with their public orientation. This may mean providing, for cost, services to other governments in the region, where to ensure that these services are relevant the commercialising body establishes ties to the 'customers' which educate its personnel in their needs and requirements. It may also mean being more open to exchanges in kind that facilitate the development of these ties, exchanges of personnel and services which enhance the knowledge and capacities of the agencies involved. These modes of public sector entrepreneurship represent infrastructural types of investment which will prove to be of great material and moral value for direct forms of capital exchange and investment.

All this is to remind us, as I shall have occasion to do again below, that economic activity is normally embedded within a moral economy (see also McDonald, 1988). It is doubtful that an anomic economic individualism and entrepreneurship—one that acknowledges no ethical obligations or social ties—can characterise anything more than short-term enterprise and relationships (see Durkheim, 1964:1 ch. 7). Weber's individuals who were driven by the protestant ethic into an entrepreneurial and highly ascetic pursuit of productively oriented capital accumulation were also oriented by this ethic to universal (non-discriminatory), lawful relationships to others. If honesty proved to be the best policy, economically speaking, this revealed also the dependency of successful economic activity over the long term on a shared moral orientation of the various parties to economic interaction: investors, producers, workers, managers, customers. This point is made in a different way by Peters and Waterman (1984) in their stress on the value-orientation of the successful US capitalist firms they studied: this orientation declared itself in a strong sense of mission, a commitment to quality and to closeness to the customer.

The discourse of restructuring poses the question of what are likely to be the national value orientations most likely to foster enduringly successful economic enterprise. If in Australia these must now involve an inclusivity that transcends the historical legacies of gender, racial and ethnic discrimination, it is important to acknowledge the barriers that will have to be overcome for this to occur. The most significant of these is the absence of a tradition of citizenship within Australian society. It can be argued that 'multiculturalism' is the first time that the concept of citizenship as a bundle of economic, social, political and cultural rights and obligations has been elaborated in Australian society, or, perhaps more accurately, that multiculturalism, feminism and the Aboriginal movement for self-determination have all contributed to the development of this discourse of citizenship. However, the problem with this distinctively Australian citizenship discourse is precisely that it has been elaborated on behalf of those excluded from the modal type of Australian who is white, Anglo and male. If the overseas success of the movie *Crocodile Dundee* has played its part in contributing to a positive trade balance, the personage of Mick ('Crocodile') Dundee was one that we probably did not need to reinvent at this time. Or perhaps unconsciously, and with some of Mick's own brand of irony, we have done so in order to remind us of the points Marx makes at the beginning of 'The Eighteenth Brumaire of Louis Bonaparte':

> Hegel remarks somewhere that all facts and personages of great importance in world history occur, as it were, twice. He forgot to add: the first time as tragedy, the second as farce.... Men make their own history, but they do not make it just as they please; they do not make it under circumstances chosen by themselves, but under circumstances directly encountered, given and transmitted from the past. The tradition of all dead generations weighs like a nightmare on the brain of the living. And just when they seem engaged in revolutionising themselves and things, in creating something that has never yet existed, precisely in such period of revolutionary crisis they anxiously conjure up the spirits of the past to their service and borrow from them names, battle cries and costumes in order to present the new scene of world history in this time-honoured disguise and this borrowed language.

THE GLOBAL CONTEXT OF AUSTRALIAN RESTRUCTURING

The global context which is generating the pressure for the restructuring of the Australian economy is complex. Interpretations of the nature of these pressures vary according to how particular national economies are situated in relation to them. It is inevitable, given Australia's historical association with the trans-Atlantic national economies and with the 'developed world' at large, that Australian interpretations of these pressures are influenced by those which arise in the United States, the United Kingdom and other European national economies.

Before, however, I enumerate some of the types of national response to the current pressures of the global economy, it is important to say that the nature of the global economy itself is under dispute. To make this point it is necessary to refer no further than to two very different neomarxist perspectives on the global economy. The first offers a conception of 'global capitalism', which suggests that there is a new global division of labor driven by the mobility of transnational corporations, and their interest in relocating production in regions or states which offer cheap labour, low or no tax liability, and possibly various forms of subsidy as well (see Nash, 1983; Ross, 1987). The effects of this are: a relative deindustrialisation within erstwhile developed, industrial economies; a decrease in the bargaining power of labour within these economies, in part because of increasing unemployment; a declining public revenue base for the polities in such economies because multinational corporations are able to use their overseas investments to reduce their tax liability; and the consequent erosion of redistributive social provision within these polities (Nash, 1983:14). Ross (1987:249) sums up the principal thrust of global capitalism: 'industrial location becomes a buyers' market. Among the matters subject to explicit or implicit bargaining between location buyers and local sellers are aspects of local public policy.'

In this perspective, as Doreen Massey (1987:122) argues, the 'impetus for restructuring has come in an immediate sense from capital'. Massey is discussing the changing geography of employment and industry in Britain. This has involved a loss of manufacturing jobs in the cities, the concentration of management hierarchies and of financial, legal and other services in London and the Southeast, and the relative decentralisation of production itself 'both within individual regions, outwards from cities, and from the Southeast and Midlands of England to the regions of the north and west' (1987:113). Massey interprets much of the impetus for restructuring from capital to be 'a response to, and attempt to break, established elements of labor movement organization' (1987:122). However, she points out in the same passage that the cities are far from dead politically, however much they might be losing jobs. The fact of decline, together with their changing social structure, has been a basis for some of them to become the seedbeds of a new kind of politics, based around new coalitions and attempting a restructuring more on labour's terms. In a very interesting discussion of the urban economy of New York City, Sassen-Koob (1983:175–205) makes a similar argument, namely that capital recomposition occurs at the end of a cycle which begins with capital emigration from this urban environment, and a resulting decline of light manufacturing and the office jobs associated with this type of manufacturing. Recomposition of capital in New York city has occurred through two associated processes: first, 'the transnationalization of capital [has] generated a pronounced expansion in the international demand for advanced specialized services', where the 'production of these services is disproportionately concentrated in a few old centers at the core, such as London and New York City' (1983:176); second, there is a new migration to the city of low-cost and unorganised labour from the Caribbean and Asia, and it is these immigrant communities who provide cheap services to the high-income professional workforce and their workplaces, who contribute to 'the survival of declining industries' by providing cheap labour, and who, additionally, undertake low-cost forms of urban renewal in their neighbourhoods (see Sassen-Koob, 1983:198–201).

Massey's and Sassen-Koob's remarks work in different directions. However, they are enough to indicate that, if the global capitalism and new international division of labour perspective is adopted, structural developments do not proceed independently of the agency of those who are constituted in this process as collective actors sharing an interest in influencing the direction and shape of capital recomposition and its relationship to infrastructural investment. It is the case, however, that this perspective appears to underemphasise the role of the state in the development of an active industry policy, where tax incentives for example may be used to induce productive investment and thereby to promote the (re-) development of a region or nation. This tendency may not be surprising given the national economic locations of the exponents of this perspective: the United Kingdom, and the United States, both national polities which under Thatcher and Reagan respectively have deliberately eschewed an explicit, tripartite (as it has to be) industry policy.

The second perspective is offered by the US neomarxist economist David Gordon (1988). He takes issue particularly with the general thrust of the global capitalism perspective which confers on capital investment a fairly unrestricted transnational mobility which is directed primarily by the availability of cheap labour costs. Necessarily, such an emphasis leads to a pessimistic evaluation of the capacity of labour to effectively organise to extract concessions from capital, and it generally maintains the traditional marxist assumption of a zero-sum relationship between the interests of capital and labour.

Gordon argues two general points: first, patterns of investment in the 1980s have been influenced by the relative lack of growth—'decay', as he calls it—in the postwar global economy, a development that needs to be seen in the context of long-term business cycles; second, patterns of transnational capital investment are not determined by the factor of cheap labour costs, and there are indeed more decisive factors which determine the direction and location of capital investment. Since his points provide a salutary corrective to some of the assumptions which govern the global capitalism perspective, let us take these in turn.

Gordon provides data which support his argument that the 'recent shifts of industrial production toward the LDCs [less developed economies] and the NICs [newly industrialised countries] are not particularly large by relevant standards' (1988:37). He continues: 'These recent shifts are not nearly as large as the gains made by the LDCs during the Depression and World War II and have served essentially to recoup the losses in the LDC share which those countries experienced between the late 1940s and the mid-1960s.' All the newly industrialising economies have been affected by the same slow-growth or recession tendencies that have affected the developed market economies, as Gordon terms them.

Gordon emphasises the general state of decline, stasis or no-growth that has been the rule rather than the exception since the collapse of the long post war boom in the advanced capitalist economies. He argues that it is because of the relative stagnant and unstable features of the global economy that there has been a shift away from productive towards short-term financial investment:

> When economic conditions are prosperous and stable, financial capital flows help support and even foster productive investment. But when the economy has become stagnant and unstable, investors tend to move their capital out of productive investments—because of increasingly cloudy longer-term prospects—and into short-term financial investments. The investment climate becomes increasingly speculative. The past fifteen years appear to have illustrated the latter dynamic. As the rate of return on fixed investment in plant and equipment has declined and as global economic conditions have become increasingly volatile, firms and banks have moved toward paper investments. The new and increasingly efficient international banking system has helped to foster an accelerating circulation of liquid capital, bouncing from one moment of arbitrage to another. Far from stimulating produc-

tive investment, however, these financial flows are best understood as a symptom of the diminishing attractiveness and increasing uncertainty about prospects for fixed investment (1988:54–55).

Gordon's second point concerns the determinants of the locations of direct foreign investment. He cites a study which shows that 'the combined importance of the size of the home-market, price/exchange rate stability, and political/institutional stability was fifteen times greater than the influence of relative wage costs and skill levels'. The reasons for this are the following:

> First, in many commodities, labour costs are a relatively small proportion of total costs; proximity to large home markets will matter much more than variations in wage-costs, at the margin, among possible investment sites. Second, particularly in recent years, exchange rates have varied with much greater volatility than wages, so those countries with relatively stable price and trade horizons are much more exceptional than those with relatively low labour costs. Third, and probably, most important, investments in plant and equipment must be amortized over the medium run—say ten years—while larger investments in infrastructure and distribution systems must be recouped over even longer periods. What matters most, for those kinds of investments, is the general institutional climate and its prospective evolution over a decade's time, not simply current unit labour costs (1988:59).

What Gordon glosses and does not explore is the significance of the changed terms of competition between the developed market economies and the shift away from the dominance of two giants (the US and the UK) in the direction of a plurality of strong, competitive economies: 'Between 1960 and 1984, for example, the US and UK share of the total stock of foreign direct investment declined from 65.4 per cent to 53.3 per cent while the share accounted for by Germany, Japan, Switzerland, Canada and Sweden increased from 9.6 per cent to 25.6 per cent in 1981' (Gordon, 1988:42).

The changed terms of competition correspond with two other trends. The first concerns the intensification of the dependence of the developed market economies on international trade: 'Among the OECD countries ... exports as a percentage of GDP increased from 11.8 per cent in 1951 to 18.6 per cent in 1979' (Gordon, 1988:44). The other involves a shift in international trading patterns 'away from a trans-Atlantic to a trans-Pacific pattern of trading specialization': 'Out of total world trade, trans-Atlantic trade fell from 13.1 per cent in 1970 to 8.7 per cent in 1983 while Pacific Basin trade increased from 10.2 per cent in 1970 to 14.2 per cent in 1983' (Gordon, 1988:58).

What these trends suggest is that something besides a relative slump or stagnation in productive investment is going on. There is an important intensification of competition, an increase in the number of competitors, and a shift away from the erstwhile epicentres of capitalist development. In this context, the UK and US literature about global capitalism may be seen as an echo within the circles of the left intelligentsia of the shock which has reverberated through both the UK and US national economies in the wake of lost financial and commercial hegemony. It makes sense that the effects of this shock would be destabilising in an economic sense.

NATION-STATE RESPONSES TO RESTRUCTURING

This global economic context presents both advantages and disadvantages for the Australian national economy. Australia's situation within the economically dynamic Pacific Basin is a decided advantage. However, it shares in the disadvantages of what become evident in this context as an historical overreliance on the export of commodities and an overprotected manufacturing sector (see Ergas and Lee, 1988). While Australian foreign debt is not 'of the crisis proportions of indebted developing countries' (Australian Council for Overseas Aid, 1987:28), alongside the relative undevelopment of a competitive manufacturing sector and the continuing reliance on commodity exports, it is enough to require careful government management. However, it is worth noting that most of the Australian foreign debt (about 75 per cent) is private and is not subject to government management, in contrast to Latin American and African foreign debt which is mostly sovereign debt.

There is a further advantage which the Australian national economy enjoys, and this is an historical association with statecentric modes of national economic management. Why, however, is this an advantage?

State-led national economic management is a crucial variable which influences the location and shape of productive investment and capital flows (see Evans, 1985; Katzenstein, 1985). This is one of the critical variables in determining patterns of multinational investment mentioned by Gordon (1988:60–61, 63–64). Increased competition among multinationals may have increased the leverage of national governments in relation to them, although increased competition between nation-states for multinational capital investment is likely to offset this leverage in the other direction. Political stability and the delivery by governments of infrastructural supports, labour skilling and various institutional supports are very important in attracting multinational investment:

... what seems especially striking about the NICs [newly industrialising countries like Taiwan, South Korea and Singapore] is the increasingly political and institutional determinations of production and trading relationships. TNCs [transnational corporations] negotiate with each other and host countries for joint production agreements, licensing, and joint R & D contracts. They search among potential investment sites for institutional harbours promising the safest havens against an increasingly turbulent world economy (Gordon, 1988:56).

There have been generally four different categories of nation-state response to the challenges of increased global economic competition (see Reich, 1983:25–32, from whom I have adapted this classification). There are first the responses of the nation-states like the US which have sought to block change by resort to various measures of protectionism (see Reich, 1983:29–30). This has been accompanied by an ostrich-like head-in-sand *insouciance* in relation to the changed terms of competition, indicated, among other things, in an uncontrolled rising public deficit fuelled by tax cuts introduced by the Reagan administration in 1981. Second, there is the response of nation-states like the UK, which under Thatcher has combined privileged access to the protectionism of the European Common Market, and to the foreign earnings of North Sea oil, with a *laissez faire* encouragement of market competition within the national economy at the expense of asserting the obligations of capital to the national community with which it is symbiotically entwined. Third, newly industrialising nation-states like Singapore, Taiwan and South Korea—not to mention the exemplary newly industrialised Japan—have pursued top-down institutional change which has provided a favourable climate for productive investment, and effective trade competition (for Taiwan, see Amsden, 1985). As Reich (1983:30) remarks about these cases, 'Rapid industrial change ... is relatively easy to achieve when the leaders who plan it have no serious worries about [the claims by interest groups and social movements on] politics, when economic planning is made by stable elites who simply need not take account of how the burdens of economic change are borne by the less advantaged'. The fourth response is a social democratic response, where a democratically oriented tripartite and state-led approach is undertaken to modernise industry and labour in order to make the national economy more competitive. This response is associated especially with Sweden, but it is also evident in the other Scandinavian state-societies, Austria, and to some extent, West Germany.

This classification of nation-state responses to the challenges of increased global economic competition is not definitive. It refers only to the range of nation-states which have sufficient command over resources to enjoy some leverage in attracting capital investment to promote their economic growth. Nonetheless, such a classification makes the point that is the one to emphasise in this context, namely, that where a national economy is already industrialised and integrated with developed markets, there is a mutual symbiosis between the state and capital investment, and accordingly the determinants of investment patterns rely heavily on political-sociological variables. It is states and their institutions which determine the specificity of how capital, labour and property markets within their jurisdictions operate. While states have become more rather than less involved in macroeconomic policy, it is increasingly the case that they are becoming involved also in microeconomic policy areas which cover the development of specific strategies for industry restructuring and processes of bargaining with particular firms over production and investment agreements.

It is important to appreciate that a stable political environment and intelligent state planning are crucial features in establishing an attractive investment environment. Accordingly, where this stable political environment is informed by the democratic expectations of citizens, while it is true that these democratic expectations require economic development to be answerable to redistributive requirements of social justice and to civilised standards of health, work and consumption, this may attract rather than deter capital investment in search of a safe, stable investment context.

The revival of economic liberalism as a metapolicy framework has very little to do with investors seeking a return on their capital. Its contemporary success is owed to a cluster of conditions which work together to favour the relevance of the invocation of free (deregulated) markets. These are: 1. the persistence of clumsy and insensitive state bureaucratic practices and taxes which obstruct and even discourage entrepreneurial risk-taking, and which tend to make productive forms of investment less attractive than short-term speculative forms of investment; 2. an enduring and inevitable tension between the claims of regulation and public accountability on the one hand, and those of freedom of initiative on the other; 3. the renewed salience of markets and of market-oriented activity which has followed in the wake of the development of a decentred and more competitive global market economy; 4. the failure of centrally planned economies, and their current efforts to reintroduce a market principle or to introduce some form of entrepreneurship within state-owned enterprise; 5. the exploitation of these developments by the parties or ideologues who are identified symbolically with the claims of the market as opposed to the claims of the state.

Just how out of step these ideological and politically motivated invocations of the freedom of the market may be with empirical developments is illustrated by a newspaper article which discusses the increasing activity of the South Australian (Labor-led) state in raising venture capital and in seeking to find equity partners for undercapitalised, innovative companies. In this article, (*The Advertiser* 21 September 1988:21) the following paragraph appears: 'The SA Chamber of Commerce has not objected to the moves, although its economist, Mr Rod Nettle, says that philosophically it is opposed to any government intervention in the marketplace.' At the same time it would be unwise to ignore the exploitation of the renewal of economic liberalism for political capital by genuine ideologues on behalf of those who seek to enjoy and to enhance their class position unfettered by the claims of those with whom they are placed in a series of complex interdependencies. There are proto-fascist ideologues who oppose justice in the name of deregulation and who seek to disestablish all aspects of state activity which represent the accountability of capital to public standards of occupational health and safety, and of what it means to live in a civilised community. However, it is important to understand that while such an ideologue and a capital investor may come together as apparently congruent *personae* of the same individual, the logic of developing this kind of proto-fascist political ideology and of seeking a return on capital are quite different.

This is an important point to understand for those who are committed to the development of a social democratic type of state response to the current challenges of restructuring. If they are to make this response viable, they need to understand the current practicalities of capital investment and to make state modes of intervention those which facilitate productive capital investment. In Australia it is likely that the development of public entrepreneurs, i.e. entrepreneurs of commercialising activities within the public sector, will provide a critical learning experience for the state by making its personnel aware of the kinds of regulative frameworks and infrastructural supports which facilitate rather than hinder entrepreneurial activity.

AUSTRALIAN PUBLIC POLICY AND THE ETHOS OF RESTRUCTURING

The Labor-led administrations of the Australian federal state and of the States of South Australia, Victoria and Western Australia are contributing to what may be loosely described as a social democratic type of state response to increased global economic competition and the ensuing challenges of restructuring. The question I want to return to here is whether their response is social democratic enough.

I suggested above that economic enterprise depends on an ethos which motivates this activity. This ethos has cultural and normative features. The former concern how the world is portrayed so as to make economic enterprise appear a sensible response to a plenitude of opportunities for creative entrepreneurial initiative. This portrayal is often one of 'new' opportunities, suggestive of entirely new contexts of activity and initiative which no one (yet) has thought of exploiting. The normative features concern how this enterprise is made to appear worthwhile, worthy, of value, not just to the entrepreneur but to those who work with the entrepreneur and who buy her products or services. If the entrepreneur is to seize and exploit new opportunities, the success of her endeavours will depend on them being regarded as relevant to the needs of others with whom she is placed in relationships of interdependence. When this shared relevance is strong, there is a moral community shared between entrepreneur, those working with her, and their customers. It is this moral community which constitutes much of the inspiration for the entrepreneur's creative efforts, which are indicated in exciting modes of problem-solving pragmatism.

Naturally, my use of the feminine personal pronoun to refer to the entrepreneur is intended to jar the Australian sense of reality, and to problematise features of current Australian response to the challenges of restructuring. Let us return to one of the advantages which Australia enjoys in relation to these challenges: its location in the Pacific Basin. But how can Australian society realise this advantage unless it embarks on the kind of cultural learning it needs to do to understand that a white, male character of the type that Crocodile Dundee portrays is not the modal type of human being? And who within Australia is likely to lead this process of learning? Surely not those who inherit this identity through privilege of gender, race and ethnicity, but those who do not.

There is some evidence, as indicated above, that the Australian Labor-led governments have some awareness of this. However, since they comprise the (albeit overeducated) inheritors of the white, Anglo, masculine legend of Australian justice ('mateship'), their awareness is blocked by their entrapment within this legend and its ritual invocations.

This point has been made by Frank Castles, in his recent book *Australian Public Policy and Economic Vulnerability* (1988). He adopts Ibsen's metaphor of 'ghosts' to indicate that the long-established and unique institutions of what he calls the Australian state 'politics of domestic defense' haunt the current policy options and tend to skew them in the direction of conservation of these past practices. The institutional complex he identifies comprise the following: 1. a tradition of protection of manufacturing industry through tariffs and other trade restrictions; 2. the centralised state wage-fixing institution of Conciliation and Arbitration which ensures the provision of a living wage to those who fall under its jurisdiction, namely organised wage-workers, whose advocacy in this arena comes from their centralised union structure, the Australian Council of Trade Unions; 3. the control of immigration so as to ensure that organised labour is not undercut in its bargaining power in relation to conditions and wages; 4. a residual system of income maintenance for those who fall outside the labour market (1988:91–93). As Castles argues (here, and in his previous book, 1985), the political trade-off between protectionists and labour which is expressed in this complex of institutions was established at the end of last century.

In both books Castles argues that this trade-off had the consequence of making Australia a relatively backward society as far as the provision of welfare and social services goes. Since the wage settlement was originally a 'family wage' settlement, it was the amount of the wage which was to afford individual workers the private capacity to maintain the welfare of those dependent on them, women and children. Later, it became possible to legitimise a progressive taxation system, including the taxation of wage-incomes, in return for the introduction of widow pensions (1942), and unemployment, sickness and special dependency benefits in 1944 (see also Watts, 1987:chs 2, 3, 4). However these services were conceived in a strictly residualist way, and were intended to complement rather than to compromise the principle of private need provision. Castles' analysis cannot be bettered:

> Like the liberal corporatist countries, with which it has in common both early industrialisation and a strong liberal tradition, Australia's philosophy of compensation was directed to the individual, whether through wages—what I have called elsewhere the 'wage-earner's welfare state'—or through transfer payments. Like the social corporatist countries [such as Sweden], with which it has in common the fact that the historic compromise was shaped in a context where the political arm of the labour movement was at the point of achieving dominance, Australia's strategy of social protection took a *statist* form in the sense that domestic defence or compensation was effected by state agency, whether through regulatory control to make individuals conform to rules embodying the 'general interest'—the Arbitration Court, the tariff board, etc.—or public intervention to create organs of collective consumption. The circumstances and timing of Australia's historical compromise made for a strategy of social protection which was both *statist and private*, the seeming contradiction between the two being underwritten by the utilitarianism which legitimated state action for the population as a whole (1988:129, emphases in the original).

It is not the centralised wage system that is regarded as problematic from the point of view of the reproduction of inequalities in Australian society. As the National Pay Equity Coalition Submission to the 1988 National Wage Case (1988:4) argues, 'A centralised wage system should apply, since industry and enterprise bargaining disadvantages less well organised and less industrially powerful groups'. The problematic features concern the trade-off of wage-earner welfare against the development of services and structures of collective consumption which materially and symbolically underwrite what T.H. Marshall (1977) termed 'social citizenship'.

The effect of this tradition of privately oriented corporatism has been the absence of an Australian discourse of citizenship. The discourse of citizenship is an inclusive one, which when extended to welfare, tends to favour universal services which express the shared community of citizenship to which individuals belong. The labour movement has never been willing to support such services through taxation.

Indeed, under pressure from its trade union constituency the Hawke Labor Government promised tax *cuts* in 1989. It is clear that tax cuts can only be accompanied by even stricter forms of selective targeting of the beneficiaries of publicly funded income maintenance. Under current policies, income support is tied increasingly to an active labour market policy, where there will be strong encouragement, if not some form of coercion, operating to get income support beneficiaries into either employment, education or training. This could be a desirable step in the direction of developing a labour market structured by the claims of citizenship. However, it is hard to imagine that effective structures of an active labour market policy can be developed under the public funding conditions of tax cuts, and of an undeveloped public system of needs provision. It is also hard to imagine that individuals who are subject to the 'poor law' features of our public income support system are likely to identify their life chances with access to mainstream institutions of employment, education and training.

The mainstream masculinist structures of union awards and the structures of either public income maintenance at poor-law rates or non-unionised, part-time and casual labour markets together constitute a dual structuring of Australian society. This duality is very pervasive, as two examples may indicate. First, a standard form of acknowledgment of need to do something about the legacy of the historical exclusion of women from unionised labour markets, and awards, is the proposition that, with the support of equal opportunity and anti-discrimination legislation, women must be encouraged to enter these 'non-traditional' areas of training and employment. Necessarily this entry is predicated on an exceptionalism which maintains the segmentation of the labour market. Second, when there is acknowledgment of the importance of integrating Australians of non-English-speaking background—estimated at about 20 per cent of the Australian population (see Jupp, 1986:41–42)—into mainstream structures of Australian society, this is done usually in the spirit of lumping them in with 'special needs' groups. This is what occurs with publicly funded childcare centres (see Yeatman, 1988c:55–56), and it maintains the binary classification of those who stand for the (English-speaking-background) norm and those who do not.

The majority of Australians lie outside the traditional Labor institutions. These institutions cannot provide the basis for the resources of citizenship and moral community that Australians need to share if they are to produce creative responses to restructuring that are effective over the medium to long terms.

Nor is it likely that these institutions can provide the kinds of vision and leadership which are necessary to reframe Australia's relationship to its Pacific Basin environment. Another ghost which lurks is the labour movement's 'White Australia' policy which lasted until the early 1970s, and which is indicated in the current policy which confers access to citizenship in the white Australian community if the non-white in question has the capital or skills deemed as effective surrogates of a white skin. This sense of conferral of privilege is marked in the recent Fitzgerald report, *Immigration: A Commitment to Australia* (1988:12): 'As worldwide competition to immigrate to Australia increases, becoming Australian should be seen as the final achievement of a challenging process.'

Productive investment, as distinct from speculative investment, is difficult to encourage unless there are fairly long-term ties of mutual dependency between investors and the communities in which these investments are to be located. Such long-term ties are creatures of the development of a shared vision of where an economy is heading and who it includes. There are many in Australia who are ready to build this shared vision, one that will require intercultural exchange and learning with the other societies in the Pacific Basin region. Whether their entrepreneurship can combine to bring about the development and restructuring of the Australian economy depends on whether social democrats in Australia can mediate their Labourist heritage and commit themselves to a universal culture of citizenship, supported by a more developed system of providing public needs and by a developed system of intercultural exchange with other societies in the Pacific Basin. It is not likely that they will do this independently of the struggles of those who are excluded from the Labourist heritage.

As will be clear, the task of restructuring is a new one for Australian society, demanding cultural innovation and moral development. Here I am in agreement with Kevin McDonald's (1988:43) argument that 'new patterns of economic development will not be the result of technical improvements to economic development, but will result from public life being renewed by new social conflicts and social movements'. McDonald's argument that investment is not an economic variable but 'a social project' influenced the exploration of a sociology of investment that I have offered in this chapter. McDonald's argument suggests that the current 'decline in investment is not a matter of economic technique' but a 'decline of a form of social organisation', a decline precisely of the polarised politics of energies of a two-class capitalist/worker system.

7 Feminism and the 'crisis' of the welfare state

There is now a considerable literature on the 'crisis' of the welfare state. Most of this literature is non-feminist in orientation. At the same time feminist analyses of the welfare state have tended to neglect this 'crisis' as an object for analysis, or at least to subsume it within what they consider to be the normal workings of the welfare state. It is not that feminist analyses overlook the empirical referents of this so-called crisis, for example, cutbacks in public expenditures leading to a decline in publicly provided services, which means an absolute decline in the overall level of services and the reprivatisation through the commodification of some of these erstwhile public services; the increasing impoverishment of women who are sole supporting parents with their children; and the reprivatisation of caring activities by requiring a good deal more of family-based care in supporting and caring for the sick, the aged and the young. Rather feminist analyses tend to consider these phenomena without necessarily regarding them as symptoms of a crisis.

In this chapter I want to consider why this is so. I want to inquire whether the diffidence of feminism towards the 'crisis' of the welfare state can be justified and whether in addition it indicates a fundamental ambivalence towards the welfare state which precludes clear direction for analysis and political action.

THE CRISIS OF THE WELFARE STATE

The concept of the crisis of the welfare state can be misleading. To the extent that the welfare state represents the administrative and fiscal management by the state of needs arising out of lack of direct access to market-related incomes—the needs of those who are unemployed, sick, disabled, old, etc.—there is no doubt about the need for this type of management.

If there is fundamental dispute about how this management is best done and how far it should go, there is no dispute between most neoconservatives, modern liberals, social democrats and, it is necessary to add, feminists, regarding the functional necessity of such providing for people's needs through the state in modern capitalist societies. How then is it possible to speak of the crisis of the welfare state? The crisis concerns the *ideal* of a welfare state. This ideal has two features: 1. the idea that a safety net must be provided so that individuals are not forced by want into legal or illegal market activities which deny their humanity and status as persons; 2. the idea that those constituting a national polity have a communal responsibility for all who belong to that polity, and that this responsibility is to be expressed in, among other things, a progressive system of taxation which funds the provision of public services which all who belong to that society may enjoy. The ideal may be more or less elaborated: it can be expressed in minimalist and maximalist ways. Most of the so-called welfare state societies had by the end of the Second World War committed themselves to the minimalist dimension. This comprised such things as labour legislation regulating hours and safety, the development of a public infrastructure of municipal services like roads, sewerage, water, lighting, libraries, and parks, and the provision of public education ranging from primary schools to tertiary institutions. Anyone who has watched the deterioration of the municipal infrastructure of cities like New York City and London over the last decade is aware that this minimalist dimension is no longer a safe object of public commitment.

Logue's (1979) concept of the welfare state expresses what used to be the most widely distributed and minimalist ideal of the welfare state. We may term this the safety-net ideal. He constitutes the welfare state and why it came into existence as follows:

> Empirical studies before and after the First World War indicated that the principal cause of poverty was loss of employment income. The primary focus of the welfare state has been the provision of income security measures to protect the living standards of those forced out of employment temporarily by sickness or by unemployment, or permanently by age or disability. A major secondary cause of poverty was found to be the poor 'fit' between employment income and family size, and steps were taken to improve the position of those with large families and small incomes through family allowances, housing subsidies, subsidized day care, and similar measures. Some services, most notably medical care and education, are provided outside the market on the basis of need to the particular benefit of the economically worst off. The weakest members of society—the elderly, the handicapped, and children—are the beneficiaries of a range of special measures; in fact the level of aid to the weak has become a new norm for evaluating the conduct of the state. (1979:71)

As Logue and Mishra (1984:7–8) reminds us, the welfare state is a principle of need provision which *complements* the market principle of need provision. It does not 'attempt to tamper with distribution of income *inside* the market' (Logue, 1979:71, emphasis in the original). Rather it represents a principle of need provision for those who cannot meet their needs through market activity either because this activity does not afford a subsistence income or because they cannot get access to market modes of distribution of goods and services. The acknowledgment of the necessity for a complementary statist principle of need provision represented historically a 'genuine reformation of liberal capitalism' (Mishra, 1984:8).

The complementary character of welfare state provision has ensured that the relativities of the distribution of wealth have remained unaltered. As Mishra (1984:23) remarks, this became evident in the 1960s when the 'rediscovery' of poverty led to renewed scrutiny of this distribution: social welfare, it turned out, 'was a system of horizontal redistribution which involved intra-class rather than inter-class transfers'. Typically, these are transfers from those who are earning to those who are not, from those without children to those with children, and from those who are healthy to those who are sick or disabled. However, it is necessary to point out that if the relativities of the distribution of wealth have been left fairly undisturbed, this has not precluded significant redistributive effects.

At present, it is not only the maximalist dimensions of the welfare state ideal which are under attack. The maximalist dimensions are bound up with the social democratic ideal of citizenship. This ideal requires public modes of need provision not only to pick up on individual needs which have been left unmet by market modes of provision but also to extend the cultural capacities and collective services of all considered as a community of citizens. The safety net dimension of this ideal is also under attack by, in particular, neoconservatives who have revived the ideology of *laissez faire* liberalism. These concede that there must be a safety net of some kind, but they seek to restrict its scope, especially where it allegedly interferes with the workings of the market. Theirs is a radically selective and residual safety net, which becomes in effect the less than adequate protection of a new underclass. This underclass is defined by these conditions of state-sponsored dependency and is sharply distinguished in the lack of choice which follows on this dependency from the classes who can enjoy the freedoms of the market activities of capital speculation and investment, consumption, and work.

As we are discovering at the moment, there is nothing in the acknowledgment of a statist principle of need provision per se which necessarily takes us beyond old poor-law principles of community-based need provision. Such provision may be directed only to those who possess what is regarded as genuine need in such a way as to ensure that they have access to a bare minimum, while at the same time universally accessible services are either withdrawn or run down, and there are sustained efforts to preclude welfare fraud and cheating. The current rationing of social services and cash transfers, the increased restrictiveness of criteria of eligibility to receive these, and increased surveillance and control of potential cheats, all indicate that the concepts of the 'deserving poor' and 'undeserving poor' are back with us. Neoconservatives and New Right ideologies have introduced the concept of 'genuine poverty', thereby carving out a field of non-genuine poverty.

The neoconservative advocacy of a retreat from the welfare state takes the form of advocating a more restrictive safety net. Neoconservatives raise fundamental questions about statist modes of providing for need when the modern state itself has become complex, bureaucratised, all-pervasive and monolithic. However, since it counterposes to state provision the classical liberal principle of market provision, the neoconservative 'small-government' discourse has to reinvoke a residual, compassionate and efficient statist principle of need provision. Thus, in an article which presciently foreshadows all the revisions of the welfare and social security systems by the Hawke Labor Government since the 1987 May Economic Statement, Hendrie and Porter, from the neoconservative Centre of Policy Studies, talk of the necessity for 'equity, efficiency and targeting' in the provision of welfare. They argue:

> While we consider that social security expenditure should be targeted (thus minimising the efficiency costs of providing income support), we do not advocate a rolling back of the safety net provided by pensions and benefits. Given the compromise to be made between equity and efficiency we suggest that welfare policies should be designed to provide:
> • adequate support for those unable to provide for themselves;
> • little or no help to those who can have access to other means of earning income, or can engage in training;
> • strong incentives to become self-supporting, helped by matching labour market reforms.

Accordingly, they advocate an end to unemployment benefits for sixteen- and seventeen-year-olds because this benefit 'allows for the payment of benefits to unemployed recipients who live at home and whose family has considerable means' (1987:25), and argue for a deregulation of youth wages because 'artificial wage awards' 'place obstacles in the way of youth employment' (1987:26). The more inclusive safety net that has existed is to be privatised in two directions: to deregulate in favour of market activity, and to withdraw public need provision in favour of private familial provision.

It is noteworthy that, while the neoconservatives talk of small government, they do not question the basic division of labour between the market, the state and the family which structures the whole framework of modern, masculinist theories of society. Essentially they claim that activities best left to the market or the family have been inappropriately taken over by the state. This has happened either because interest groups have captured parts of the state and used its power to give them services or goods which they did not really need (the problem of 'middle-class welfare') or because the functionaries of the state itself have sought to extend their sphere of influence by extending the scope and reach of the state (see Hendrie and Porter, 1987; Antcliff, 1988). Overprovision by the state have allowed 'families' to shirk their responsibilities:

> Single parenthood, widowhood, divorce and separation represent changes in family composition which can change significantly the economic status of families. In the absence of adequate support by non-custodial parents, cash transfers during these crisis periods are an important function of social security and assist families while adjusting to changed circumstances. Nevertheless, it must be acknowledged that at present taxpayers are meeting much of the cost of caring for other people's children. Public provision of income transfers ultimately has the effect of reducing individual responsibility for maintaining family income (Hendrie and Porter, 1987:27).

The neoconservative critique represents an attempt to restore liberal capitalism, unfettered by the ideal of the welfare state. It neither questions the structure of domination inherent in the modern division of labour between market, state and family (see Yeatman, 1988a; Olsen, 1983) nor finds state definition of needs problematic when these are accepted as requiring extramarket provision.

The neoconservative approach to the welfare state, however, has radical consequences if it both informs the policy agendas and determines the ideology of the government. Both the Reagan and Thatcher governments have revised the safety-net concept of the welfare state by refusing to accept the principle established in the New Deal and Beveridge welfare state: that every individual is to be guaranteed a minimum level of security so that they are protected against the capriciousness of market forces, and are not forced into forms of earning a crust which may not provide an acceptable level of subsistence by modern standards and which may place them at risk of relationships which contravene modern values of individual freedom and equality: e.g. begging, unofficial forms of labour which not only lie beyond the reach of taxation but also beyond minimal standards of occupational safety and employer decency. By setting up a distinction between the genuine and non-genuine poor, and by insisting that the latter are those who choose not to work and that there should be no social security or welfare incentives which encourage them out of the labour market, both the Thatcher and Reagan administrations have rolled back the welfare state (see Krieger, 1987; and Block, Cloward, Ehrenreich and Piven, 1987). Thus, for example, one Thatcher initiative has been to disqualify striking workers or those locked out as a result of a trade dispute 'from both unemployment and supplementary allowance or pension (unless they demonstrate non-participation or no direct interest in the dispute or their unemployment follows from the loss of some bona fide source of employment secured after the stoppage began)':

> A spouse or unmarried partner of a striker is assessed for benefit as a single householder. Although the requirements of the striker are thereby ignored, the striker's union strike benefits are treated as income to be taken into account in the usual way in reducing benefits for the other members of the household unit. Moreover a set amount (£17 weekly from November 1985) is deducted *even if no union strike benefits or other income is actually received*. (Krieger, 1987:184, emphasis in the original)

The Reagan administration has not challenged the contributory and universal social security system, but has cut the means-tested programs for individuals with no (or insufficient) contributory coverage (see Krieger, 1987: 188–91). Krieger (1987:189–90) argues that the decline in the real value of the benefits concerned (Aid to Families with Dependent Children, Medicaid, Supplementary Security Income, food stamps, etc.) was a trend established during the 1970s, and that in this respect the Reagan policies have not been particularly radical. Indeed, 'the average annual decline of $13 per month payment during the early Reagan years represents in fact only a very small increase (of roughly fifty-cents per month on average) over the pattern of decline in the real value of household AFDC and food stamp benefits during the decade of the 1970s'. The radical features of the Reagan Administration's attack on the welfare state reside in the sustained and effective efforts to pare down the welfare rolls and to force AFDC recipients into forced work programs (workfare). Block, Cloward, Ehrenreich and Piven (1987) make a convincing case that the intent behind all this is to reduce the bargaining power of labour in relation to capital by developing a labour market on terms favourable to capital. They state:

> ... the business community ... has launched a broad attack on working-class standards of living, including intensified union-

busting, demands for concessions in wages and benefits, and the imposition of a greater tax burden on the poor and the middle class relative to the rich. At the same time, business has accelerated the decline of American industry by recklessly diverting capital away from productive investments and into financial speculation. As a result, the class contours of American society have begun to change for the first time in the post-world war era: the affluent control a greater share of wealth and income than ever before; the poor are becoming both poorer and more numerous; and the middle class, faced with stagnating wages and diminishing middle-income employment, is shrinking. (1987:xii)

The crisis of the welfare state has several dimensions, and they cannot be reduced to the single factor of such an attack by the business community on working-class standards of living. However, there can be little doubt that increasing doubts in many quarters about the efficiency and wisdom of bureaucratised, statist need provision has helped to create a legitimate ideological space for this business-class response. This has occurred in Australia as elsewhere.

Femininist critiques begin to problematise the division of labour between family, state and market by bringing out the gender politics of this division and the gender politics of the substitutability of one domain for another. It is not clear that this problematising goes all that far since, as we shall see, and for good reasons, feminists tend to privilege the public principle of need provision in relation to private, especially familial, types of need provision. Here, since public need provision has become conflated with statist need provision, feminist approaches to the welfare state form a mirror-image to neoconservative approaches. Where the latter tend to invoke the freedom and private discretion of markets and families, the former tend to invoke the positive construction and sanctioning of rights by the state (see Yeatman, 1988b). To the extent that this is so, feminist critiques of the welfare state are a good deal less concerned with issues arising out of the increasing size and complexity of the state.

There is then wide agreement about the functional necessity of the complementary principle of state provision of needs. The debate begins in the concern as to how far this principle should be developed. The crisis in the welfare state is, as Mishra (1984) puts it, a crisis of the *legitimation* of the welfare state. As we have seen, the postwar consensus on the safety-net function of the welfare state has broken down to the extent that neoconservatives propose the withdrawal of this safety net for those who are able to work but who for some reason 'choose' not to, especially if they can rely on the alternative income provided by such things as sole supporting parent benefits or (as it was before the Australian 1987 May Economic Statement) an unemployment benefit for sixteen- and seventeen-year-olds. At the same time there has been a greater withdrawal of commitment from the social democratic conception of the welfare state as a civilised state in terms of criteria of justice, freedom and equality. Social democrats themselves, at least those who have inherited the traditions of modern social democracy within Labor parties, have proved to be a weak and divided defender of this conception. The social democratic approach to the welfare state is best encapsulated in the idea of 'social citizenship'. Here the welfare state is seen as the vehicle of the extension of social citizenship to all individuals who belong to the society concerned. This means that not only do they all have access to a basic minimum of civilised living, which is guaranteed by the public provision of universal services, but that this access ensures that each individual enjoys an *equality of status* with every other. T.H. Marshall (1977) is the theoretical exponent of this concept of equality of status.

Marshall argued that social citizenship did not mean or require the overcoming of class or income inequalities. These would remain. What social citizenship meant was the extension *via* the state of social forms of needs provision so that all members of the society had access to the same substance of civilised living, namely 'a general reduction of risk and insecurity, an equalisation between the more and less fortunate at all levels—between the healthy and the sick, the employed and the unemployed, the old and the active, the bachelor and the father of a large family' (Marshall, 1977:113). This would bring an equality of status, predicated on full membership of the same citizen community. Equality between citizens could thus be juxtaposed with inequality between members of different market-income classes.

As Castles (1978:72–73) argues, the idea of social citizenship permits a clear distinction to be made between provision through *social security* and that through the *welfare state*. The former provides the 'safety net' for market activity. Such a safety net is expressed either in a contributory social security system as in the United States or in a taxation-funded social security system as in Australia. There are no egalitarian messages positively embedded in the safety-net conception, or, to put it another way, it may be a condition of the conception of social citizenship, but there is no need for it to be elaborated. As Castles (1978:68–72) shows, high percentages of GNP devoted to social security expenditure are not necessarily correlated with high expenditures on welfare where indices of welfare expenditure are taken to be current revenue of general government as a percentage of the GNP, public spending on education as a percentage of the GNP, and deaths in first year per thousand of live births.

Social democratic welfare state provision tends to favour universal rather than social services, and to use taxation as well as contributory principles to fund this provision. The tendency towards universal modes of provision—a high-quality and universally accessible public education system for example—arises out of the orientation to equality of status. Needs are equal with respect to an equality of status shared by all individual citizens. Accordingly, there must be a universal sharing in the funding for the provision of these needs (hence a developed taxation system) and universally accessible services which sustain and uphold this equality of status. Education and health are viewed as two fundamental goods which are to be distributed as equally as possible, particularly because they are construed as essential conditions of the self-determination which equality of status fosters.

It is clear that this idea of equality of status is fundamentally opposed to all aristocratic, racist and class ideologies. Such ideologies draw their force from the idea that people live differently because they are different in their needs, capacities and tastes. Accordingly there should be no interference with how these differences become expressed in different modes of access to, and in different degrees and types of, need provision. At least there should be no interference up to the point of requiring a safety net. Class ideologies are logically expressed in the combination of individual, market-oriented preferences (the user-pays principle) and specially directed services (the safety net for the deserving poor).

The crisis of the welfare state concerns the crisis of this social democratic 'image of society' (Castles, 1978:96–97). Castles argues that this image has been elaborated to become the 'image of society purveyed through the agencies of political socialization' only in Scandinavia where the 'dominant political class' is the Social Democratic party. The Scandinavian welfare states, however, are subject to the same structural strains as are occurring elsewhere, namely: 1. an increasing dependency ratio as a consequence of an increasingly ageing population, increasing numbers of female-headed households, and, (to a lesser extent than in the US, Britain and Australia) increasing unemployment; 2. the impact of worldwide recession on economic growth; 3. public deficits and negative trade balances; 4. increasing political strains following from the intensification of state-centric mechanisms of decision-making and resource distribution. The result of these structural strains has been 'cutbacks and restrictions in the welfare programmes' in all the Scandinavian countries (see Marklund, 1988). However, it is still the case that the social democratic image of society has largely survived there and that these state-societies have handled the structural strains of the welfare state in ways largely consistent with that image.

It may be true that equality of status has been actualised to any degree in very few of the welfare state-societies. It is important to acknowledge that the discourse of social citizenship, while often subjugated to the class-bound *noblesse oblige* of the safety-net idea, became an important discourse in the 1960s. The normative orientation to citizenship became a focal point for a number of important social movements—the civil rights movement in the USA, and the women's movement—while national struggles for liberation in Vietnam and elsewhere were assimilated to the rhetoric of citizenship and self-determination. In this context the actual welfare state structures in the US, UK, Australia and elsewhere were measured and found wanting. The upshot was an extraordinary elaboration of the discourse of social citizenship in ideas like 'the war on poverty', 'Headstart' (a program designed to provide specially designed educational stimulus within a multiracial mode to poor black children, and which became embedded in the curriculum of 'Sesame Street'), and a variety of seeds of what later became known as equal opportunity and affirmative action programs.

At the same time ideas of self-determination and participative modes of decision-making and social organisation were also being elaborated. They were not entirely new but this time they had new cadences. Self-determination was now an idea informed by the concept of self, a notion indicating the uniqueness of each individual and the importance of him or her authorising his or her needs and identity. Participative modes of decision-making became not only a point of normative rejection of most centralised liberal democratic structures of authority (e.g. the party machines and the way in which they controlled political debates and dialogue) but of the centralist and Stalinist components of the socialist and communist political traditions.

Democratic theory itself was recast. Pateman (1970:1) began what was then a definitive treatment in *Participation and Democratic Theory* by remarking, 'It is rather ironical that the idea of participation should have become so popular, particularly with students, for among political theorists and political sociologists the widely accepted theory of democracy (so widely accepted that one might call it the orthodox doctrine) is one in which the concept of participation has only the most minimal role'. The retreat from a participatory to an elitist theory of democracy was elegantly expressed in Schumpeter's 'realist' construction of democracy: 'That institutional arrangement for arriving at political decisions in which individuals acquire the power to decide by means of a competitive struggle for the people's vote' (quoted by Pateman, 1970:4). Schumpeter's version of democracy is one which emphasises private, self-interested motives: 'Schumpeter compared the political competition for votes to the operation of the (economic) market; votes like consumers choose between the policies (products) offered by competing political entrepreneurs and the parties regulate the competition like trade associations in the economic sphere.' Citizenship is replaced by a political version of the rational economic activity of individuals. Schumpeter thus anticipated the public-choice theories which became popular in the 1970s and 1980s.

The renewal and development of a participatory democratic discourse in the 1960s carried over into the proliferation of the 'new social movements' in the 1970s. Various arms of the women's movement, an ecological movement, a peace movement, and the increasing presence in progressive politics of ethnic and racial plurality, all combined to represent challenges to stable structures of party competition and compromise. The challenges were not direct. The real challenge lay in the way in which the new social movements could not be contained within these established structures of political control where the party in power together with the peak bodies of employers and unions managed the political agendas of the welfare state societies.

The response to this challenge has been a fundamental shift away from the language of citizenship at large, and away from the language and claims of social citizenship in particular. While the structural strains attendant on publicly funded welfare and collective services have become evident in all the welfare state societies over the last decade, different welfare state traditions have led the societies concerned to respond to these strains in different ways (see Castles, 1987; Marklund, 1988). Where the ethos of social citizenship had only a slender hold on the administrative culture and political management of a particular welfare state, the easier the scuttling of this orientation to welfare claims could be. It is perhaps not surprising that in these state-societies where strongly marked race and class ideologies and ensuing race and class segregation are established, the disestablishment of the claims of social citizenship was systematic and deliberate. I refer of course to the Reagan and Thatcher administrations (for the Reagan Government, see Piven and Cloward, 1982; Block, Cloward, Ehrenreich and Piven, 1987; for discussions of the Thatcher Government, see Wilson, 1987; Schwartz, 1987; for comparison of both governments, see Krieger, 1987).

Indeed Krieger (1987) takes the case of these administrations as evidence against generalising from Offe's influential 'compatibility' thesis of the welfare state. Offe (1984) argues that the distinctive identity of the modern state resides in its role in steering the contradictions and tensions between two necessary claims on it: the claims of the working class for incorporation into the structures of citizenship; and the claims of the capitalist accumulation process for support by the state. Offe argues that the task of the welfare state is to make these two distinct and often conflicting agendas compatible.

Krieger (1987:178–79) argues that the Thatcher and Reagan governments present evidence of welfare states where the policy agendas seem to have been shaped by the inverse of the 'compatibility' problem. These 'social policy agendas have become part of broader state efforts to exacerbate and strategically manipulate *incompatibilities* between previously sanctioned demands by working class and underclass constituencies and the perceived exigencies of budgetary, financial and labour market policies'. The thrust of this argument is the proposition that the compatibility problem frames the social policy agendas only when there is an enduring tradition of welfarist-egalitarianism.

In two respects the new social movements have contributed to the crisis of the welfare state ideal. First, their participative conceptions of democracy have helped to discredit the bureaucratised, statist modes of delivering the services of the welfare state. Second, precisely because they were not containable within the institutions of compromise between the political claims of labour and capital, they implied that these institutions could not be the basis of a culture of common citizenship. In different ways both the social democratic defenders of the welfare state ideal and its liberal critics have sought to reinstate these traditional institutions of modern citizenship. The former have embraced the citizenship of capital, labour and the state within corporatist forms of decision-making, while the latter have embraced the citizenship of common access to the institutions of the market. These, however, are defensive and backward-looking orientations which cannot preempt the fundamental challenges which the new social movements represent.

ARE WE MOVING TO A POST-WELFARE STATE SOCIETY?

It is clear that the historic compromise between the claims of labour and capital that the welfare state represented has broken down. It is no longer the 'major peace formula' that Offe described for the 'advanced capitalist democracies' after the Second World War.

Let me summarise how the breakdown of this peace formula has been expressed. First, there has been a process of disestablishment of the legitimacy of social citizenship and its claims. This has happened in different degrees depending on the particular welfare state society involved and its historical traditions. Second, the safety net that the welfare state income support and benefit provisions were to provide for individuals who could not get access to labour markets, or who were unable to work, has become more restrictive. Increasingly, the trend is in the direction of structuring income support and benefits so that individuals are forced back into labour markets even if this means into highly exploited and poorly paid ones. Third, there has been a sustained tendency to marginalise the new social movements and the democratising forces that they represent. This has been done principally through denying their universal significance and making them appear vehicles of particular sectoral interests. The other form of marginalisation has been to constitute the new social movements as lying on the outer limits of the norm: they become (where this is an appropriate attribution) disadvantaged groups for whom special provision is to be made.

All three trends are evident in the policies of the Hawke Labor Government which came to power in Australia in 1983, and which entered its third term in 1987. In the rhetoric of this government there has been a progressive shift away from the discourse of citizenship in general and specifically away from the discourse of social citizenship (see chapter 1). This is marked when the rhetoric of the Whitlam Labor Government (1972–75) is recalled. This was a rhetoric shaped by the ethos of social citizenship as is indicated in Whitlam's retrospective characterisation of the program of this government (1983:2–3):

> For a party of social democracy, however, the program required a philosophical relevance. I strove to relate the principal elements of the program to what I have called the doctrine of positive equality. This concept does not have as its primary goal equality of personal income. Its goal is greater equality of the services which the community provides. This approach not merely accepts the pluralistic nature of our system, with the private sector continuing to play the greater part in providing employment and growth; it positively requires private affluence to prevent public squalor.

The retreat from the construction of the welfare state in terms of the logic of social citizenship is indicated in the progressive shift over the course of the Hawke Government away from universal, publicly provided services or benefits to specifically directed benefits or services with the corollary of requiring those no longer receiving the benefit or service to make appropriate private provision or to go without. Two examples will suffice. In 1987 the Hawke Government abolished the universal family allowance, and substituted an income-tested family allowance, with a family allowance supplement for the poorest families. It is relevant to point out that about 75 per cent of recipients of the non-income-tested family allowance had incomes which fell below the equivalent of a couple without children of $28 000 a year (an Institute of Family Studies calculation, cited by Disney, 1987:16; and see Antcliff, 1988:66). This moved the rationale for the family allowance away from the notion that those who are childless should support through their taxes those who are

131

bringing up children because they are doing this on behalf of us all to the idea that children are a function of a privately exercised preference and should be the private responsibility of all those who have the capacity to pay for their upkeep.

The second example concerns access to higher education. It is in keeping with its subscription to the ideas of social citizenship that the Whitlam Government in 1974 abolished fees in what were then the only types of higher-education institutions: publicly funded ones. The Hawke Government indicated its intent to renege on this commitment by first reintroducing a fee, albeit a minor one, the Higher Education Administrative Charge (HEAC) in 1987, and then by committing itself to some variant of a graduate tax. This is a change away from the universalistic equal opportunity thrust of removing fees as a barrier to higher-education access towards the inevitably class-bound consequences of introducing a user-pays principle. The latter may provide a structural basis on which the newly emergent private universities can establish themselves and enter into successful competition with the increasingly run-down public higher-education institutions.

The trend to make the welfare safety net more restrictive is expressed in the trend toward the specific directing, or 'targeting', of social services and benefits. Julian Disney (1987:16) comments: 'It is notable that since the Hawke Government took office the proportion of the population which is receiving pensions and benefits has fallen. This stems largely from the introduction of the assets test and the fall in unemployment from the heights of 1982–83.' The abolition of the non-income-tested (universal) family allowance will have reduced the proportion of the population receiving pensions and benefits even further.

The Hawke Labor Government's alliance with the peak trade union body, the ACTU, has constrained its options for cutting back state provision of services and benefits as recommended by the pro-free-market economic rationalists. For example, even though Pusey's (1988a) work shows that two-thirds of the 215 SES officers he interviewed favour deregulation of the labour market, it is clear that, if this view is finding its way into the policy advice these senior public servants are giving the Hawke Government, it is advice likely to go unheeded. At the same time it is possible to argue that this Government is prepared to consider certain modes of privatisation of income support and services.

As argued already, the tendency under this Government has been to reinstate the residualist traditions of the Australian welfare state (see Castles, 1988: especially ch. 7). There has also been some tendency to withdraw public need provision in favour of private familial need provision, a particular kind of privatisation. This is evidenced in the child support proposal (discussed in ch. 5), and in the abolition of the junior unemployment benefit for sixteen- and seventeen-year-olds in the May Economic Statement, 1987. Sixteen- and seventeen-year-olds are eligible if unemployed for the Job Search Allowance which, in 1988, provided a flat rate of $25, and an additional income-tested rate of $25 for those who are not 'homeless' and therefore still living with their parents. If they continue to complete the post-compulsory years of schooling, as the government is encouraging them to do, these sixteen- and seventeen-year-olds are eligible for Austudy on an income-tested basis, providing also for a maximum (in parental home) rate of $50. These maximum rates not only involve the residualist principle of 'targeting', but they are predicated on the assumption that these young people are receiving substantial private parental support. It is clear from the conditions of eligibility for the away-from-home ('independent', 'homeless') rates that there is no encouragement in these for young people to leave the parental home (see Yeatman, 1988d).

Finally, the Laborist-corporatist orientation of the Hawke Government has coloured the way in which it has adopted an 'active-system' approach of public income support programs, where there will be a tendency to tie income support to participation in labour market programs, training or education. This is a form of public sponsorship of transition to privatised forms of income support, and there is some similarity to the Thatcher Government's adoption of income support tied to labour market programs for young people and adults. The Hawke Government's active system approach has now been applied to sole supporting parent beneficiaries, who will be encouraged into labour market programs, training or education with the hope that this will reduce the number on benefits. This active-system approach in the Australian context occurs in a situation where there is no tradition of industry or employer commitment to provide ongoing employment to individuals after they have undertaken a labour market program or training-related work experience. If there is no commitment to ongoing employment there is even less commitment to ongoing employment with built-in career ladders. In this context it is all too likely that an active system will contribute to the development of relatively unregulated and poorly unionised part-time and casual labour markets. This permits income support to be wholly or partially privatised, and a corresponding reduction of numbers of public beneficiaries and payments.

Where the Whitlam Labor Government doctrine of 'positive equality' was contrary to the residualist traditions of Australian welfare state provision, and committed Labor in a non-residualist direction of social protection which, in Castles' (1988:129, 149) terms, is 'both statist and public', the Hawke Labor Government has reinstated the residualist tradition of a strategy of social protection which is 'both statist and private'. The likelihood of this Government succumbing to the ACTU demands for tax cuts for low and middling tax payers is high, and this will be a further Labor version of strategies of privatisation.

The trend to marginalise the new social movements has taken the form of a distinctively social democratic mode of constituting them special-interest groups, outside the corporatist mainstream. They are recast not as movements with emancipatory thrusts for the whole society but, where this is appropriate, as specially disadvantaged groups. This incorporates the Aboriginal struggle for self-determination, the multicultural vision of Australians from non-English-speaking backgrounds, and the feminist struggle for the liberation of women. These become deconstructed as components of debate about the shape and direction of the Australian national polity and society, and reconstructed as the claims of disadvantaged groups which require special access and equity strategies and programs. These are 'special-needs' groups. Accordingly, even the rhetoric of access and equity loses the cadences of universal citizenship and becomes assimilated to the non-citizenship approach of 'targeting'.

Where it is not possible to consign a new social movement and its politics to the ghetto of disadvantaged groups, as in the case of the environmentalist-green movement, it is constituted as an interest group competing with the claims of other interest groups (the logging industry and its employees, for example). The Government then assumes the classical liberal role of honest broker between the competing claims.

Finally, the Hawke Government's Labor strategy of corporatism has reinstated the traditional primacy of the older political contestants: the organised trade union movement and the employers' associations. In so doing, the new social movements have been rendered not simply marginal but made to appear as irrelevant to the real and urgent issues of the day.

These trends represent the renegotiation of the nature and boundaries of the welfare state in a context where the terms of power have become very much more favourable to capital. This has occurred largely because of the development of a global economy and international division of labour. These developments have had the following implications: 1. the restructuring of the terms of trade competition between national economies, with the dominant and successful postwar economies becoming vulnerable to increased and effective competition; 2. this trend has been heightened by the collapse of a nexus between capital and national economies: capital moves offshore to find cheaper labour and lower taxes and leaves behind it the structural dislocation and sudden unemployment of thousands of manufacturing workers with all that this implies for the revenue base of the city and region within which they are situated; 3. accordingly, the terms of the labour market have changed profoundly for the working classes within the erstwhile welfare state societies: no longer is it meaningful for them to organise to regulate the terms of the bargain between capital and labour *within* the boundaries of their society because that bargain is influenced by the availability of cheaper and less well organised labour in societies where historical expectations about standards of living, equality of status and the legitimacy of open political struggle are much lower or nonexistent.

The collapse of a nexus between capital and national economies is not only inherent in the general trend for capital to break out of all local restrictions (Marx and Engels, 1968) but was an inevitable consequence of the end of empire which deprived capital in the imperial nations of its protected and militarily guaranteed international sphere of operation. Once nationhood itself became universal, capital freed from its old imperial allegiances could not only facilitate the development of the new nations but was free to explore the world unfettered by national loyalty.

All of this guarantees a long, slow and painful revenue crisis for the old welfare states. It means that the burden of taxation is thrust more and more onto the middling and lower groups who are trapped within national economic boundaries. If this analysis is correct, it is not surprising that most progressive political tendencies have been slow to construct its structural features and to appreciate how much is at stake. It is clear that the challenges posed for the development of a new forward-looking and *globally* oriented progressive politics are profound given the specific histories of the class and democratic struggles which have informed that politics in the past.

THE RESPONSES OF THE LEFT TO THE CRISIS OF THE WELFARE STATE

The response of the left to this crisis is indicative of how difficult these challenges are proving to be. For the purposes of this discussion, I am using the term 'the left' to refer to the political forces which have inherited the socialist and marxist revolutionary tradition.

The left has been ill placed to defend the idea of social citizenship in the face of its progressive disestablishment for two fundamental reasons. First, in general, the left has not accorded the democratic developments and ideas within capitalist state-societies any status or autonomy of their own. The exceptions to this rule are the left-democratic exiled critics of the Soviet state-societies such as Agnes Heller (1988), and Georg Konrad and Ivan Szelenyi (1979), and democratic neomarxist theorists like John Keane, Pierre Rosanvallon and Alberto Melucci (see their contributions in Keane, 1988). It is noteworthy that the exceptions are recent developments belonging to the 1970s and 1980s: they have been influenced profoundly by left-democratic criticism of Soviet state socialism and they are linked into advocacy of the new social movements. Democracy in a capitalist society has been mostly viewed by the left as a set of ideological and institutional practices which function to incorporate, pacify and disarm the working class, and which legitimise the real power-brokering of the most powerful class interests in relation to state policies and agendas. This position has deprived the left of any capacity to anchor its own egalitarian vision in the ways in which the idea of equality of status have been actualised, albeit in what have proved to be increasingly ephemeral ways.

Second, the unwillingness of the left to accord democratic developments and ideas respect in their own right has made it very difficult for it to understand or to embrace the new social movements, as they have come to be called. All these social movements share the project of democratisation of society, even if their relationship to this project is variable. It is true that some of the younger, erstwhile 'New Left', voices in the left are attempting to correct this deficit in both analysis and practice. This statement in Stuart Hall's analysis of the emergence of the British interventionist state 1880–1920 (1984:25–26) is instructive:

> Some of the new forces had no clear-cut character and are better defined as 'social movements': the suffragettes were perhaps the best example of the latter. We have considered them all part of the democratic forces because their ultimate effect was to expand the power and influence of the popular classes and other unrepresented social strata.

These tendencies in the left are often inclined to accord a privileged place to the new social movements in the dynamics and trajectory of current progressive and oppositional politics. For example, Claus Offe takes the promise of the new social movements very seriously, and Ian Gough, at the end of an analysis of the crisis of the welfare state, argues:

> There is an urgent need to create an effective, coherent political alternative to the ideology of the new right. The Keynesian welfare state did provide an alternative in the 1940s, but it is vital today to resist the temptation to seek refuge in liberal Keynesianism and social democratic reformism.
> What is the political basis, then, on which to construct a 'third alternative'? It is to be found in the new social movements of the last decade—notably the women's movement and the peace move-

ment, but also including the numerous groups struggling in and against the state'. These all provide a rich source of ideas, nonoppressive practices, and prefigurative forms of welfare provision. (1983:476)

However, after lauding the new social movements in this manner, it is a feature of such analyses to move immediately to state allegiance to 'reality', namely some version of traditional left institutions and practices: 'In my view these movements are not enough; they need to relate to sections of the labour movement, and both need to find expression in a political party which has a realistic chance of forming a government.' It is clear in this kind of statement that the seriousness accorded to the new social movements operates according to the logic of inversion: marginal forces are given the role of a cutting edge in relation to what is taken as an indivisible given: the traditional institutions of the labour movement. It is precisely this indivisible status of these institutions, their imperviousness to integration of the new social movements, that represents a fundamental weakness and crisis of conscience of the left.

The resistance of 'old' left analysis is equally instructive as this statement by Ralph Miliband and Marcel Liebman in the *Socialist Register 1985/6* indicates: 'However useful and effective other elements of pressure in the political system may be—trade unions, movements of women, blacks, ecologists, peace activists and many others—they cannot and do not for the most part wish to fulfil the main task of socialist parties, which is to inject a "stream of socialist tendency", by word and action, into the political system and culture of their societies.' In this statement, Miliband and Liebman ignore the fundamental problem posed by the integration into the labour force of women, and non-ethnically/racially dominant groups who are not represented in the socialist parties, their strategies or their analyses. Here Ross and Jensen's analysis of the changing character of the labour force since the postwar compromise of the welfare state is useful. They argue that not only has there developed a stratum of marginal workers, but

> Alongside such marginal workers were large numbers of service-sector operatives in new or greatly expanded sectors of clerical work, tourism (food, travel, lodging) and merchandising. Here one found numbers of feminised occupations in which, because of this fact and because unions found it persistently difficult to organise in such areas, working conditions, job security and wage levels were inferior to those in the blue-collar unionised sphere. The class conflict implications of such class fragmentation depended upon its specific national structures.... In general, however, one found working classes divided between those to whom socialists and unionists referred rather hastily as 'the workers', full participants

in the post-war compromise, and those who fell outside it in one or another way. *In some places this latter group grew large enough to present a challenge to labour's right to speak on behalf of 'all the workers'.* (1986:26—27, emphasis in the original)

Thus the traditional left institutions and parties have lost credibility and legitimacy in claiming to represent a mass base and universal progressive force.

Third, this problem has been underlined by the inability of the left to come to terms with the application of class analysis to the theories which have informed its politics and to the theoreticians (the intelligentsia) who have produced these theories. The construction of the intelligentsia as a 'New Class' with its own class project and aspirations to power (see Gouldner, 1979; Konrad and Szelenyi, 1979) is an important challenge to the internal democratisation of the left which it has not accepted.

Fourth, this inability to surrender the illusion of operating from an archimedean point in class terms has to be seen in relation to the deep embarrassment of the left confronted by the association of left visions and ideals with highly statecentric and state-dominant modes of social control. Much of the left is willing to articulate this embarrassment, and there is a readiness to understand that the left must fail to attract a wide and continuing popular base until it is able to come to terms with the issues that are involved in the democratisation of the modern, complex state (see Panitch, 1986, for example).

Finally, not only is the revolutionary ideal for all the reasons offered above a less than compelling one nowadays, but at present the left is deprived of its historic role in the dialectic or dialogical relation between reform and revolution. The exponents of reform have largely vacated the stage. If the left does not defend the democratic, social-citizenship features of the welfare state ideal who will? If some individual adherents of social democracy attempt to defend threatened gains inch by inch, the *framework* for a defence will not come from the exponents of incremental reform and of the inevitable compromises of a mixed economy, however ethical and serious their commitments are. In this context, Block, Cloward, Ehrenreich and Piven (1987:xiv) make an interesting observation which, with necessary qualifications, would apply to many social democrats operating in Hawke's Australia as well as to liberal progressives operating in Reagan's America:

> In general, liberals have offered only timid and infrequent rebuttals to conservative attacks on the welfare state. Instead of advancing a strong and principled defense of the welfare state, liberals seem to have fallen into theoretical and moral disarray. Part of the problem

lies with the liberal intelligentsia, who were totally unprepared for a re-emergence of conservative opposition to the welfare state. They had, we believe, succumbed to a kind of complacency bred by theory. Most analysts, whatever their other disagreements, had come to take for granted that expanded welfare state programs were an inevitable concomitant of economic growth and urbanization. Consistently, and not unreasonably, a good deal of the work done by left and liberal social welfare analysts was critical of the programs, fastening on their inadequacies and neglecting their achievements. This critical tradition—which certainly had its place in periods of social welfare expansion—left many of the liberal intelligentsia unprepared to respond to the conservative assault with a strong defense of the welfare state.

THE FEMINIST RELATIONSHIP TO THE CRISIS OF THE WELFARE STATE

Feminists have been no different from anyone else in discerning the wider structural issues and broad patterns involved in the crisis of the welfare state. That is, such discernment has been fairly slow in coming. As in the case of the left, this discernment has been hindered also by the ambivalence of feminists towards the welfare state.

I have argued above that the crisis of the welfare state is a crisis of the welfare state ideal, and that this crisis has permitted a serious erosion of gains made on behalf of a welfare safety net and social citizenship. I suggested also that these gains are subject to the contingencies of struggles for democratisation, and that such contemporary struggles confront new structural conditions of intensified problems for national polities in controlling and commanding sufficient economic resources to permit a welfare state society, even one where statist and bureaucratised forms of public need provision have been checked by the involvement of local communities in such need provision (see Rosanvallon, 1988).

By and large feminists have not distinguished themselves from the left in attempting to defend and refurbish the welfare state ideal. In general feminists are not especially tempted to defence of what have been existing institutions and traditions because of the way in which they are structured by the modern patriarchal gender division of labour. Specifically, feminists have not found the discourse of social citizenship to be particularly favourable to women, and have neglected its possibilities for the development of feminism. Like the left, feminism has tended to be sceptical of the democratic claims of modern welfare states. Rather than developing a positive and radical embrace of the democratic tradition, feminism has tended to lock its own critiques and commentaries into an exclusively oppositional relationship to the deployment of this tradition as apologia and legitimation for dominant and masculinist political and economic classes.

Elizabeth Wilson's analysis 'Thatcherism and Women: After Seven Years' brings out a tendency in feminist responses to the crisis of the welfare state to discern continuities rather than discontinuities. She argues that the British postwar settlement did not extend social citizenship to women; 'to restrict women's right to equal access to paid work was seen quite cynically as the only way to ensure that women carried on with their traditional duties in the home.' (1987:202) Wilson's analysis shows that the Thatcher administration has not introduced new inequalities as far as women relative to men are concerned. Indeed, the Thatcher Government is an up-to-date equal opportunity government that has welcomed advances that women have made as successful individuals participating in the newly deregulated markets. If it is a government that uses the ideology of familism to justify the reprivatisation of certain services and caring activities ('community care', see Finch, 1984), this resort to familism does not distinguish it from its opponents or from preceding governments.

The important effect of the Thatcher Government's policies has been to develop class differences between women: 'the employment policies pursued by the Conservative government for the past seven years have not affected all women uniformly, but have actually widened the gap between better off women and those at the bottom of the employment hierarchy, and this is in large part due to the loss of women's jobs in the manufacturing sector' (Wilson, 1987:206). Wilson argues that the structural tendencies prompting the increasing integration of women into the labour force are well established, and are accepted parameters of government policies. The mode of integration is of a kind to develop the gender segmentation of the labour force and to sequester the majority of women workers within the poorly paid, part-time labour market segments. Wilson concludes:

> It is perhaps too simple ... to see Mrs Thatcher's Toryism as having a clear cut commitment to the subordination of women. Rather, women are to be treated primarily as members of their class, with some hopes of advancement for the women of the business and professional classes who have for many years formed the backbone of Tory grassroots support but with prospects of ever-increasing poverty and repression for working women, poor women and women from the black community and ethnic minorities. (1987:223)

The implications of this analysis are that feminism will have to link up a gender with a class and race/ethnic analysis. No longer can it be assumed that women share the same gender-determined position of dependency in relation to the state and the economy. It is clear also that Wilson does not consider it meaningful to resurrect an historical tradition of welfare statism which has excluded women from social citizenship and which was predicated on a racially and ethnically homogeneous society.

Two recent feminist analyses of welfare state societies indicate clearly the essential features of feminist critique of the welfare state. The first of these is Nancy Fraser's 'Women, Welfare and the Politics of Need Interpretation' (1987). Her object of analysis is the welfare state society of the United States, with particular reference to the Reagan Administration's cutbacks and attacks on welfare clients. Fraser argues that 'women have become the principal subjects of the welfare state':

> On the one hand, they comprise the overwhelming majority both of program recipients and of paid social service workers. On the other hand, they are the wives, mothers and daughters whose unpaid activities and obligations are redefined as the welfare state increasingly oversees forms of caregiving. Since this beneficiary-social worker-caregiver nexus of roles is constitutive of the social-welfare arena, one might even call the latter a feminized terrain. (1987:91)

Fraser supports this proposition by bringing out clearly the gendered character of the binary division in the US welfare state between the 'masculine' social welfare programs, the social insurance types of programs, and the 'feminine' relief programs. The former are understood as program entitlements for right-bearing individuals, individuals who have participated in labour markets and who have paid their contributions to a system of social insurance in the event of sickness, unemployment and the like. The latter are stigmatised as 'welfare', i.e. unearned relief for households which lack effective access through a masculine head of household to income derived from the labour market.

Fraser reserves 'social citizenship' for the predominantly male participants in the social security system, because this is a social insurance scheme which positions recipients 'primarily as rights-bearers'. While these entitlements are administered by the state, they are done so in ways which preserve the dignity of the beneficiaries, do not require continued proof of eligibility, and which are 'far less subject to intrusive controls and surveillance' than the feminine sector of the social welfare system. These relief programs are financed out of tax revenues, with the bulk of this financing coming not from the federal but the state governments. This means, that unlike the federal social security system, relief programs are variable between states, and the less progressive states are relatively free to treat their welfare populations with neglect and administrative abuse. These 'welfare' programs are administered in ways that emphasise the lack of rights of the recipients: they 'require considerable work in qualifying and maintaining eligiblity; and they have a heavy component of surveillance'.

Fraser's analysis represents an interesting and appropriate construction of the distinction between contract and tutelage in liberal democratic capitalist societies as a gendered distinction. The less an individual is able to be oriented as a freely contracting individual the more he or she is placed in a client relation to the state and placed under the tutelage of the state. This is a loss of masculine types of freedom and represents a necessary identification with what are classed as feminine types of dependence. Thus, while many households on 'welfare' in the US contain male individuals, these males lose access to masculine rights and become subsumed under the symbolic association of these households with 'welfare mothers' (for the ramifications of this, see Liebow, 1967; Stack, 1974). Some years before Fraser's analysis, Donzelot (1980) explored the same territory using French case data, and argued that access to the principle of contract defines middle-class status, whereas dependency on the principle of tutelage defines working-class status. Donzelot did not discern the gendered features of this distinction, while Fraser understates its class and race features.

Fraser's use of the term 'social citizenship' is a rather esoteric one: its meaning is quite different from the one intended by Marshall (1977) and which is the one generally current. Her argument suggests that citizenship in the United States is tied to participation in the status of a market-oriented possessive individual (Fraser, 1987:95–96). This is not 'social citizenship'. Perhaps it ought to be termed 'market citizenship'. This would not deny the point of Fraser's argument: namely, that market citizenship is the type of citizenship which predominates and which entails a degree of freedom and power that other types of citizenship do not. For instance, it is possible to argue that market citizenship is dominant in relation to political citizenship, the right to vote and to stand for election. This is particularly evident in the US where voting is not compulsory, and where to be an effective candidate for election the market value of the candidate has to be very high, in the millionaire category. Moreover, it is the case that what Marshall meant by social citizenship is not expressed in the welfare relief system in the US. In the past it used to be expressed in the incorporation of the traditions of progressivism in the municipal services and institutions that had developed in Minnesota, New York and some of the other eastern and mid-western states.

Fraser's analysis is important for its ability to explain how and why the welfare state has become symbolically identified increasingly with feminine forms of dependency as, at the same time, there has been a renaissance of the free-market principle tied to the greater efficacy of market citizenship in a transnational capitalist economy. It loses potency to the degree that she forgets that feminine is as feminine is constructed within the discourse of modern gender and that it covers not just those who are deemed 'naturally' feminine but all those who cannot lay effective claim to masculine freely contracting status. Indeed, it is clear that many deemed naturally feminine can buy their way out of feminine dependency through effective access to market citizenship. The new liberalism, as Elizabeth Wilson (1987:205–7) points out, prides itself on its 'modern' acceptance of this extension of market freedoms to those women who can claim them.

Fraser's analysis agrees with that of Wilson's primarily in the shared feature of each which emphasises how market citizenship overrides the other kinds of citizenship and has become the central marker of citizenship in Reagan's United States of America and Thatcher's Britain. In this respect these analyses are to be contrasted with Carole Pateman's analysis of the welfare state, which represents accurately the ambivalence of most feminists towards the welfare state. Pateman (1987) accepts the argument by Elizabeth Wilson (1977) and others that the welfare state reconstitutes women as dependent on patriarchal authority, in this case the authority of the state. However, she reminds us that feminists, especially first-wave feminist social reformers, fought for many aspects of what later came to be institutionalised as the welfare state, a point that begins to complicate the critique of the patriarchal character of the welfare state. In addition, Pateman argues that welfare benefits have helped to make it possible for many women to be independent of individual men, and there is one crucial difference between the 'construction of women as men's dependents and dependence on the welfare state'. She elaborates:

> In the former case each woman lives with the man on whose benevolence she depends; each woman is (in J.S. Mill's extraordinarily apt phrase) in a 'chronic state of bribery and intimidation combined'. In the welfare state each woman receives what is hers by right, and she can, potentially, combine with other citizens to enforce her rightful claim. The state has enormous powers of intimidation, but political action takes place collectively in the public terrain and not behind the closed door of the home, where each woman has to rely on her own strength and resources. (1987:35)

The implication of this argument is that social citizenship does have significance for women in extending to them a public status and public rights. That these are obviated to some extent by the patriarchal features of women's dependency on the state Pateman concedes, but her point concerns the contestability and visibility of public dependencies in contrast to the invisibility and capriciousness of private dependencies. It is clear that Fraser's analysis of women's client status is at odds with Pateman's. Fraser is arguing that the very construction of that client status takes it out of the political domain and thus out of the public domain. Instead, it is placed within the domain of the administration of welfare, where administrative and professional discretion, in accordance with technical and professional conventions, depoliticises the decisions and processes involved. She argues that both the privileged social security system and the welfare relief system in the US are depoliticised through their subsumption under a 'juridical-administrative-therapeutic state apparatus' (JAT). This means that even the social citizenship which is tied to social security rights tends to be a 'degraded and depoliticised one. It is a form of passive citizenship in which the state preempts the power to define and satisfy people's needs'. This is the point that Fraser wants to emphasise, namely the state's management of need satisfaction, to which she contrasts a politics of need interpretation. When the state administers need satisfaction, there is substitution of 'monological, administrative processes of need definition for dialogical, participatory processes of need interpretation' (Fraser, 1987:150).

Fraser's analysis of the JAT tables a feature often missing from feminist analyses of the welfare state, namely the problematic features of a state-administered and statecentric system of welfare. It is not clear that state activities necessarily fall within the public domain and there is a good deal of evidence that many aspects of the administration of welfare are kept out of public scrutiny and debate. There is an increasing tendency for this to be true as the safety net is made more restrictive with increased surveillance of potential welfare cheats and a marked shift away from the administrative reform measures of administrative appeals and freedom of information. It is arguable, however, that state activities are always potentially public in liberal democratic parliamentary systems where a question in parliament may open up for public scrutiny and thereby politicise state administrative practices and policies. However, some of the same difficulties attend this process of politicisation as they do the bringing to light of the relations of patriarchal domination inherent in the private world of family life. Both state administrative practices and patriarchal familial domination conform to deeply engraved and largely unexamined assumptions about power, who has it and who has not: bureaucrat and client, professional and client, parent and child.

Nonetheless it is possible to conclude that Fraser's and Pateman's analyses converge in the desirability and importance of politicising state need provision and thereby bringing it into the public domain. Neither analysis takes the next step, namely identifying the norm or ideal in relation to which this positive political action might be developed.

Ambivalence towards a much more advanced welfare state than is evident in Britain or the United States comes out also in feminist Scandinavian analyses of the Scandinavian welfare states. Siim's (1987:256) summary of the argument is apt. On the one hand the Scandinavian welfare state, by making developed provision for childcare and other policies, has made possible women's integration into the labour market to a fuller extent than has occurred in other advanced capitalist societies. In this respect the state has contributed to altering the privately based gender division of labour and to increasing gender equality between men and women. On the other hand, relative to men, women have been excluded from the most decisive political process which occurs within the highly centralised, corporatist structures of the Scandinavian state. Hernes (1987: 78–80) develops this argument, and adopts a variant of Boris and Bardeglio's (1983) argument for the US that the development of the welfare state means a transformation from familial to state patriarchy. Hernes argues that women's integration into the labour market tends to be dependent on the expanding field of public sector employment, and on the public services which underwrite this expansion of public employment. Women's status as citizens, however, remains tied to the sphere of reproduction even though this sphere has become restructured by state policies and by state-sponsored forms of shifting reproductive labour from private households to paid, public employment. Women are still identified with a dependency status, because the sphere of reproduction is constructed as dependent on the sphere of market-oriented production. Men enjoy a privileged relationship to the sphere of production. Thus, when men become identified with the state-sponsored corporatist politics of managing relations between employers and unions so as to foster effective accumulation in the national economy, this type of dependency on the state does not qualify their provider status but emphasises it. There is thus a dual and gendered state structure in Scandinavia, where men enjoy more access to political power, more effective state support and more rights than do women.

Hernes (1987:72), argues that 'while feminists from other Western countries often look upon Scandinavian women with a certain mixture of envy and admiration, a closer analysis reveals patterns of under-representation, discrimination and subordination very similar to those elsewhere'. Hernes focuses her attention on the patterns of women's participation in the political domains, both that of the legislature and that of the corporatist decision-making bodies. As anyone who knows the Scandinavian political system will be aware, the latter of these two domains is much the more powerful and generally dominant (see Heclo and Madsen, 1987). It is thus significant that while women's parliamentary participation has increased remarkably, especially in the 1970s, they tend to be absent from the corporatist domain of decision-making:

> Corporatism as a mode of interest intermediation, redistribution and policy formation is a male world of civil servants, organizational leaders and technical-professional experts which defines an ever increasing part of the public interest. It is also an institutionalized form of group access rather than individual access to politics. As a matter of fact these 'groups', i.e. organizations and professions with political clout, have very clear gender profiles, which helps to explain women's small chances of getting into the political power network. The organizational gender profile in Scandinavia, where we find men in economic and professional organizations with representation in the corporate bodies such as commissions and boards and women in humanitarian and volunteer organizations without political access, is politically more consequential than in other less corporate systems. Powerful organizations and institutions rather than voters and political parties have become the central gatekeepers in the Scandinavian state system and have not been in focus in the same manner as political parties in terms of their willingness to recruit women or take up women's issues. Of all the channels of access to the political decision-making centers the corporative one is the least 'participative', the most hierarchical and oligarchical, and the most elitist (Hernes, 1987:75-76).

Hernes concludes that 'the Scandinavian state form' is 'a tutelary state for women, since they have had a minimal role in the actual decision-making process concerning the distribution process' (1984:31). This conclusion is remarkably similar to Fraser's, a convergence all the more noteworthy given the gulf between the developed Scandinavian type of welfare state and the relatively undeveloped US type (see Castles, 1987).

Borchorst and Siim raise relevant questions about the extent of women's integration into Scandinavian labour markets. They argue that, from a feminist perspective, a central feature of Danish and Swedish welfare state development has been the 'development of a partnership between the state and the family in relation to human reproduction, especially care for children, the sick, the elderly and the handicapped'. 'The expansion of public responsibilities for care work', which was a prerequisite of the integration of women into the labour force, was based, they argue, 'on an institutionalization of women's double role as mothers and wage-earners' (1987:128).

Women's labour force participation is compromised still by their domestic responsibilities, an inevitable structural consequence of the maintenance of a dominant male norm in working conditions. Thus, while the Scandinavian countries have the highest participation rates for women, they also have very high rates of part-time work. Borchorst and Siim (1987:141) claim also that from 1977 'women have been relatively harder hit by unemployment than men, and sex differences in unemployment have been widening since then'.

Borchorst and Siim remark two trends which are of particular resonance to Australian feminists living under the Hawke Government. First, while the public provision of childcare is very much more developed in the Scandinavian welfare states than in the other types of welfare state—in 1984 42 per cent of 0–2-year-olds and 57 per cent of 3–6-year olds were enrolled in public daycare and childcare institutions in Denmark—childcare became one of the favourite targets for public spending cutbacks in the 1970s:

> At first there was no fundamental break with the incentives of the 1965 legislation, and the number of places in daycare and childcare institutions still rose, but gradually educational standards deteriorated and care gained higher priority, whereas pedagogical purposes are rarely mentioned in government notices. What has also happened is that admission to childcare facilities has been still more closely linked to the employment situation of the parents (Borchorst and Siim, 1987:139–140).

They also remark that since the 1970s there has been increasing official effort to break down labour market segmentation by gender by integrating women into the so-called non-traditional occupations. They comment:

> As far as we can see only those strategies for sexual equality which are acceptable from a male point of view are carried through. This means that attempts to change the male-dominated areas so that girls' and women's values and experiences are integrated are doomed to fail. Instead the problem is perceived as the failure of women to choose the right education and jobs, and the strategy is mostly based on attempts merely to integrate women in the male-dominated areas. (1987:143)

It will be clear that if the breaking of the nexus between capital and national polities underwrites a tendency for market citizenship to become the dominant form of citizenship, any social groups locked into dependence on the state and public forms of revenue are particularly vulnerable. It is clear that the feminist critiques of the welfare state table for concern the asymmetry in power between market-established capacities and state-derived capacities. In so doing they place fundamental questions against what may be called the classical,

Marshallian tradition of social citizenship. Feminist critiques also refuse to leave unquestioned the relationship between the market, state and family, and thereby bring to light another set of silences and exclusions which resided in this classical tradition of social citizenship. To this degree, their critiques contribute to the crisis of the ideal of the welfare state.

There is, however, a fundamental difference between the direction of their contribution and that of the neoconservative, New Right and corporatist disestablishers of the ideal of social citizenship. Where the former are struggling towards naming the new conditions and rhetorics of contemporary struggles for democratisation, the latter represent a counterrevolution in relation to the revolutionary reforms which the ideal of social citizenship opened up.

8 The politics of discourse and the politics of the state

> Once the state has been founded, there can no longer be any heroes. Hegel, *Philosophy of Right*

Heroes depend for their existence on belief in origins myths. Whatever the form of myth, in some sense the hero comes down from the mountain armed with god's word and is a hero precisely because he has been privileged to receive this special and direct communication from the source—the source of reality, truth, word and law. We are not too keen on heroes these days. We have become suspicious of their claims to represent some archimedean point from which they can assess the rest of us and the validity of what we do. We have good reason to be suspicious of their claims. For many of us these suspicions arise out of our increasingly emancipated awareness that we belong to those silenced by the Word (see Threadgold, forthcoming, where she discusses how women and blacks are admitted but never as their own voices, only as the projections of the spokesmen of the Word). We cannot have a voice of our own for that would be to disrupt and to contest the monocentric and monological features of the universe that is created by the Word.

If those of us who are women, gay, black, ethnic, non-metropolitan, are discovering and contesting our exclusions from the various versions of the Word that we encounter, there have been important disaffections among the inheritors of the Word. Milan Kundera, for example, a Czech who has forsworn his particular inheritance of the Party Word, writes poetry in order to make a critique of poetry, the generic site of 'the lyric attitude', in his wonderful novel *The Unbearable Lightness of Being*. The lyric attitude is the poetic or youthful hero's orientation to receiving (being given) the Word. Kundera indicates why he finds this attitude so deeply suspect:

> Starting with Dante, the poet is also a great figure striding through European history. He is a symbol of national identity (Camões, Goethe, Mickiewicz, Pushkin), he is a spokesman of revolutions (Béranger, Petöfi, Mayakovsky, Lorca), he is the voice of history

(Hugo, Breton), he is mythological being and the subject of a virtually religious cult (Petrarch, Byron, Rimbaud, Rilke), but he is above all the representative of an inviolable value which we are ready to write with a capital letter: Poetry.

But what has happened to the European poet in the past half century? Today his voice is barely audible. Without our being quite aware of it, the poet has passed from the great, noisy world scene. (His disappearance is apparently one of the symptoms of that dangerous time of transition in which Europe finds itself and which we have not yet learned to name.) Through a kind of satanic irony of history, the last brief European period when the poet still played his great public role was the period of post-1945 communist revolutions in Central Europe.

It is important to stress that these peculiar pseudo-revolutions, imported from Russia and carried out under the protection of the army and the police, were full of authentic revolutionary psychology and their adherents experienced them with grand pathos, enthusiasm, and eschatologic faith in an absolutely new world. Poets found themselves on the proscenium for the last time. They thought they were playing their customary part in the glorious European drama and had no inkling that the theatre manager had changed the program at the last moment and substituted a trivial farce.

I witnessed this era 'ruled hand in hand by the hangman and the poet' from up close. I heard my admired French poet Paul Eluard publicly and ceremonially renounce his Prague friend whom Stalinist justice was sending to the gallows. This episode (I wrote about it in *The Book of Laughter and Forgetting*) hit me like a trauma: when an executioner kills, that is after all normal; but when a poet (and a great poet) sings in accompaniment, the whole system of values we considered sacrosanct has suddenly been shaken apart. Nothing is certain any longer. Everything turns problematic, questionable, subject of analysis and doubt: Progress and Revolution. Youth. Motherhood. Even Man. And also Poetry. I saw before a world of shaken values and gradually, over many years, the figure of Jaromil, his mother and his loves took shape in my mind. (from the Preface to *Life is Elsewhere* v–vi)

Kundera's novel is about Jaromil, his mother and his loves. Among other things, the novel shows how the symbiotic yearnings of a silenced voice (Jaromil's mother) helped to create Jaromil and his entrapment within the lyric attitude. Symbiotic tyrannies of this kind are fostered when the Word is still dominant, whatever its particular guise (Poetry, Reason, Science).

This chapter is about the emergence of the politics of discourse, a politics which is predicated on the heroic attitude losing credibility among (most of) us. This politics is tied into both the politics of the contemporary 'interventionist' state and into the dispersed and barely emergent politics of the new global society, in ways that I shall discuss below. The fundamental thrust of this chapter is to argue that a self-conscious embrace of the politics of discourse is an important contribution to the democratisation of our shared conditions of life. It is one which must lead those of us making this embrace to refuse to share in the monological, monovocal and monocentric constructions that non- and anti-democratic individuals, groups and parties currently practise and even promulgate. In the global, post-colonial universe we now inhabit, this refusal needs to be made explicit (see Haraway, 1987).

AN ANECDOTE

I was born in South Australia in 1948, the child of a mother whose first husband had been killed in the Second World War in Egypt (*El Alamein*), and whose second husband (my father) had gone to war and served as a medical officer in North Africa and New Guinea. One of my paternal great-aunts had been imprisoned in Changi, the Japanese POW camp in Singapore. Some of the central discursive parameters of my history—and that of others like me—have concerned this War, its protagonists, the Holocaust, the Atom Bomb and Hiroshima, and the legacy of suspicion about the vanquished Japanese and their imperial vision of regional dominance within white Australian society. I need not remind Anglo-Australians of my generation or of our parents' generation of the plenitude of stories about 'the Japs', and their legendary cruelties towards (white, European) prisoners of war.

I hasten to add that I am not questioning the veracity of these accounts. My point is that they are inscribed within a discursive universe which permits inversion as the only alternative to the proper order of things (white, metropolitan, western civilisation) (see Threadgold, forthcoming).

Consider now the force of the disruption that programs shown on SBS television (the 'multicultural' channel in Australia) represent for this discursive universe. One program in particular illustrates this. This was the first episode of a Japanese documentary called 'Showa', which is about the development of Japanese participation in international power-broking and diplomacy between the First and Second World Wars. This episode focused on the attempt of the Japanese delegation to get a clause about racial equality inserted into the Treaty of Versailles, the treaty which marked the truce and territorial carve-up which the victors imposed on the vanquished at the end of the First World War. This attempt of the Japanese legation was shown against a context already established in this program: the silence of the Japanese diplomats in the ongoing negotiations of the various powers, their deep embarrassment and anguish at a silence enforced, their memoirs suggest, by lack of familiarity with European and Trans-Atlantic diplomacy and issues, by lack of confidence in this context, and by their discursive exclusions from the white, European and Trans-Atlantic club of the 'Big Three' (Britain, France and the United States led respectively by Lloyd George, Clemenceau and Wilson).

In this context, it was (the program suggests) an act of courage for the Japanese to persist in their insistence that the final treaty include a racial equality clause. The program indicated that such persistence was fruitless in the face of the implacable opposition of the Big Three. The British delegate made it clear that such a clause could not be included, especially, he argued, since none of the other similar types of inclusions had been accepted such as recognition of women's rights for example, and it was critical not to include anything which might introduce grounds for conflict among the signatories. The final comment offered was: you (Japan) have been accepted as a Great Power. The implication of this comment was clear enough: such acceptance should be enough, it brings you into the club of heroes, so be good chaps, don't insist on us recognising you as equal to us, that would upset the whole apple cart, namely the constitution of a small, imperial pantheon of great powers licensing each other in their respective imperial claims. For racial equality implies an end to the order of Great Powers, and the discursive entry of a plurality of voices, hitherto silenced and confined within the category of Other.

The Japanese delegation dropped their insistence on the racial equality clause 'in return for'—as the Big Three interpreted it—recognition of their imperial claims to the Chinese province of Shantung. Robert Lansing, the US Secretary of State and part of the US delegation, stated in his memoir that he and the other Europeans viewed this as demonstrating the insistence on the racial equality clause to have been a ploy, a blackmailing tactic, to force this outcome. One direct consequence of this outcome was that China refused to sign the Treaty.

For someone of my discursive history, it is quite a remarkable experience to be offered access to a Japanese perspective that is so disjunctive and contrapuntal in respect of the mythologies with which I grew up, not least of them being the legend of the generous internationalism and global vision of Woodrow Wilson as evidenced in the processes which produced the Treaty of Versailles and the League of Nations. It is one of those ironies of such a discursive history that the next day in *The Australian* (23 August 1988) I read the executive summary of the Liberal Party's policy on immigration, released the day before. The first paragraph of this summary read as follows: 'The next Liberal-National Party government will foster the ideal of One Australia where loyalty to Australia, our institutions and our values transcend loyalty to any other sets of values anywhere in the world.'

ENTERING THE POLITICS OF DISCOURSE

The politics of discourse is a politics that can be developed only under certain conditions. One condition concerns the development of a modern structure of statecentric modes of political, economic, social and cultural management because, as Durkheim (1957:ch. 7) argued so long ago, the state problematises by naming, and thereby bringing to the surface, features of our lives within the national boundaries that define the jurisdictional scope of any one state. The thrust of the state is to denature reality, to 'conventionalise' it by constituting it as subject to state agency or intervention (for development of this argument on 'conventionalisation', see Connolly, 1984).

Statecentric modes of management subject these features of our lives to 'policy', i.e. to reflective, rational, deliberative and purposeful discursive interventions, such as the White Paper on Higher Education (*Higher Education: A Policy Statement*), circulated by the Minister for Employment, Education and Training and published by the Australian Government Publishing Service in July 1988. The opening paragraph of this policy document is: 'This Policy Statement sets out the Commonwealth Government's strategy for the long-term development of Australia's higher education system. It marks a new era of growth and opportunity for our higher education institutions, with potentially significant benefits for all Australians.' Compare the introductory paragraph of the report of the Committee for Stage 1 of the Review of Migrant and Multicultural Programs and Services, *Don't Settle for Less*, published in 1986:

> All of us, whether born here or coming as immigrants, are part of Australia: our present is determined by the nature of Australian society and our future is tied to the nation's destiny. The strength of the nation is the strength of its members, and it is in our common interest to ensure that each person can use their skills, their talents and their abilities to the fullest. In part this Review is about how to ensure that one section of our population—those born overseas and their families in Australia—can achieve this potential. But it is also about the entire society, as each person's life is affected by the nature of the society in which they live.

While the status of these two policy 'texts' is different—the former reflects a policy that the Government has accepted, and the latter is a report for consideration by the Government—it is clear that they both make problematic aspects of what it means to be an Australian. The former (and the Green Paper on Higher Education which preceded it) has thrust publicly funded higher-education institutions into the domain of state management and has thereby forced conscious consideration of and debate about the social purpose and functions of higher education (for a similar point, see Coady, 1988:15). The latter is a policy which constructs Australia as a 'multicultural' society, a definition in relation to which the Liberal Party's policy of 'One Australia' needs to be seen as riposte and counterpolicy.

It is not just the emergence of statecentric modes of management which have required the production of policies. The proliferation of policies at the present time is a response to the increasing complexity of society. This complexity results from, as it creates, a plurality and fragmentation of voices which seek to be heard within the policy process. Thus there is no longer the political theatre of contest within the legislature between the party representatives of the two great class protagonists: the bourgeoisie and the proletariat. There is a multiplication of interests which express how different identities are created and framed by the increasingly complex relationships of a post-colonial global society. For example, the specific conjuncture of white Australian patriarchal sexuality with the gender politics of poverty in the Philippines creates a specific claimant on and interest group within the Australian policy process: Filipina brides, women who have been bought out of poverty, sometimes as mail-order brides, by relatively affluent Australian men.

This is a social complexity which precludes the new social movements adopting an essentialist conception of their identity, even as the old class-linked parties cling to the essentialism of the traditional rhetoric of class conflict. The women's movement in the US, UK and Australia has had to abandon an essentialist construction of what it means to be a woman oppressed by patriarchal rule, and to accept that there are irreducible differences between women that position them quite differently in relation to gender politics. At the same time this movement has begun to express and explore a politics of difference whereby women of colour, Third World women, lesbians, women of non-English-speaking background constitute their own versions of feminism. How this politics of difference is constituted depends on the specific historical coordinates of gender, race, ethnic and class division within a particular society. The different versions of feminism are not reducible to a single version, they cannot be synthesised, but they become so many distinct versions of feminism within the specific context to which they belong. To emerge they have to be discursively constituted: they have to be named. Once named, they enter potentially into the politicised domain of policy consideration and policy formation.

Melucci (1987:251), then, is right to suggest that political relationships have never been so important as they are now: 'Never before has it been so necessary to regulate complexity by means of decisions, choices and "policies", the frequency and diffusion of which must be avowed if the uncertainty of systems subject to exceptionally rapid change is to be reduced.' Melucci thus defines a political relationship as 'one which permits the reduction of uncertainty and the mediation of opposing interests by decisions'.

If politics involves the reduction of complexity by means of decisions and policies, the field of political activity comprises all those who seek to affect and to contest how the agendas of policy-making get framed. Political activity itself becomes preeminently a politics of contest over meaning: it comprises the disputes, debates and struggle about how the identities of the participants should be named and thereby constituted, how their needs should be named and thereby constituted, how their relationships should be named and thereby constituted. This is a politics where, for example, it is of critical importance whether the term 'families' or the term 'parents' constitutes the core label for the policy at issue. Where 'families' imply a reified unit whose needs have to be satisfied, and a norm concerning how that unit is to be defined, parents imply the needs of specific persons who parent. The policy discourse is directed accordingly: policy outcomes in relation to 'families' can be vaguely swathed in ritual and rhetoric, while, in respect of individuals who parent, outcomes have to take on specific and concrete form as assistance to persons who parent.

This is a politics of discourse, or what Haraway (1987:30) calls 'language politics': 'Contests for the meaning of writing are a major form of contemporary political struggle.' They can bring to light the domination which is inscribed in institutional practices and procedures, mass media communication, government policies, and so on. These contests are not oriented simply to demystifying (debunking) these inscriptions of power: they are oriented to substituting an alternative meaning. Discourse is the power to create reality by naming and giving it meaning. As Foucault (1984) argues, this power to create is always a distributive politics. It selectively constitutes what is to be counted as real and true, and, in so doing, discourse determines a politics of inclusion and exclusion. Thus, for example, feminist discourse authorises women as speaking subjects at the same time as it delegitimises men as speaking subjects. The distributive politics of discourse explains why Foucault proposes that 'discourse is not simply that which translates struggles or systems of determination, but is the thing for which and by which there is struggle, discourse is the power which is to be seized' (1984:110).

Politics comes to be appreciated as a politics of discourse when social complexity reaches the point, as it has now, where it becomes impossible to maintain old ideals of reconciling opposing interests within a single standard of justice. A feminist orientation to the politics of difference means that a particular feminist accepts that her complex of placings vis-à-vis the world, what one might call her 'positionality' as, for example, a white, English-speaking, non-metropolitan, university-educated, post-Holocaust feminist leads her to develop a specific version of feminism which makes sense in terms of that positionality but not another. Her construction of justice is accordingly made in terms of these partial standpoints, and is no less valid than any other construction for being so. It is, however, only one of the versions of justice which contest the policies which bear on justice.

Once political actors begin to comprehend how their positionality constructs their political ideas and visions, they are ready not only to accept a place within a multiplicity of contesting ideas and visions, but also to understand that their own positionality is not fixed or even coherent. They may discover that their subjectivity has been located between, or across distinct and even contradictory discourses of identity. Thus, for example, many feminists of my generation have been positioned across the contradictory identities of 'women' and 'professional'. For this generation, these identities were understood as discursive configurations which could not be easily fitted together. More subtle cross-positioning of identities is possible: for example that of the identities 'South African', 'white', 'Jewish' and 'woman', which is explored, to some degree at least, by Nadine Gordimer in her last novel *A Sport of Nature*. The cross-positioning of these identities means something quite different at the point of the consolidation of the white state politics of apartheid with the 90-day Detention Act in the early 1960s from what they do at the point of development of a military alliance between Israel and South Africa in the 1970s and 1980s. Identities are not fixed, although they become archaeological sites of past subjective experience. While the subjectivity of an actor who witnessed and participated in the domestic protest politics of the Vietnam War in Australia does not dissipate, what it means to this actor changes and shifts with new historical and life-cycle experiences. As Teresa De Lauretis (1986:8) puts it: 'Self and identity ... are always grasped and understood within particular discursive configurations. Consciousness, therefore, is never fixed, never attained once and for all, because discursive boundaries change with historical conditions'.

The potential for such a statement as this to become a vacuous truism is checked when we think more deeply about why it is that, at present, many political actors are self-consciously exploring their subjective relationship to the politics of discourse. In *A Sport of*

Nature I think it is clear that Gordimer is inquiring into the reach and limits of how post-Holocaust, Jewish ethics in South Africa construct an emancipatory politics of white communist alliance with a black movement of self-determination. Gordimer writes about the consciousness which produces the need for alliance when she constructs the character of her protagonist's aunt, Pauline. She makes it clear in how she develops Pauline through the course of anti-apartheid politics and the deepening official terrorism of the South African state in the 1960s and 1970s that Pauline (as she, Gordimer) has to confront a point where the universalism of this emancipatory politics of alliance is no longer adequate to the difference between black and white anti-apartheid politics.

Gordimer actually fudges this shift into the politics of difference by casting her protagonist, Hillela, in the role of 'a sport of nature'. This gives her the qualities of a changeling who can defy the ritual and regimes of South African race politics, and makes it possible for her to end up as the wife (and comrade) of an eminent black nationalist president of a newly independent African state. She has a child from this interracial union, a child which (for Gordimer) represents synthesis, indeed, the utopia of South African race politics. Gordimer thus holds onto her universalistic politics of emancipation, a politics which authorises white appropriation of black struggles. It is arguable, however, that the fairy tale of Hillela does not carry the weight that Pauline's story does.

Gordimer, as many of us, has been forced to explore some of these issues of a politics of difference, not because of the truism 'consciousness is never fixed', but because of the era in which she, and we, live. This is a post-colonial era. It is also an era of the multiplication of struggles for emancipation from various essentialist principles of domination. Preeminently an era such as this is one of contested identity, where old essentialist understandings of identity crumble into dust. Such an era ensures that our consciousness of who we are keeps changing, and that these personal pronouns 'our' and 'we' become both fundamentally problematic and contested.

The politics that this kind of consciousness informs is a politics of lateral connections, of permeable boundaries between contexts, and of the multiplication of relevant contexts. Its discursive requirements are relatively easy for those who have been 'outsiders', especially for all groups who have been placed in positions of receiving, mediating and interpreting the communications of monocentric modes of domination. These requirements are quite different from the older traditions of monocentric discursive mastery. The master of classical rhetoric has to surrender his erstwhile privilege. His rhetoric now appears as the mobilisation of certain metaphors, situated in particular styles of discourse, which he has learned in the corridors of white, Anglo, metropolitan and masculine power. For the first time since the seventeenth century, this is no longer a politics which privileges the participation of lawyers.

In Australia, two contemporary political/social analysts, Beilharz and Watts, have adopted the deconstructionist and Foucaultian approaches to power in constructing as an object for analysis the discourse of 'Labourism' that has been the dominant discourse in the Federal Government of the Labor Party under the leadership of Robert J. Hawke in the 1980s (see Beilharz and Watts, 1986). This permits them to argue such things as the following:

> What we find in reading these pieces of policy from the Accord to Social Justice, is a massive discrepancy between minimum and maximum programs, between incremental administrative politics and reforming aims and objectives which have very little to do with them. The fundamental text rules. This fundament is labourist, masculinist, reading 'people' as 'workers' and 'workers' as 'men', rather than conceiving a policy around the actual rights of different people understood as citizens. It sets up its own case as superior or 'obvious', through the use of the dualisms associated with the rationalist tradition and the manipulation of shared or persuasive values such as those of growth, prosperity and 'full' employment. (Beilharz, 1987:398)

The thrust of this analysis is that the 'language of labourism' is generally taken to be unproblematic because it expresses the dominant discourse of the political forces of the left in Australia. The discourse operates to constitute who is a legitimate member of the left, and what count as expressions of left politics. Beilharz's point in the article cited above is that this discourse constructs policy agendas, and determines how they operate. Thus, if a 'social justice strategy' is adopted, the meaning of these key terms or values (social, justice, strategy) is determined by the logic of labourist discourse. It turns out that a social justice strategy is a set of policies designed specifically for those whom labourist discourse excludes from mainstream modes of participation and distribution: currently these are conceptually constituted as 'disadvantaged groups'. When social justice is in this way discerned as a discursive strategy it then becomes possible to ask whether it is a strategy which maintains, and even *develops* through discursively reconstituting, the exclusions which are built into the dominant labourist discourse.

Beilharz's specific concern in this article is to emphasise that social policies represent the power of specific dominant discourses. Social policies, it becomes clear, are not responses to social problems already formed and 'out there'. Social policies constitute the problems to which they seem to be responses. They are involved in problem-setting, the setting of agendas. Here Beilharz borrows the language of Schon (1979) in making this point. As the title of his article indicates—'Generative Metaphor: a Perspective on Problem-Setting in Social Policy'—Schon is insisting on the metaphorical qualities of social policies. His term 'metaphor' is just another way of saying that reality is as we constitute it through language. This constitution of reality is variable, and, as Beilharz insists, potentially contestable. Schon's approach is clear in the following statement:

Problem-settings are mediated, I believe, by the 'stories' people tell about troublesome situations—stories in which they describe what is wrong and what needs fixing. When we examine the problem-setting stories told by the analysts and practitioners of social policy, it becomes apparent that the framing of problems often depends upon metaphors underlying the stories which generate problem setting and set the directions of problem solving. One of the most pervasive stories about social services, for example, diagnoses the problem as 'fragmentation' and prescribes 'coordination' as the remedy. But services seen as fragmented might be seen, alternatively, as autonomous. Fragmented services become problematic when they are seen as the shattering of a prior integration. The services are seen something like a vase that was once whole and now is broken (Schon, 1979:255).

Beilharz is arguing that many participants in social policy production in Australia are naive practitioners of policy arts because they do not discern nor are they required to debate and to justify the problem-setting frameworks or metaphors which they deploy. This is especially problematic for Beilharz (1987:388) since 'In Australia, a Left largely given to the pursuit of socialist science in the 1970s has now itself become deeply involved in the production and advocacy of policy'. At the end of his article, Beilharz (1987:404) makes a plea for debate: 'Now is the time for debate, for contestation, difference, articulation as well as "aggregation"—because politics comes before policy.'

It is important to ask to whom is Beilharz addressing this appeal. By the placement of the article (in the *Australian and New Zealand Journal of Sociology*), and by the rhetoric which begins and closes his argument, it would appear that he is addressing (left) social theorists.

Beilharz does not ask why social theorists might want to open up the politics of discourse to democratic and dialogical modes of participation. After all engagement in social theorising as though it were a *meta*-discourse (a discourse that rises above ordinary discourses, a discourse that is more than a discourse)—a *heroic* discourse is a claim on monopoly rights which often works depending on how the claim came to be licensed and where.

To contest social policy as a set of discursive practices and to do so with practical objectives in mind—namely the revision or rejection of a particular policy or set of policies—requires the contestant to relinquish a heroic posture and to enter into the decidedly unheroic politics of discourse. By this I mean that the participant who wants to discursively contest policies as texts must come to understand how discursive practices operate, how they distribute power and constitute power, and how discursive interventions are possible. This will apply no less to their own discursive practices, including their own policy recommendations, as to those of others.

It is true that social policy is expressed in texts which conform to the requirements of the genre of policy documents. Within this general genre there are a number of subgenres: e.g. White Papers, Green Papers, documents that express government policy, documents that represent the tabling of issues for consideration by the government, documents that generate data sets which bear on areas of public expenditure which have been constituted as problematic, documents which elaborate the rhetorical commitments of a government but which do not bind it (e.g. *National Policy on Languages*), and so on.

The feature which all these have in common as instances of the policy genre concerns the way in which the interest of the state in the *management* of issues means that the policy text is written in such a way as to deny the politics of discourse (a politics of contested meaning). As Beilharz (1987:389) brings out, the central feature of the genre of policy texts is the use of language to make the problem which is to be tackled appear as self-evident, thereby rendering invisible the construction of this agenda by those who produce the policy and the politics which informs this construction. As Beilharz (1987:389), using Habermas' distinction, puts it: 'communicative action is collapsed into strategic action.' This is a necessity built into the policy genre. It is one reason why the myth of public service as an administrative rather than political activity, as the proficient practice of technical knowledge rather than value-oriented agency, must be maintained.

If the denial of the politics of discourse inheres in the conventions of the policy genre, this does not prevent social theorists like Beilharz and other political activists from deconstructing a particular policy text and permitting its politics to emerge. This of course is what Beilharz is encouraging his fellow social theorists to do, and thereby to explore also the interconnections (the 'intertextuality') between academic social science and practitioner social policy.

What Beilharz does not develop is the possibility that self-consciously political policy producers may deploy the conventions of the policy genre in ways which are conducive to dialogue and debate. This is possible and even likely at a point when the scope of the state has widened to embrace a wealth of issues and has brought into policy-making circles a plurality of interests and identities. Consider the possibilities indicated in the following examples. A visiting professor of public administration offers a class on policy and program evaluation to senior/middle-level public servants and proposes that there are different functions of evaluation: to establish control so as to effect cost-cutting; to generate information in order to defend the program; to generate feedback to improve the program. A social semiotician who has the theoretical knowledge that permits the analysis of the contradictions which are inherent in any text, uses this theoretical knowledge to 'produce' (i.e. to enhance) the contradictions within a committee report so as to provide ways in for those who want to mobilise those contradictions. A leading reformer in public administration, who combines practitioner and academic identities and who has been one of the most senior public servants within the Labor-led administration of the Commonwealth Government, emphasises in his book of essays the thrust of the 'new' public administration which is to propose that it is a myth that policy (= politics) and administration (= management techniques) can be separated: values always inhere in administrative practices and values are the subject of policy decisions (Wilenski, 1987).

If development of the politics of discourse as a politics of the state is to occur, our understanding of what the politics of discourse involves needs to be more than a value-orientation to debate and more than an intuitive grasp of the possibilities of discursive action. It is important both to clarify the nature and the significance of that value-orientation, and to become theoretically more aware of the possibilities and constraints of discursive action. The next section is given to indicating some contemporary theoretical work which contributes to the achievement of these tasks.

WHAT IS THE POLITICS OF DISCOURSE?

Clarification of a value-orientation to the politics of discourse requires something different from the classical liberal position explicated by John Stuart Mill and others that out of open debate 'truth' emerges. Here the work of William Connolly is useful. Connolly is a political theorist working in the United States who titled one of his books *The Terms of Political Discourse* (1983), and who may be termed a theoretical advocate and exponent of the politics of discourse.

Connolly begins his book by arguing that when political scientists or political theorists attempt to produce a concept that is shorn of areas of dispute or the alleged fuzziness of a layperson's imprecision, they are denying the nature of politics itself. It is impossible to develop a technical concept of 'power', or a concept of power which distils the elements common to all uses of the term. Attempts at this may be made, but it turns out that the concepts so generated can be and are contested by those who think of power in a different way. The point about 'power', 'democracy', 'rights', 'class' for Connolly is that these are contested concepts. It is the discursive politics of those contests which constitutes the field of meaning which is what 'power', 'democracy' and so on are.

Thus Connolly (1983:1) proposes: 'The language of politics is not a neutral medium that conveys ideas independently formed; it is an institutionalized structure of meanings that channels political thought or action in certain directions.' Here he is rejecting what Threadgold, Poynton, Martin and others (after Reddy, 1979) have termed the conduit model of language.

According to the conduit model, language functions simply as a conduit for concepts, ideas, truths already existent. Thus it is simply a matter of determining the linguistic modes and terms which best correspond to those concepts, ideas, truths. The conduit model of language depends on the privileging of an indivisible knowing subject (god, reason, the proletariat, the party) who sends messages which, in order to be received properly, must be coded properly. Thus socialism needs scientific revolutionaries, namely trained interpreters of the class-consciousness of the proletariat, who, according to scientific method, translate this consciousness into appropriate policies of a one-party state. Connolly's own way of rejecting this conduit model of language and the depoliticised world it authorises is worth citing:

> To say that a particular network of concepts is contestable is to say that standards and criteria of judgment it expresses are open to contestation. To say that such a network is *essentially* contestable is to contend that the universal criteria of reason, as we can now understand them, do not *suffice* to settle these contests definitively. The proponent of essentially contestable concepts charges those who construe the standards operative in their own way of life to be fully expressive of God's will or reason or nature with transcendental provincialism; they treat the standards with which they are intimately familiar as universal criteria against which all other theories, practices, and ideals are to be assessed. They use universalist rhetoric to protect provincial practices. (Connolly, 1983: 225–26, emphases in the original)

The implications of Connolly's position are the following. First, contests over concepts like patriarchy, class, multiculturalism etc. constitute the *politics* of patriarchy, class and multiculturalism. Second, the contestants share the ground that they are contesting. Third, the dispute cannot be resolved through appeal to some transcendental criterion (god, reason, science, nature), although it may come to be resolved in a certain sense if the concept concerned becomes less contestable and recedes from view. Fourth, if the contestants are willing to acknowledge the intrinsically dialogical nature of the contested concept they are likely to welcome the contribution of their opponents as a contribution to the development of the politics of contestable concepts.

Connolly's position encourages and welcomes a 'discursive multiplicity' (Kress's term, 1985:11), which not only dethrones a putative source of indivisible truth but opens up the way for an understanding of the identity of the contestants as itself multiple, contradictory, and changing over time. Thus there is no reason for the political actors themselves to require their own discursive interventions to be the same over time or to be singular rather than multiple. In short the politics of discourse permits a dialogical and discursive relationship to one's own identity that is likely to permit the individual actor much more pragmatic space and flexibility as well as much greater acceptance of the diverse and multiple selves of other actors.

Connolly's exposition of the politics of discourse is that of a democratic theorist. The substance of his position is matched perfectly by the implications for a discursive politics that follow from the work of a particular school of social semioticians, some of whom are working in Australia. This school involves the followers of Michael Halliday, and his approach to 'language as social semiotic'. This approach permits the synthesis of the work of Foucault, Bernstein, and of linguists who have tended to be oriented to language as a social semiotic. Threadgold points out the convergence in this direction of the work of Volosinov, Bakhtin and Eco:

> For all three language as semiotic must be seen as interacting with the other semiotic systems within the culture. There is a parallelism between verbal and non-verbal forms of behavior which makes language and culture mutually dependent. The relationship between system (codes) and process (communication/dialogue/interaction) in language is situated for them all in dialogic interaction with speaking others, and thus 'text' as the basic unit produced through this interaction ... (Threadgold, 1986b:109)

This approach views language 'as a meaning potential capable of realisation under the constraints of the text-context dialectic' (Threadgold, 1988:41–42). Threadgold continues: 'This involves a view of language which sees the micro-structures of texts (their lexico-grammar) as in some sense a realisation of, a metaphor for, social structure and culture—and thus as realising, constructing, transmitting and changing the ideologies, the social meaning making practices, and the systems of ideas and beliefs that constitute the culture, the social system and speaking subjects.'

Gunther Kress (1985) provides a clear exposition of the premises of this social theory of linguistic-discursive practices. Following the work of Foucault, Kress defines 'discourses' as 'systemically-organised sets of statements which give expression to the meanings and values of an institution':

> Beyond that, they define, describe and delimit what it is possible to say and not possible to say (and by extension—what it is possible to do and not to do) with respect to the area of concern of that institution, whether marginally or centrally. A discourse provides a set of possible statements about a given area, and organises and gives structure to the manner in which a particular topic, object, process is to be talked about. In that it provides descriptions, rules, permissions and prohibitions of social and individual actions. (Kress, 1985:6–7)

Discursive reality is not determined by any one discursive system because discourses depend on active subjects for their realisation and these subjects are always positioned interdiscursively. That is, each subject is positioned across several discourses, and this positioning provides multiple points of identification and discursive differences which ensure that the tendencies for a discourse to become a genuinely as distinct from an illusorily closed system are never realised. The subject's interdiscursive position ensures that when he or she speaks within a particular discourse contradictions and incompatibilities are introduced which reflect that position, and which change the discourse. Moreover, the subject(s) may mobilise more or less reflectively the tensions and contradictions of their interdiscursive situation so that they proceed actively to contest a particular discourse.

Kress (1985:11) elaborates the discursive multiplicity which constitutes the identity of any one individual: for any member of a social group discursive multiplicity, contestation, and difference is both a description of their history and an account of their present social position at any given moment. The individual's history is composed of the experience of a range of discourses, passing through the intimate relations of the family and its discourses of authority, gender, morality, religion, politics; into school and its discourses of knowledge, science, authority, aesthetics; to work and adulthood. The discursive history of each individual therefore bears the traces of the discourses associated with the social places which that individual has occupied and experienced. These form, like sedimentary layers, the linguistic experience and potential of the speaker. If all discourses, depending as they do for their realisation on the discursive agency of complex subjects, are always dynamic, these dynamics will be the more pronounced as those who have been subjugated and silenced within particular dominant discourses establish their own voice and contest these systems of domination. The current active mobilisation of these voices is often referred to as the 'new social movements'. These represent the emergence of black, feminist, environmentalist, gay, and non-metropolitan voices. Their very emergence disrupts the monocentric discursive world that prevailed up to this point. Some of the participants in these new social movements understand this and have committed themselves to exploring and legitimising a discursive multiplicity that precludes any tendency to return to monocentric constructions of reality. The work of these social linguists to which I am referring needs to be seen as a theoretical expression of this commitment, and to be located as part of the emergence of Australia as a multicultural society within a global and post-colonial context.

The emphasis on the discursive multiplicity of each individual informs us how these theorists understand the production and reading of texts. Kress (1985:12) suggests that it is unresolved tensions of an individual's discursive history which motivates him or her to produce a text, where this text becomes a 'site of attempts' at resolution of these tensions and contradictions.

Texts, then, are dialogical in character. Because they arise out of discursive difference, they always contain contradictions which can be mobilised by readers who are discursively positioned to do this. For example the White Paper *Higher Education: A Policy Statement (1988)* is a text which brings together the official discourses of 'access and equity' and 'economic restructuring'. The uneasy coupling of these discourses reflects dominant discursive binary assumptions that 'economic' and 'welfare' are about different things and obey different logics. For feminist readers of this policy document, the following statement from it stands out as contradictory, and permits them to proceed to argue that this is the case:

> Priority in the allocation of additional intakes will be directed to areas of strong demand from students and industry, having regard to the likely future needs of the economy and labour market. The Government will continue to give high priority in the 1989–91 triennium to the fields of engineering, science and technology, and business and management studies.... Achieving improved rates of transfer to technology-based courses in particular will require increased participation in mathematics and science at the secondary level. The Government is concerned that the proportion of Year 12 students, particularly girls, currently taking such subjects remains low (p. 17).

For feminist readers positioned as they are in a discursive tension between their experience of lack of access to these fields of engineering, science, technology, business and management, and their commitment to equal educational opportunities for girls and women, this policy text mirrors this tension. Government rhetoric asserting the desirability of getting girls at school into 'non-traditional' areas for girls recreates gender inequality by discursively constructing the problem of getting 'girls' into 'non-traditional' areas. Moreover, the Government's continuing to give funding priority to engineering, science and technology means less funds for the areas of professional training and higher education into which women do go, and from which they enter the labour markets that are open to them.

A text, then, can become a site of struggle. As such, 'texts are the sites of linguistic and cultural change' (Kress, 1985:32). It is important to emphasise that just as a text reflects and articulates 'the contradictory discourses of social heterogeneity and conflict' (Threadgold, 1986a:48), this polyphony of the text remains latent until the point where it invites the attention of those who are positioned in ways that motivate them to openly mobilise these tensions within the text and to make it a site of struggle.

If 'texts give material realisation to discourses' (Kress, 1985:18), they are determined also by the conventions of a particular 'genre' to which they have to conform. For instance, a novel and policy document are quite different genres. Policy texts are produced in conformity to the rules which govern the genre of a policy document, and within this genre there are a number of subgenres. The genre corresponds to and expresses the conventions of the social occasion to which it belongs: for example, there are specific policy text subgenres which belong to the occasions of a parliamentary sitting, a formal government inquiry, a party conference, and a program evaluation.

Thus the same discourse may be expressed in different genres. The distinction between discourse and genre makes it possible to appreciate the difference between discursive closure/openness and generic closure/openness. Discursive closure in broad terms refers to the tendency built into particular discourses which leads them to construct the world in a monocentric fashion, to totalise their own terms of operating, and thus to colonise other discourses. Generic closure refers to particular genres which operate to maintain power differences by privileging the power relations which conventionally structure the social occasion. This, as in the case of the lesson which Kress (1985:26) discusses, means that the content of the exchange takes a back seat in relation to how it functions to maintain the ritual features of the power relation. This is illustrated clearly in the case of the university lecture: the spatial architecture and acoustics of the lecture theatre guarantee that the lecturer reproduces the ritual of power which separates the lecturer and the students, keeps the former talking (discursively powerful), and the latter silent (discursively passive). Generic openness requires reciprocal discursive power. This means, Kress argues, that formality and ritual must be backgrounded and that content be foregrounded. The genre which is most unlike the lecture in this respect is, Kress points out, conversation. Policy documents tend to conform to generic conventions which maintain the power of the state in relation to the individual. Thus they use the conventions of power to which Kress refers when he discusses distancing strategies which maintain, by obscuring, the source of power: 'Generally, the strategies are of two kinds: a retreat into an institutional impersonality, or a retreat into individual invisibility. The effect in each case is to make the sources of power or authority difficult to detect, and therefore difficult or impossible to challenge' (1985:57) Kress proceeds to discuss bureaucratic language, a genre which is not the same thing as policy genres although these often share some features.

For Kress bureaucratic language is about as far from ordinary reciprocal forms of dialogue as can be. It appears as the impersonal voice of authority, where propositions assume the features of fact, formal principles of order are fundamental to shaping the text, and there are no indications of process, uncertainty or contest. If debate is admitted it is referred to as the 'consultations' which inform the final version of the policy. Thus, for example, the White Paper *Higher Education* (1988:4–5) acknowledges the raging debate which the Green Paper provoked by terming it 'The Community Response'. This section begins with the positive claim that 'the great majority of responses to the Policy Discussion Paper supported the broad objectives underlying the Government's proposals', and it ends with this paragraph:

> Within this framework, however, the Government readily acknowledges the legitimacy of concerns expressed by many respondents. To the extent that the Policy Discussion Paper sought to emphasise the need for change without also explaining the associated need for maintenance of valuable traditions, it may not have given an adequate impression of the Government's intentions. The Government takes the opportunity provided by this statement to present its objectives in a broader context.

Discourses and genres distribute access, making it more possible for some than others to participate in them. It is the interaction of monocentric discourses and power-oriented genres which maintain structures of discursive domination. The contribution of social semiotics to the politics of discourse lies in the semiotic emphasis on the impossibility of closure within even the most closed of texts. The contestation of discursive dominance needs to be oriented not only to the mobilisation of discursive contradictions and the reassignment of meanings but must contest generic structures of dominance. The latter can occur when unauthorised and non-dominant voices (the voices of the other) establish their own access to discourses.

It is possible to overstate the extent to which the impersonal and institutional features of bureaucratic and policy genres work to maintain the structures of discursive domination. It is often the case that the impersonal styles of bureaucratic and policy discourse open up discursive space for dialogical constructions of needs as claims on statecentric modes of distribution.

For example, consider the bureaucratic and official discourse of 'needs-based planning' in contemporary Australian statecentric cultures. As I understand the discursive history of this concept, it arose in relation to the perceived inequities of the Commonwealth Government's distribution of childcare services in relation to effective submissions from groups sufficiently organised and equipped with relevant, professional knowledge to make effective submissions. The submission basis of funding was considered by many within the childcare bureaucracy to favour 'middle-class' claimants on the system. The alternative proposed and adopted was the needs-based planning approach. This requires the identification of areas of greatest need, where the identification is made on the basis of combining census data, relevant Commonwealth, State and Local Government information and data sets, and relevant academic demographic research. This approach is to complement this quantitative/hard data with qualitative investigation of perceived needs and wants within a particular geographical area. This latter type of investigation requires communication and interaction with community groups, potential users of the service, and the establishment of what type of service they would like. Thus, if the area is ethnically variable, this component of needs-based planning requires the planners to talk with the various ethnic groups and to determine with them what the service would need to look like if it is to be culturally sensitive (for descriptions of this planning approach, see Hurford, 1987:5; Coleman, Gallagher and Thame, 1987:10; for an elaboration of this approach see Cameron's, 1983:5–8, discussion of the planning stages of developing a 'community profile').

This is a compelling example of how bureaucratic and policy discourse can lend themselves to the admission of dialogical and multivocal constructions of needs. In this case it is the very impersonality of the discourse that permits these democratic features of the planning orientation. In other instances of bureaucratic and policy discourse, we should not automatically assume that their surface appearance of lacking any dialogic features precludes the play and mobilisation of contradictions that develop a politics of meaning in those instances.

Those who have been acculturated as indivisible individual subjects whose subjectivity is expressed only as it is marked as their own singular authorship—namely the possessive individuals of modernist metropolitan masculine culture—find bureaucratic modes of discourse antagonistic to this type of subjectivity, and, with Kress, tend to want to restrict their scope. These 'individuals' accordingly find it difficult to be oriented to the play and politics of the dialogical potential and possibilities of bureaucratic and policy discourse. Those who can mobilise this play and politics tend to be those who have been excluded from this culture of 'individuality' and who can express their multiple subjectivities within this play and politics.

THE POLITICS OF DISCOURSE AND THE POLITICS OF THE STATE

I proposed above that the emergence of the politics of discourse is tied into the politics of the contemporary 'interventionist' state and into the dispersed and barely emergent politics of the new global society. As the new global society develops with its plethora of communications networks, and its relative lack of clearly identifiable institutional centres of policy determination, the boundaries of the politics of the state will become highly permeable. Jurisdictionally specific policies will become driven increasingly by non-jurisdictionally bounded global discourses. Until now the modern state has been the institutional centre of the discursive processes which have conventionalised phenomena and thereby made them subject to policy. This has entailed a strong identification of such conventionalised phenomena with legally constituted phenomena.

In this context, the 'interventionist' state can be viewed as one phase, and a passing phase at that, of the development of the politics of discourse. The development of the modern 'interventionist' state extended the scope of conventionalised phenomena, i.e. phenomena which are understood to be subject to construction by policy, the corollary of which is to bring them into the politics of the making and distribution of claims (see Peattie and Rein, 1983). This is why the modern state is regarded by many, who for various reasons resist this process of conventionalisation, as the 'interventionist' state.

Increasingly, it will be difficult to identify the structures and processes of conventionalisation with the conventional legal order instituted and elaborated by the modern sovereign state. This is the state theorised by the great modern political theorists of sovereignty: Hobbs, Rousseau and Hegel. Melucci also proposes that 'as a unitary agent of intervention and action the state has dissolved. It has been replaced from above by a tightly interdependent system of transnational relationships and subdivided from below into a multiplicity of partial governments, defined both by their own systems of representation and decision-making and by an ensemble of interwoven organisations which combine inextricably the public and private' (1988:287). This dissolution of the sovereign state is expressed in a dispersal of the state and in the plurality of discursive forums which the different aspects of state activity create; for instance, the politics of welfare is almost completely uncoupled from the politics of fiscal policy. The former implicates a different set of interested parties and different levels of government from the latter: for example, welfare politics involves the local and provincial levels of government in a way that fiscal policy does not. Instead, fiscal policy involves preeminently the national level of government. This is why, as Melucci argues, contemporary 'public spaces are characterised by a great fluidity.' (1958:259) They are a 'mobile system of instances kept open by creative confrontation between collective action and institutions'.

To give an example of what I mean by the modern state extending the scope of conventionalisation and the politics of claims, let us take the example of the discursive construction of child abuse as a social problem. This discourse problematises a relationship which was previously thought to be 'natural' in character. This is the parent–child relationship, which the discourse of child abuse conventionalises by constituting the norms and practices which should govern that relationship. Indeed the discourse of child abuse comes close to introducing the parent–child relationship into the conventional sphere of the polity by focusing on the power differential between parent and child and raising the question of what constitutes legitimate modes of parental domination over children. In this respect, the relationship loses its erstwhile 'private' status, and becomes a matter of 'public' interest. The discourse of child abuse constitutes new 'claims' on the political process, claims by various different kinds of advocates on behalf of children, claims by parents and others resisting this politicisation of parenting, and, although this is a potential development still largely unrealised, claims by children (see Yeatman, 1988e). In constituting these claims, the discourse constitutes the claimants making the claims.

Evidently the state does not monopolise 'discourse', but the discourses to which I am referring here concern those which extend the state's discursive and conventionalising power. The discursive field which develops in relation to any particular set of claims involves complex negotiation and struggle between various parties concerning which meanings are incorporated into official policies. These parties cannot be simply thought of as 'the state' and the social movements, or interest groups, outside the state who are pressing the state to adopt their construction of legitimate claims and claimants.

A good deal of negotiation and struggle goes on within the state itself, where advocates of particular claims and claimants may press their case in a subtle combination of intrabureaucratic politics, the invocation of strongly felt citizen or consumer views, and reference to 'neutral' social scientific exercises in evaluation and planning which establish the 'needs' which inform those claims. Accordingly, when the politics of discourse and the politics of the state flourish, there is an important degree of interpenetration of the state and civil society. Civil society comes into the state to the degree that the politics within the state is structured in part by advocacy on behalf of interests, groups and movements in civil society. The state penetrates civil society when, in admitting interest groups, advocate lobbies and social movements into the discursive politics of the state, it effectively constitutes them by shaping the mode and distribution of leadership of these groups, the substance of their claims and their style of discursive action. Offe terms this process the 'attribution of public status to interest groups', and he remarks:

> Policies that provide status to interest groups, assign certain semi-public or public functions to them, and regulate the type and scope of their activities are, under conditions of advanced capitalist social and economic structures, far more important factors affecting on-going change in the system of interest representation than factors that have to do with changes of either ideological orientations or socio-economic structures. Interest representation, for a number of reasons ..., tends to become predominantly a matter of 'political design' and thus, in part a dependent rather than independent variable of public-policy making. (1985:223)

The development of the state as a site and producer of discursive practices has been interpreted by Daniel Bell and others (see Bjorklund, 1987:20) as entailing the 'expansion of the political arena'. This has encouraged the proliferation and pluralisation of claimants on the statecentric political process. It is against this backdrop that the 'new social movements' and the kind of plurality which ethnic group politics represents have developed.

The state's management of the discursive proliferation and development of claims can be more or less controlling. One response of the state is to develop various rationing strategies with regard to claims and claimants. These rationing strategies can take the form of sophisticated discursive practices, e.g. the discourse of more effective 'targeting' of social welfare.

With regard to highly empowered discursive producers, as in the case of the professional educators within the publicly funded school system or the higher-education system, the state has developed a different type of response. It has embarked on subtle strategies of containment of the claims generated by these masters of discursive production. The general thrust has been in the direction of corporate management whereby, in the current general environment of declining public resources and services, and as legitimised by the discourse of decentralisation (letting the managers manage, etc.), the management of reduced budgets is given over to the units closest to the coalface. Thus State Government departments of education devolve this authority to individual schools, and the Commonwealth Government to individual institutions of higher education; and, within the latter the central administration devolves the management of the reduced budget to faculties. This means that claims and claimants are brokered much lower down the line, and it becomes all the more difficult for their advocates to elaborate them into generalised and generally visible discursive maps and claims. When managers close to the coalface are required to manage reduced budgets, which in a climate of restructuring bring with them acutely intensified competition between claims and their advocates, they can do little more than retreat into control modes of management which favour the existing distributions of discursive power and resources (see Blackmore and Kenway, 1988:44). Meanwhile the state continues to encourage the production of highly elaborate curriculum design (within the schooling system) or access and equity objectives (for the higher-education system), which seem to promise extraordinary and creative developments which are oriented to the needs of individuals and disadvantaged groups within education. This discursive production eats up the energies of the creative and innovative advocates of change within education circles only to contain this creativity within a particularly ornate form of symbolic window dressing.

The Australian state under the leadership of the Hawke Labor Government has incorporated into policy making many of the Labor/new social movement–oriented intellectuals (higher-education-credentialled) who are masters of discursive production. This state has encouraged and funded the production of elaborate discourses of access and equity. These discourses function to either legitimise particular forms of rationing (e.g. 'the new graduate tax' for participants in the public system of higher education) or to throw up symbolic smokescreens around material developments like the reduction, under the Hawke Government, of the proportion of the population receiving pensions and benefits at a time of relatively high unemployment (see Disney, 1987:16).

This is a complex, discursive politics, where agendas of control and rationing threaten to discredit central values like access and equity, and, in their modes of usage, to turn them into a form of Orwellian doublethink (see the discussion of Orwellian linguistics by

Hodge and Fowler, 1979). Under these conditions—and they bear some similarity to the Soviet states which constructed their policy agendas in terms of the discourse of scientific socialism—for those who want to restore substance to these values of access and equity, and to locate them with reflective debates, their crucial contribution lies in empirical investigation of what is happening to real people and their needs in relation to the distributive politics of claims.

Historically, there have been two fundamental limits to the politics of discourse and the politics of the state. One is terror: state-sponsored terror represses even while it can never entirely vanquish the politics of the state and the politics of discourse. A recent case is the Junta's coup against the democratically elected government of the socialists led by Salvador Allende in Chile, and the ensuing regime of terror. The other limit involves the recommodification of claims, the taking of them out of the political arena and placing them within the market. This has the effect of disaggregating claims, and thereby making it very difficult to establish a full picture concerning different groups of claimants, their needs and how the distribution of claims is operating to advantage some relative to others. The commodification of claims has the effect of privatising them, and in turn this has the effect of restricting the scope of the politics of discourse.

Historically, liberal democratic capitalist states have not had the option of using terror as a means of limiting the politics of discourse and the politics of the state, and they have had only partial resort to the option of the commodification of claims. Since their legitimacy is considerably bound up with tolerance if not encouragement of the politics of discourse, it is inevitable that many claims are successfully made as public claims which it is the business of the state to meet.

In the context of the development of the welfare state and of the proliferation of public claims, both actual and potential, these states have become practised in using a mix of strategies to restrict the scope and development of the politics of discourse. This mix involves different balances, themselves reflecting the ideology of the government in power, of the following strategies: 1. the conversion of core values like equity or choice into ritual litanies to be invoked on all symbolic occasions, where the values themselves lose discursive and reflective meaning and become situated as a form of doublethink fuzz; 2. the subjection of claims to technicist modes of administrative rationality where a claim is accorded legitimate existence only if it accords with tightly controlled criteria, the value-orientation of which is thoroughly hidden within the smokescreen of technical rules and norms; 3. the commissioning of grand works of discursive policy statement by intellectuals, which assume a sort of life of their own, but this life tends to be confined within the highly restricted social circles of the state-oriented intelligentsia and rarely receives wider exposure and debate (most of the pro-multiculturalism policy documents are of this kind); 4. the commodification of claims by turning them over to the market, and thereby rendering them subject to market-oriented discourse rather than to political discourse.

THE POLITICS OF DISCOURSE IN A GLOBAL CULTURE

Above I suggested that a statecentric politics of discourse may become to some degree anachronistic as state sovereignty becomes increasingly diluted and penetrated both by global and local discourses. It will be the nature of the latter that they emanate from many centres of discursive production. In this context those who want to develop and elaborate the politics of discourse will need to develop a global, local and national awareness and orientation.

It is clear that a global orientation is not the same thing as an 'internationalist' orientation. The latter presupposed the universal elaboration of a monocentric construction of humankind, wherein it made sense to use abstract universals like 'Man', 'the human family', and so on. As Haraway (1987:15) proposes, 'It is no accident that the symbolic system of the family of man—and so the essence of woman—breaks up at the same moment that networks of connection among people on the planet are unprecedentedly multiple, pregnant, and complex'.

It is this context that is likely to develop the potential of the politics of discourse for encouraging the proliferation of discursive interventions, of different forms of deconstruction, and of different languages themselves. For those of us who are committed to the substantive possibilities of the politics of discourse for the surfacing of claims, for debate and struggle over the distribution of claims, for the exploration of the 'intertextuality' of differences among the many differently voiced claimants, and for the decoding and deconstruction of discourses of domination, we need to understand that we are in a new era. It is an era of emancipation from the iron embrace of an indivisible subject of history and of invitation to those who have been silenced within this iron embrace to speak. If the systems of control are likely to be polycentric, to be both everywhere and nowhere, so too will be the politics of discourse.

Appendix A
Financial accountability mechanisms

Excerpt from *Managing Change in the Public Sector: A Statement of the Government's Position*, Government of Western Australia, June 1986, pp. 8–9.

The traditional approach: achieving financial accountability through micro-controls

Government financial accountability in the past has been typically based upon micro-controls, with responsibility for certain expenditures, generally those perceived as more vulnerable to extravagance or error, being retained at a central level. The chief executive officers of the public service departments are accountable for retaining expenditure within approved limits in defined areas. The same structures are not necessarily applied to all statutory authorities although their work is also conducted on behalf of government in accordance with legislation enacted by Parliament.

Micro-controls fragment responsibility, inhibit flexibility and, hence, get in the way of seeking the most economical means of achieving results. They are costly to maintain and fail to lend themselves to the functional costing now sought by Government. More pertinently, the evidence emerging from the work of the Functional Review Committee has indicated that they are not necessarily effective.

Ineffectiveness arises partly because many costs of specific departmental operations are difficult of determine. Chief executive officers who wish to establish the costs associated with a particular function, find the task extremely difficult. Despite changes in recent years general expenses, buildings, motor vehicles, superannuation, building maintenance, rates and charges and the services of central Government agencies tend to be accounted for separately.

Put simply, a way in which a chief executive officer can best do the job is to acquire as many of these resources as possible. Economy is neither established nor called for in present reporting arrangements and, consequently, the management focus too often moves to one of achieving the task without criticism rather than achieving it with optimum economy. The Government is concerned to avoid placing too much reliance upon micro-controls as it moves to develop efficient structures.

Achieving financial accountability through macro-controls

The general trend within public sector operations in Australia appears to be to achieve financial accountability by use of fewer and broader financial control mechanisms in the expectation that these will be more effective. Such mechanisms have been called 'macro-controls'. Their purpose is to enable chief executive officers to turn their attention from procedural controls towards a more results-oriented approach in which the major objective is to meet their commitments on time and within budget.

The achievement of financial accountability within a results-oriented context requires clarification of the roles of Government and of chief executive officers. In general it is the role of the Government to provide to chief executive officers:
— clear policy directions;
— broadly defined operating guidelines; and adequate financial resources.

For their part, chief executive officers have the responsibility to:
— achieve the required results effectively and economically;
— adapt their strategies as circumstances require;
— stay within their overall budget allocation; and
— provide financial information to Government in a form which allows for the setting of 'whole of Government' priorities.

The Government will give consideration to proposals designed to achieve these objectives, including those concepts put forward in the remainder of this chapter:
— performance agreements;
— organisational profiles;
— counter-acting the 'year by year' budget syndrome; and
— rewarding economy.

Performance agreements

The Government plans to explore the concept of 'performance agreements' to be prepared on an annual basis by public sector organisations. Such agreements would contain:
— a statement of the relevant Government priorities;
— the identifiable targets for achievement by the organisation during the year;
— the management strategies proposed;
— the approved level of resource allocation;
— appropriate standards to measure financial performance; and
— the planned organisational profile.

Performance agreements would carry the commitment of the chief executive officer and the Board or Commission where appropriate, as well as the approval of the Minister. They would provide a basis for reporting to Government on actual performance, including documentation of actual organisational profiles and financial performance. The concept of performance agreements will be thoroughly explored in consultation with all interested parties.

Organisational profiles

The Government is interested in the use of organisational profiles as a means to enhance flexibility in staffing structures, while still maintaining overall control. The concept of organisational profiles involves placing broad limits upon the number and classification levels of staff. Flexibility is allowed provided that the overall budget is not exceeded nor the profile unduly distorted. The degree of flexibility can be varied as appropriate.

Organisational profiles require the development of guidelines, standards and systems of review which, on the one hand, maintain an acceptable level of consistency throughout the public sector yet, at the same time, leave accountability and an appropriate degree of flexibility with chief executive officers. The Government proposes a closer examination of the concept with a view to implementing it in this State.

Counter-acting the 'Year by Year' budget syndrome

Despite the existence of three-year Capital Works Programs and forward estimates of revenue and expenditure within the Consolidated Revenue Fund, the fact remains that most public sector budgets must be determined on a year by year basis. As a consequence, by the time public sector managers and executive officers are aware of the level of funding for a current year, it is already a quarter gone and the expenditure which they incur in the final weeks of the financial year is formally brought to account in the following year. Hence, the period of fully informed financial management is considerably less than one year.

Beyond that, however, the system encourages public sector managers to ensure that the expenditure of their organisations reaches at least the budgeted figure. The attitude prevails that a slight excess will appear to be evidence of a general endeavour to operate within a budget which was, in fact, too tight: hence increased allocation is appropriate in the following year. Economies are not rewarded since they tend to result in a reduction in the level of funding in the following year when, for one reason or another, similar economies may not be possible. Hence, public sector managers often act on the premise that it is better to play safe and ensure that funds are spent, regardless of the relevance of such expenditure in terms of broad Government priorities. The Government will examine means of counteracting the unwanted attitudes that arise from the 'year by year' budget syndrome, while recognising that annual budgets will continue to be a permanent feature of Government.

Rewarding economy

More generally there is a need to adapt the motivational system for public sector managers so as to reward successful efforts to manage with less. It is generally true at the present that the total number of staff supervised has an influence on the level of remuneration. Hence, the manager who reduces staff receives no reward for that contribution to Government while the person who indulges in 'empire building' may well be rewarded by increased classification. The classification of individual employees should place relatively greater emphasis upon function and less upon the number of staff supervised. In addition, management performance will be assessed against the achievement of results economically and on time.

Appendix B

Excerpt from *Senior Executive Management Program 1987 Design Specification* Senior Executive Development Branch, Public Service Board, February 1987.

6. *SEMP Streams*

(a) The critical difference between senior executives and middle managers is that SES managers can no longer rely on achieving results through their own subject matter competencies but need to achieve results through other people.
(b) Industrial relations is no longer regarded as a narrow skill to be practised by a small number of experienced experts, instead dealing with unions is expected to be a central skill of most SES managers.
(c) The Government's reform program requires managers to make government work as efficiently as possible for Australia by:
   — doing more with less
   — focussing on outcomes and results
   — managing change better

The most recent reforms, the 1986 streamlining measures, are about giving more power and responsibility to managers at all levels and helping them to exercise that power responsibly.

A core component of SEMP will be a focus on values, attitudes and behaviours in managing self and others to achieve results (Personal and Interpersonal Competence Stream).

Industrial relations will be a core component of SEMP. This component will include values clarification and skill-building elements as well as information input. Skill-building will focus on participative management and industrial relations negotiating skills. (Refer to Industrial Relations design specification for details.)

Managing organisational change will be a core component of SEMP. This component will include values clarification and skill building elements as well as information input. (Refer to SEMP Managing Organisational Change stream design specification for details.)

Managing for results, equity and managing change will be integral elements of each SEMP stream.

Bibliography

Advisory Council for Overseas Aid (1988) *Towards a National Agenda for a Multicultural Australia: a Discussion Paper* Canberra: AGPS

Affirmative Action Resource Unit (1985) *Affirmative Action Implementation Manual: Higher Education Edition* Office of the Status of Women, Department of Prime Minister and Cabinet, Canberra: AGPS

Amsden, A. (1985) 'The State and Taiwan's Economic Development' in P. Evans, D. Rueschemeyer and T. Skocpol (eds) *Bringing The State Back In* Cambridge: Cambridge University Press

Antcliff, S. (1988) 'Behind the Rhetoric—a closer look at the New Right' *Australian Quarterly* 60: pp. 63–70

Ashenden, D. (1988) 'Who's Unskilled?' *Australian Society* May, pp. 23–28

Australian Council for Overseas Aid (1987) *Life After Debt: Australia and the Global Debt Crisis* Development Dossier No. 23

Baldock, C. and Cass, B. (eds) (1988) *Women, Social Welfare and The State* 2nd edn, Sydney: Allen & Unwin

Barron, R. and G. Norris (1976) 'Sexual Divisions and the Dual Labour Market' in D. Barker and S. Allen (eds) *Dependence and Exploitation in Work and Marriage* London and New York: Longman

Beale, R.D. (1985a) 'Public Service Reform—A Progress Report' *Canberra Bulletin of Public Administration*, 12, 2, pp. 116–119

—— (1985b) 'Strategies for Management Improvement in the Commonwealth Public Service' *Australian Journal of Public Administration* 44, 4, pp. 376–84

Beilharz, P. (1987) 'Reading Politics: Social Theory and Social Policy' *Australian and New Zealand Journal of Sociology* 23, pp. 388–407

Beilharz, P. and R. Watts (1986) 'The Discourse of Labourism' *Arena* 77, pp. 97–110

Bjorklund, U. (1987) 'Ethnicity and the Welfare State' *International Social Science Journal* 111 pp. 19–31

Blackmore, J. and J. Kenway (1988) 'Rationalisation, instrumentalism and corporate managerialism: the implications for women of the Green Paper in higher education' *Australian Universities Review* 31 pp. 42–49

Bledstein, B. (1976) *The Culture of Professionalism: the Middle Class and the Development of Higher Education in America* New York: W.W. Norton

Block, F., R. Cloward, B. Ehrenreich and F. Piven (1987) *The Mean Season: The Attack on the Welfare State* New York: Pantheon

Borchorst, A. and B. Siim (1987) 'Women and the advanced welfare state—a new kind of patriarchal power?' in A. Showstack Sassoon (ed.) *Women and the State: The Shifting Boundaries of Public and Private* London: Hutchinson

Boris, E. and P. Bardaglio (1983), 'The Transformation of Patriarchy: The Historic Role of the State' in I. Diamond (ed.) *Families, Politics, and Public Policy* New York and London: Longman

Boxer, M. (1986) 'Protective Legislation and Home Industry: The Marginalization of Women Workers in Late Nineteenth – Early Twentieth-Century France' *Journal of Social History* 20, pp. 45–66

Bradley, D. and D. McCulloch (1985) 'South Australia: a question of commitment?' in M. Sawer (ed.) *Program for Change* Sydney: Allen & Unwin

Bryson, L. (1986) 'A New Iron Cage? A View from Within' *Canberra Bulletin of Public Administration* 50, pp. 362–70 (see the longer version in *Flinders Studies in Policy and Administration* 3, 1987)

—— (1987a) 'A New Iron Cage? Experiences of Managerial Reform' *Flinders Studies in Policy and Administration* 3, pp. 16–46

—— (1987b) 'Women and Management' *Australian Journal of Public Administration* 46 pp. 259–73

Burns, A. (1987) 'Mother-headed Households: What is the Future?' *Australian Quarterly* 59, pp. 387–401

Burton, C. (1987) 'Equal Pay: A Comment' *Australian Feminist Studies* 4, pp. 107–114

—— (1987) 'Merit and Gender: Organisations and the Mobilisation of Masculine Bias' *Australian Journal of Social Issues* 22, pp. 424–35

Cabinet Sub-Committee on Maintenance (1986) *Child Support: a discussion paper on child maintenance* Canberra: AGPS

Cameron, J. (1983) 'Integrated Children's Services' *Australian Early Childhood Resource Booklets* No. 4, Australian Early Childhood Association

Cass, B. (1978) 'Women's Class in the Class Structure' in E.L. Wheelwright and K.D. Buckley (eds) *Essays in the Political Economy of Australian Capitalism* vol. 3, Sydney: ANZ Book Co.

—— (1986a) *The Social Security Review Background/Discussion Paper No. 1: The Case for Review of Aspects of the Australian Social Security System* Department of Social Security

—— (1986b), *Social Security Review Issues Paper No. 1: Income Support for Families with Children* Canberra: AGPS

—— (1988a) 'Redistribution to children and to mothers: a history of child endowment and family allowances' in C. Baldock and B. Cass (eds) *Women, Social Welfare and the State* 2nd edn, Sydney: Allen & Unwin

—— (1988b) 'Population Policies and Family Policies: State Construction of Domestic Life' in C. Baldock and B. Cass (eds) *Women, Social Welfare and the State* 2nd edn, Sydney: Allen & Unwin

Castles, F. (1985), *The Working Class and Welfare: Reflections on the Political Development of the Welfare State in Australia and New Zealand, 1890–1980* New Zealand and Australia: Allen & Unwin

—— (1988), *Australian Public Policy and Economic Vulnerability* Sydney: Allen & Unwin

—— (1978) *The Social Democratic Image of Society: a Study of the Achievements and Origins of Scandinavian Social Democracy in Comparative Perspective* London: Routledge & Kegan Paul

—— (1987) 'Thirty Wasted Years: Australian Social Security Development, 1950–80, in Comparative Perspective' *Canberra Bulletin of Public Administration* No. 51, pp. 41–47

Child Support: A Discussion Paper on Child Maintenance (1986) AGPS

Chilton, P. (ed.) (1985) *Language and the Nuclear Arms Debate: Nukespeak Today* New Hampshire: Frances Pinter

Coady, C. (1988) 'The Academy and the State' *The Australian Universities Review* 31, pp. 15–20

Coleman, M., P. Gallagher and C. Thame (1987) 'Some Distributional and Equity Issues in Financing Community Services' *Australian Journal of Early Childhood* 12, pp. 9–13

Commonwealth Public Services Board (1987) *Senior Executive Management Program 1987 Design Specification*

Connolly, W. (1983) *The Terms of Political Discourse* 2nd edn, Princeton: Princeton University Press

—— (1984) 'Introduction: Legitimacy and Modernity' in W. Connolly (ed.) *Legitimacy and the State* New York: New York University Press

Considine, M. (1988) 'The Corporate Management Framework as Administrative Science: A Critique' *Australian Journal of Public Administration* 47, pp. 4–19

Coombs, H.C. (1981) *Trial Balance* Melbourne: Macmillan

Cooper, T.L. (1984) 'Citizenship and Professionalism in Public Administration' *Public Administration Review* 44, pp. 143–50

Corkindale, D. (1988) The Role of Marketing Thinking and Practice in the Public, Human Services, revised version of paper delivered to Australian and New Zealand Management Educators' Conference, University of Western Australia

Cullen, R.B. (1986) 'The Victorian Senior Executive Service: A Performance Based Approach to the Management of Senior Managers' *Australian Journal of Public Administration* 45, 1, pp. 60–74

—— (1987) 'Business, Government and Change: Managing Transitions in the Public and Private Sector' *Australian Journal of Public Administration*, 46, pp. 10–20

Curthoys, A. (1988) 'Equal Pay, a Family Wage or Both: Women Workers, Feminists and Unionists in Australia since 1945,' in B. Caine, E. Grosz, M. de Lepervanche (eds) *Crossing Boundaries: Feminisms and the Critique of Knowledge* Sydney: Allen & Unwin

Dahlerup, D. (1987) 'Confusing Concepts—Confusing Reality: a theoretical discussion of the patriarchal state' in A. Showstack-Sassoon (ed) *Women and The State* London: Hutchinson

d'Alpuget, B. (1984) *Robert J. Hawke: A Biography* Ringwood, Vic.: Penguin

De Lauretis, T. (1986) 'Feminist Studies/Critical Issues: Issues, Terms, and Contexts' in T. de Lauretis (ed.) *Feminist Studies/Critical Studies* Bloomington: Indiana University Press

Deacon, D. (1982) 'The Employment of Women in the Commonwealth Public Service: the Creation and Reproduction of a Dual Labour Market' *Australian Journal of Public Administration* 41, pp. 232–51

—— (1983) 'Women, Bureaucracy and the Dual Labour Market' in A. Kouzmin (ed.) *Public Sector Administration: New Perspectives* Melbourne: Longman Cheshire

Department of Immigration and Ethnic Affairs (1986) *Don't Settle for Less: Report of the Committee for Stage I of the Review of Migrant and Multicultural Programs and Services* Canberra: AGPS

Department of Trade (1987) *Australia Reconstructed: ACTU/TDC Mission to Western Europe—A Report by the Mission Members to the ACTU and TDC* Canberra: AGPS

Disney, J. (1987) 'Poverty, Welfare and Tax Reform' *Canberra Bulletin of Public Administration* 51, pp. 15–20

Donzelot, J. (1980) *The Policing of Families: Welfare versus the State* London: Hutchinson

Dowse, S. (1981) 'The Transfer of the Office of Women's Affairs' in S. Encel, P. Wilenski and B. Schaffer (eds) *Decisions: Case Studies in Australian Public Policy* Melbourne: Longman Cheshire

—— (1984) 'The Bureaucrat as Usurer' in D. Broom (ed.) *Unfinished Business* Sydney: Allen & Unwin

—— (1988) 'The Women's Movement Fandango with the State: the Movement's Role in Public Policy since 1972' in C. Baldock and B. Cass (eds) *Women, Social Welfare and the State* 2nd edn, Sydney: Allen & Unwin

Durkheim, E. (1957) *Professional Ethics and Civil Morals* London: Routledge & Kegan Paul

—— (1964) *The Division of Labor in Society* New York: Free Press

Earle J. and R. Graycar (1987) 'A New Dependence' *Australian Society* February, pp. 37–39

Edwards, M. (1985) 'Individual Equity and Social Policy' in J. Goodnow and M. Pateman (eds) *Women, Social Science and Public Policy* Sydney: Allen & Unwin

Eisenstein, H. (1985), 'Affirmative Action at Work in New South Wales' in M. Sawer (ed.) *Program for Change* Sydney: Allen & Unwin

—— (1987) Women, The State, and Your Complexion: Toward an Analysis of Femocracy, paper presented at SAANZ Annual Conference, 14 July, University of New South Wales

Epstein, C. (1970) *Woman's Place: Options and Limits in Professional Careers* Berkeley, Los Angeles and London: University of California Press

Ergas, H. and T. Lee (1988) 'Industrial Competitiveness and Economic Restructuring' *Australian Quarterly* pp. 94–108

Evans, P. (1985) 'Transnational Linkages and the Economic Role of the State: An Analysis of Developing and Industrialized nations in the Post–World War II Period' in P. Evans, D. Rueschemeyer and T. Skocpol (eds) *Bringing the State Back In* Cambridge: Cambridge University Press

Evans, P., D. Rueschemeyer and T. Skocpol (eds) (1985) *Bringing the State Back In* Cambridge, Cambridge University Press

Finch, J. (1984) 'Community Care: Developing Non-Sexist Alternatives' *Critical Social Policy* 9: pp. 6–18

Fitzgerald—the Fitzgerald Report—see entry under *Immigration: a Commitment to Australia*

Fleishman, J.L., L. Liebman and M.H. Moore (eds) (1981) *Public Duties: the Moral Obligations of Government Officials* Cambridge, Mass.: Harvard University Press

Foucault, M. (1984) 'The Order of Discourse' in M. Shapiro (ed.) *Language*

and Politics New York: New York University Press
Franzway, S. (1986) 'With Problems of their Own: Femocrats and the Welfare State' *Australian Feminist Studies* 3, pp. 45–59
Fraser, N. (1987) 'Women, Welfare and the Politics of Need Interpretation' *Thesis Eleven* 17, pp. 88–107
Fry, G.K. (1988) 'The Thatcher Government, the Financial Management Initiative, and the "New Civil Service"' *Public Administration*, 66, pp. 1–20
Goldberg, G. and E. Kremen (1987) 'The Feminization of Poverty: Only in America?' *Social Policy* 17, pp. 3–15
Goldthorpe, J. (1982) 'On the Service Class, its Formation and Future' in A. Giddens and G. Mackenzie (eds) *Social Class and the Division of Labor* Cambridge: Cambridge University Press, 1982
Goldthorpe, J. and C. Payne (1986) 'On the Class Mobility of Women: Results from Different Approaches to the Analysis of Recent British Data' *Sociology* 20, pp. 531–55
Gordimer, N. (1988) *A Sport of Nature* Ringwood, Vic.: Penguin Books
Gordon, D. (1988) 'The Global Economy: New Edifice or Crumbling Foundations?' *New Left Review* 168, pp. 24–66
Gough, I. (1983) 'The Crisis of the Welfare State' *International Journal of Health Services* 13: 3: pp. 459–478
Gouldner, A.W. (1979) *The Future of Intellectuals and the Rise of the New Class* London: Macmillan
Grimm, J. (1978) 'Women in Female-Dominated Professions' in A. Stromberg and S. Harkess (eds) *Women Working: Theories and Facts in Perspective* Palo Alto: Mayfield
Gruber, J. (1987) *Controlling Bureaucracies: Dilemmas in Democratic Governance* Berkeley, Los Angeles and London: University of California Press
Guerin, Bruce (1985a) 'Setting New Directions in Management at a State Level: South Australia' *Australian Journal of Public Administration* 44, 4, pp. 384–95
—— (1985b) 'Setting New Directions at a State Level' *Canberra Bulletin of Public Administration* 12, 2, pp. 128–34
—— (1988) Address to the 'South Australia 2010' Symposium of SAGASCO Holdings Ltd, 12 August
Gustafsson, L. (1987) 'Renewal of the Public Sector in Sweden' *Public Administration*, 65, pp. 179–93
Haraway, D. (1987) 'A Manifesto for Cyborgs: Science, Technology and Socialist Feminism in the 1980s' *Australian Feminist Studies*, 4, pp. 1–43
Harrison, M. (1988) 'New Child Support Assessment Proposals' *Family Matters: Australian Institute of Family Studies Newsletter* 21, pp. 37–39
Harrison, M.L. (ed.) (1984) *Corporatism and the Welfare State* Aldershot, Hants: Gower
Hawker, G. (1981) *Who's Master, Who's Servant? Reforming Bureaucracy* Sydney: Allen & Unwin
Hawkes, D. (1988) 'The Demise of Public Service Boards ... A Pattern of Public Service Reform?' *The Australian Administration Magazine* 2, pp. 12–13
Heclo, H. and H. Madsen (1987) *Policy and Politics in Sweden: Principled Pragmatism* Philadelphia: Temple University Press

BIBLIOGRAPHY

Heller, A. (1988) 'On Formal Democracy' in J. Keane (ed.) *Civil Society and the State* London: Verso

Hendrie, D. and M. Porter (1987) 'The Capture of the Welfare State' *Canberra Bulletin of Public Administration* 51, pp. 20–30

Hernes, H.M. (1987) 'Women and the Welfare State: The Transition from Private to Public Dependence' in A. Showstack Sassoon (ed.) *Women and the State: the Shifting Boundaries of Public and Private* London: Hutchinson

Higher Education: a Policy Statement (1988) circulated by the Hon. J. Dawkins, Minister for Employment, Education and Training, Canberra: AGPS

Hodge, B. and R. Fowler (1979) 'Orwellian Linguistics' in R. Fowler, B. Hodge, G. Kress and T. Trew (eds) *Language and Control* London: Routledge & Kegan Paul

Hughes, O. (1986) 'Education for Public Sector Management' *Politics* 21, 1, pp. 104–115

Hurford, C. (1987) 'Child Care since 1983—Priorities and Achievements' *Australian Journal of Early Childhood* 12, pp. 3–9

Immigration: A Commitment to Australia (1988) The FitzGerald Report of the Committee to Advise on Australia's Immigration Policies, Canberra: AGPS

Jupp Report—see entry under *Don't Settle for Less: Report of the Committee for Stage I of the Review of the Migrant and Multicultural Programs and Services* (1988) Canberra: AGPS

Katzenstein, P. (1985) 'Small Nations in an Open International Economy: the Converging Balance of State and Society in Switzerland and Austria' in P. Evans et al. (eds) *Bringing the State Back In* Cambridge: Cambridge University Press

Keane, J. (ed.) (1988) *Civil Society and the State* London: Verso

Kelleher, S.R. (1987) 'Scrutinising a Scrutiny: Reflections on the Efficiency Scrutiny Unit Report on the Public Service Board' *Canberra Bulletin of Public Administration* 52, pp. 72–77

Kelleher, S.R. (1988) 'The Apotheosis of the Department of Prime Minister and Cabinet: Further Reflections on Administrative Change, 1987' *Canberra Bulletin of Public Administration* 54, pp. 9–12

Kelly, E.F. and R.L. Wettenhall (1975) 'Policy Analysis and the "New Public Administration"' in R.N. Spann and G.R. Curnow (eds) *Public Policy and Administration in Australia: a Reader* Sydney: Wiley

Konrad, S. and I. Szelenyi (1979) *The Intellectuals on the Road to Class Power* New York and London: Harcourt Brace Jovanovich

Kranz, H. (1976) *The Participatory Bureaucracy: Women and Minorities in a More Representative Public Service* Lexington: Heath

Kress, G. (1985) *Linguistic Processes in Sociocultural Practice* Geelong: Deakin University Press

Kress, G. and R. Hodge (1979) *Language as Ideology* London: Routledge & Kegan Paul

Krieger, J. (1987) 'Social Policy in the Age of Reagan and Thatcher' in R. Miliband, L. Panitch and J. Saville (eds) *Socialist Register 1987* London: Merlin Press

Kundera, M. (1986) *Life is Elsewhere* New York: Penguin

Laffin, M. (1987) '"No, Permanent Head": Politician–Bureaucrat Relationships in Victoria' *Australian Journal of Public Administration* 46, pp. 37–55

Lane, L.M. (1986) 'Karl Weick's Organizing: The Problem of Purpose and the Search of Excellence' *Administration and Society* 18, pp. 111–35

Levine, D. (1985) 'Political Economy and the Argument for Inequality' *Social Concept* 2, pp. 3–71

Liebow, E. (1967) *Tally's Corner: A Study of Negro Streetcorner Men* Boston: Little Brown

Lo Bianco, J. (1987) *National Policy on Languages* Canberra: AGPS

Logue, J. (1979) 'The Welfare State: Victim of its Success', *Daedalus* 108, pp. 69–89

Looseley (1987) 'How Wran Showed Labor the Way in from the Cold' *Weekend Australian* 19–20 September

Luhmann, N. (1982) *The Differentiation of Society* New York: Columbia University Press

Mannheim, K. (1936) *Ideology and Utopia* London: Routledge & Kegan Paul

Marklund, S. (1988) *Paradise Lost? The Nordic Welfare States and the Recession 1975–1985* Lund: Arkiv forlag

Marshall, N. (1988) 'The Demise of CTEC' *Australian Journal of Public Administration* 47, pp. 19–35

Marshall, T.H. (1977) 'Social Class and Citizenship' in T.H. Marshall *Class, Citizenship and Social Development* Chicago: University of Chicago Press

Martin, B. (1987) 'Merit and Power' *Australian Journal of Social Issues* 22, pp. 436–52

Martin, B. and Szelenyi, I. (1984) *The New Class and Theories of Cultural Capital*, unpublished manuscript, Department of Sociology, University of Wisconsin: Madison

Martin, J.R. (1986) 'Grammaticalising Ecology: The Politics of Baby Seals and Kangaroos' in T. Threadgold, E. Grosz, G. Kress and M. Halliday (eds) *Semiotics, Ideology, Language* Sydney: Pathfinder Press

Marx, K. (1968) 'The Eighteenth Brumaire of Louis Bonaparte' in K. Marx and F. Engels *Selected Works* Moscow: Progress Publishers

Marx, K. and F. Engels (1968) 'The Communist Manifesto' in K. Marx and F. Engels *Selected Works* Moscow: Progress Publishers

Massey, D. (1987) 'The Shape of Things to Come' in R. Peet (ed.) *International Capitalism and Industrial Restructuring* Boston: Allen & Unwin

Mauss, M. (1967) *The Gift: Forms and Functions of Exchange in Archaic Societies* New York: W.W. Norton

McDonald, K. (1988) 'After the Labour Movement: Strategic Unionism, Investment and New Social Movements' *Thesis Eleven*, 20, pp. 30–51

Meiskins, P.F. (1984) 'Scientific Management and Class Relations' *Theory and Society* 13, pp. 177–211

Melucci, A. (1988) 'Social Movements and the Democratization of Everyday Life' in J. Keane (ed) *Civil Society and the State* London: Verso

Meyer, M.W. (1987) 'The Growth of Public and Private Bureaucracies' *Theory and Society* 16, pp. 215–35

Mills, H. (1981) 'Equal Opportunities' in A. Parkin and A. Patience (eds)

The Dunstan Decade: Social Democracy at the State Level Melbourne: Longman Cheshire

Mintzberg, H. (1987) 'Grafting Strategy' *Harvard Business Review* pp. 66–76

Mishra, R. (1984) *The Welfare State in Crisis: Social Thought and Social Change* Brighton: Wheatsheaf

Mosher, F. (1982) *Democracy and the Public Service* 2nd edn, New York: Oxford University Press

Nash, J. (1983) 'The Impact of the Changing International Division of Labor on Different Sectors of the Labor Force', in J. Nash and P. Fernandez-Kelly (eds) *Women, Men, and the International Division of Labor* Albany: State University of New York Press

National Pay Equity Coalition Submission to the 1988 National Wage Case 16 June 1988

O'Donnell, C. and P. Hall (1988) *Getting Equal: Labor Market Regulation and Women's Work* Sydney: Allen & Unwin

O'Donnell, C. and Hall, P. (1988) *Getting Equal: Labour Market Regulation and Women's Work* Sydney: Allen & Unwin

O'Loughlin, M. and B. Cass (1984) Married Women's Employment Status and Family Income Distribution, paper presented at 54th ANZAAS Congress, Australian National University, Canberra, 14–18 May

Offe, C. (1984) *Contradictions of the Welfare State* London: Hutchinson

Offe, C. (1985) *Disorganised Capitalism* Cambridge: Polity Press

Office of the Status of Women (1987) *Women's Budget Statement: an assessment of the impact on women of the 1987–88 Budget* Canberra: AGPS

Olsen, F. (1983) 'The Family and the Market: a Study of Ideology and Legal Reform' *Harvard Law Review* 96: 7: 1497–1579

Ostrander, S. (1987) 'Review Essay: "Women Using Other Women"' *Contemporary Sociology* 16, pp. 51–53

Panitch, L. (1986) 'The Impasse of Social Democratic Politics' in R. Miliband and J. Saville (eds) *Socialist Register 1985/86* London: Merlin Press

Parkin, A. and A. Patience (eds) (1981) *The Dunstan Decade: Social Democracy at the State Level* Melbourne: Longman Cheshire

Pateman, C. (1970) *Participation and Democratic Theory* Cambridge: Cambridge University Press

—— (1987) 'The Patriarchal Welfare State: Women and Democracy' in Amy Gutman (ed.) *Democracy and the Welfare State* Princeton: Princeton University Press (the copy used here was in pre-publication form and incorporated only the author's revisions)

Patterson, M. and L. Engelberg (1978), 'Women in Male-Dominated Professions' in A. Stromberg and S. Harkess (eds) *Women Working: Theories and Facts in Perspective* Palo Alto: Mayfield

Peattie, L. and M. Rein (1983) *Women's Claims: A Study in Political Economy* Oxford: Oxford University Press

Peters, T.J. and R.H. Waterman (1984), *In Search of Excellence* New York: Warner Books

Piven, F. and Cloward, R. (1982) *The New Class War* N.Y.: Pantheon

Pollitt, C. (1986) 'Beyond the Managerial Model: The Case for Broadening Performance Assessment in Government and the Public Service' *Financial Accountability and Management* 2, pp. 155-71
Pomeroy, J. (1985) 'Doublespeak and the Senior Executive Service: A Regional Perspective' *Canberra Bulletin of Public Administration* 12, 2, pp. 119-24
Poynton, C. (1985) *Language and Gender: Making the Difference* Geelong: Deakin University Press
Pratt, G. (1985) 'Performance Management in the Australian Public Sector' *Australian Journal of Public Administration* 44, 4, pp. 362-67
Pusey, M. (1988a) 'Our Top Canberra Public Servants under Hawke' *Australian Quarterly* Autumn, pp. 109-123
—— (1988b) 'From Canberra, the Outlook is Dry' *Australian Society* July, pp. 20-27
Radin, B. (1988) Why do we care about organisational structure?, address to 1988 Public Management Seminar, RAIPA (Queensland Division), 14 July
Radin, B. and B. Benton (1988) 'Linking Policy and Management in Human Services' *Public Administration Quarterly* Summer
Radin, B. and T.L. Cooper (1989) 'From Public Action to Public Administration: Where does it lead?', *Public Administration Review* 49: 2: 167-170
Raymond, J. (1987) *Social Security Review Issues Paper No. 3: Bringing up Children Alone: Policies for Sole Parents*, Canberra: AGPS
Reddy, M. (1979) 'The Conduit Metaphor: A Case in Frame Conflict in Our Language about Language' in A. Ortony (ed.) *Metaphor and Thought* Cambridge: Cambridge University Press
Redford, E.S. (1969) *Democracy in the Administrative State* New York: Oxford University Press
Reich, R. (1983) 'Why Democracy Makes Economic Sense' *The New Republic* 19 December, pp. 25-32
Report of Committee of Inquiry [the 'Kirby Report'] (1985) *Labour Market Programs* Canberra: AGPS
Report of the Committee to Advise on Australia's Immigration Policies (1988) *Immigration: A Commitment to Australia* Canberra: AGPS
Roach, Sharyn (1986) The Recruitment of Men and Women Lawyers: The Interplay of Environmental, Organizational and Individual Properties, unpublished PhD thesis, University of Connecticut
Rosaldo, M. (1974) 'Woman, Culture and Society: a Theoretical Overview' in M. Rosaldo and L. Lamphere (eds) *Woman, Culture and Society* Stanford: Stanford University Press
Rosanvallon, P. (1988) 'The Decline of Social Visibility', in J. Keane (ed.) *Civil Society and the State* London: Verso
Ross, G. and J. Jenser (1986) 'Post-war Class Struggle and the Crisis of Left Politics' in R. Miliband et al. (eds) *Socialist Register 1985/86* London: Merlin Press
Ross, R. (1987) 'Facing Leviathan: Public Policy and Global Capitalism' in R. Peet (ed.) *International Capitalism and Industrial Restructuring* Boston: Allen & Unwin
Ryan, L., 'Feminism and the Federal Bureaucracy 1972-83', forthcoming in Sophie Watson (ed.) *Playing the State* London: Verso

Sahlins, M. (1972) *Stone Age Economics* Chicago: Aldine
Sassen-Koob, S. (1983) 'Labor Migration and the New Industrial Division of Labor' in J. Nash and P. Fernandez-Kelly (eds) *Women, Men and the International Division of Labor* Albany: State University of New York Press
Schacht, C. 'Labor's Modern Pioneers' *Weekend Australian* 26–27 September
Schon, D. (1979) 'Generative Metaphor: A Perspective on Problem Setting in Social Policy' in A. Ortony (ed.) *Metaphor and Thought* Cambridge: Cambridge University Press
Schwarz, B. (1987) 'The Thatcher Years' in R. Miliband, L. Panitch and J. Saville (eds) *Socialist Register 1987* London: Merlin Press
Seccombe, W. (1986) 'Patriarchy Stabilized: the construction of the male breadwinner wage in nineteenth-century Britain' *Social History* 11: 1: pp. 53–77
Sheriff, P. (1976) 'The Sociology of Public Bureaucracies 1965–75' *Current Sociology* 24, 2
Showstack-Sassoon, A. (ed) (1987) *Women and the State* London: Hutchinson
Siim, B. (1987) 'The Scandinavian Welfare States—Towards Sexual Equality or a New Kind of Male Domination?' *Acta Sociologica* 30, pp. 255–70
Skills for Australia (1987) Canberra: AGPS
Spann, R.N. (1977) 'The Coombs Doctrine' in C. Hazelhurst and J.R. Nethercote (eds) *Reforming Australian Government: The Coombs Report and Beyond* Canberra, Ripa (ACT) and Australian National University Press
Stack, S. (1974) *All Our Kin: Strategies for Survival in a Black Community* New York: Harper & Row
Stewart, J. and M. Clarke (1987) 'The Public Service Orientation: issues and dilemmas' *Public Administration* 65, pp. 161–79
Stretton, H. (1987) *Political Essays* Melbourne: Georgian House
Summers, Anne (1986) 'Mandarins or Missionaries: Women in the Federal Bureaucracy' in N. Grieve and A. Burns (eds) *Australian Women: New Feminist Perspectives* Melbourne: Oxford University Press
Szeleny, I. and B. Martin (n.d.) New Class Theory and Beyond, unpublished manuscript, Madison, University of Wisconsin, Department of Sociology
Thompson, E. (1985) 'Reform in the Public Service: Egalitarianism to the SES' 27th Annual Conference of the Australasian Political Science Association, 28–30 August, Adelaide
Thompson, G. (1987) 'The American Industrial Policy Debate: any lessons for the U.K.?' *Economy and Society*, 16, pp. 1–74
Threadgold, T. (1986a) 'Semiotics-Ideology-Language', in T. Threadgold et al. *Semiotics, Ideology, Language* Sydney: Pathfinder Press
—— (1986b) 'The Semiotics of Volosinov, Halliday and Eco', *American Journal of Semiotics* 4, pp. 107–142
—— (1988) 'Language and Gender' *Australian Feminist Studies* 6, pp. 41–71
—— (forthcoming) 'Stories of Race and Gender: an Unbounded Discourse' in L. O'Toole and D. Birch (eds) *The Functions of Style* London: Francis

Pinter

Wade, Jan (1985) The Consequences of Change in the Public Sector, address to RAIPA Conference, Menzies at the Rialto (Melbourne), 15 October, 1985

Walsh, Senator P. (1985) 'Managing the Public Sector' *Canberra Bulletin of Public Administration* 12, 2, pp. 108–111

Ward, I. (1986) A Changing ALP, paper presented to the Sociological Association of Australia and New Zealand Conference, University of New England, Armidale

—— (1987) 'Labor's Middle Class Membership: A Profile of the Victorian Branch of the ALP in the Eighties' *Politics* 22, pp. 84–92

Warwick, D.P. (1981) 'The Ethics of Administrative Discretion' in Fleishman, Liebman and Moore (eds) *Public Duties: the Moral Obligations of Government Officials* Cambridge, Mass.: Harvard University Press

Watts, R. (1987) *The Foundations of the National Welfare State* Sydney: Allen & Unwin

Weber, M. (1948) 'The Social Psychology of the World Religions' in H.H. Gerth and C.W. Mills (eds) *From Max Weber: Essays in Sociology* London: Routledge & Kegan Paul

—— (1949) '"Objectivity" in Social Science and Social Policy" in *The Methodology of the Social Sciences* New York: Free Press

—— (1958) *The Protestant Ethic and the Spirit of Capitalism* Parsons edn, New York. Scribners

—— (1968) *Economy and Society* vol. 1, New York: Bedminster Press

Weir, L. (1987) 'Women and the State: a Conference for Feminist Activists' *Feminist Review* 26, pp. 93–104

Western Australian Government (1986) *Managing Change in the Public Sector: A Statement of the Government's Position*

Whitlam, G. (1985) *The Whitlam Government 1972–1975* Ringwood, Vic.: Penguin Books

Wilenski, P. (1983) 'Small Government and Social Equity' *Politics* 18, pp. 7–26

—— (1986) 'Australia's Public Service is Proving More and More Efficient' *Australian Administration Magazine* 1, 3, pp. 8–11

—— (1987), *Public Power and Public Administration* Sydney: Hale & Iremonger

—— (1988) 'Social Change as a Source of Competing Values in Public Administration' *Australian Journal of Public Administration* 47, pp. 213–23

Wilensky, H. and C. Lebeaux (1965) 'Conceptions of Social Welfare' in M. Zald (ed.) *Social Welfare Institutions* New York: Wiley

Wilson, E. (1977) *Women and the Welfare State* London: Tavistock

—— (1987) 'Thatcherism and Women: After Seven Years' in R. Miliband, L. Panitch and J. Saville (eds) *Socialist Register 1987* London: Merlin Press

Winkler, J.T. (1981) 'The Political Economy of Administrative Decision' in M. Adler and S. Asquith (eds) *Discretion and Welfare* London: Heinemann

Wright, E. and B. Martin (1987) 'The Transformation of the American Class Structure, 1960–1980' *American Journal of Sociology* 93, pp. 1–29

Yeatman, A. (1986) 'Freedom or Self-determination? Some Comments on David Levine's "Political Economy and the Argument for Inequality"' *Social Concept* 3, pp. 40–52

—— (1988a) 'Beyond Natural Right: the Conditions for Universal Citizenship' *Social Concept* 4, pp. 3–33

—— (1988b) Contemporary Issues for Feminism and the Politics of the State, written version of paper presented to National Conference on Gender Issues in Educational Administration and Policy, 28–30 November 1987

—— (1988c) 'A Review of Multicultural Policies and Programs in Children's Services', Office of Multicultural Affairs

—— (1988d) 'Issues in Youth Income Support—Their Context and Development' *Report of the South Australian Youth Incomes Task Force* SA Youth Bureau

—— (1988e) 'The Politics of Child Abuse' *Flinders Studies in Policy and Administration* 5

Young, M. (1961) *The Rise of the Meritocracy* 1870–2033: Penguin Books

Index

administrative elite
  creation of, 11–12
  education of, 12
  promotion of, 12
administrative reform, 1–12
administrative state
  Cabinet control, 37–8
  Cain Victorian State
    Government, 37
  conditional delegation, 56–7
  democratisation, 36–58
    internal processes, 48–58
    value-commitment, 48–58
  development, 39–43
  Hawke Labor Government, 37
  organisational complexity, 43–8
  procedural respect, 52
  public orientation, 52, 55
  reflective choice, 52
  restraint on means, 52
  senior executive service, 38
  three-way partnership model,
    50–1, 53–4
  veracity, 52
Amsden, A. 111
Antcliff, S. 123, 131
Ashenden, D. 52
A Sport of Nature, 156–7
Australian Council for Overseas
  Aid, 110
Australian Development Assistance
  Bureau internal differentiation,
  viii
Australian Feminist Studies, 97
Australia Reconstructed, 87
Australian Labor Party
  political-cultural traditions, ix

Baldock, & B. Cass, 91
Barron, R. & G. Norris, 66
Beale, R.D. 8
Beilharz, P. 159–60
Beilharz, P. & R. Watts, 158
Bell, D. 171
Beveridge, W. 19
Bjorklund, U. 171
Blackmore, J. & J. Kenway, 172
Bledstein, B. 62
Block, F., R. Cloward, B.
  Ehrenreich & F. Piven, 124–5,
  129, 138–9
Borchorst, A. & B. Siim, 146–7
Boris, E. & P. Bardeglio, 145
Boxer, M. 72
Bradley, D. & D. McCulloch, 89
Bryson, L. 27, 85
bureaucratic culture
  cost-benefits, 21–2
  rational-technical orientation,
  21–2
Burns, A. 76
Burton, C. 28, 82

Cameron, J. 168
Cass, B. 1, 90–1, 93, 94
Castles, F. 90, 114–5, 126–7, 129,
  132, 133, 146
Child Support: a Discussion Paper,
  92–3
Coady, C. 154
Coleman, M., P. Gallagher & C.
  Thame 168
Commonwealth Office of
  Multicultural Affairs, 5

INDEX

Commonwealth Public Service
  functions of senior personnel, 9
Connolly, W. 153, 161–3
Considine, M. 2
contests of meaning, 155
Coombs, H.C. 19, 33, 40
Cooper, T.L. 39, 53
Corkindale, D. 56
corporate consciousness
  senior executive service, 10
credentials
  technical intelligensia, 18
Cullen, R.B. 8, 12, 37
Curthoys, 88

Dahlerup, 65
d'Alpuget, 33
De Lauretis, T. 156–7
Deacon, D. 85
delegation, 25
democratisation
  administrative state, 36–58
  control, 23–5
  line of command, 23–5
  management prerogatives, 23–5
  state, viii–ix
department heads
  devolution of powers to, 8
devolution of operating powers,
  department heads, 8
disadvantaged groups
  representation by femocrats,
Disney, J. 131, 132, 172
Don't Settle for Less, 153
Donzelot, J. 142
Dowse, S. 65, 69*, 88–9, 90
Durkheim, E. 22, 104, 153

Earle, J. & R. Graycas, 97
Edwards, M. 69, 91, 92
Eisenstein, H. 65, 69
Epstein, C. 72
equitable administration
  consumer rights, 4
  decision-making, 4
  moves toward symbolic, 11
Ergas, H. & T. Lee, 110
Ethnic Affairs Commissions, state, 5
Evans, P. 110

femocrats
  dilemmas, 80–97
  child support, 92–7
  class analysis, 62–4, 69–77
  definition, 64–9
  feminism, 77–9
  Fitzgerald Report, 103, 117
  Hawke Labor Government, 90–4
  identification, 61
  ideology, 77–9
  Office of Status of Women, 84–5
  patriarchal structuring, 82–8
  senior executive service, 83–8
  social democracy, 88
  Social Security Review, 90
Federal Cabinet
  internal differentiation, viii
financial accountability
  mechanisms
  macro-controls, 176
  micro-controls, 175
  organisational profiles, 177
  rewarding economy, 177–8
  'year-by-year' budget syndrome, 177
Finch, 140
Fitzgerald, 58
Fleishamn, J.L. *et al*, 49
Foucault, M. 155
Franzway, S. 68, 97
Fraser, N. 141, 142, 144
Fry, G.K. 37

gender politics
  educational opportunities, 166
  identity, 156
  Filipino brides, 154
Goldberg, G. & E. Kremen, 77
Goldthrope, J. 63
Goldthrope J. & C. Payne, 75–6, 77
Gordimer, N. 136
Gordon, D. 107–9, 110–11
Gough, I. 136–7
Gouldner, A.W. 18, 19, 20, 26, 28, 30, 62, 64, 78–9, 80, 138

193

Green Paper on Higher Education, 154
Grimm, J. 72
Gruber, J. 48
Guerin, B. 1, 7, 8, 54
Guerin Review, 20
Gustafsson, L. 56

Hall, S. 136
Harrison, M.L. 40
Haraway, D. 151, 155, 174
Harrison, M. 92, 94
Hawke, R.J. 33, 158
Hawke Labor Government, ix
 labourism, 158
 discursive production, 172
Hawker, G. 6, 49, 51–2
Hawkes, 8
Heclo, H. & H. Madsen, 146
Heller, A. 135
Hendrie, D. & M. Porter, 36, 96, 122–3
Hernes, H.M. 145–6
higher education, 103, 132, 153–4, 165
Higher Education Administrative Charge (HEAC), 132
Higher Education: a Policy Statement, 103, 153, 165
Hodge, B. & R. Fowler, 173
Federal Treasury
 internal differentiation, viii
Home and Community Care Department
 internal differentiation, viii
Hughes, O. 6
Hurford, C. 168

immigration, 103, 117, 153
Immigration: a Commitment to Australia, 103, 117, 153
internal differentiation
 Australian Development Assistance Bureau, viii
 Federal Cabinet, viii
 Federal Treasury, viii
 Home and Community Care Department, viii

Prime Minister's Department, viii

Jupp, 117

Katzenstein, 110
Keane, J. vii
Kelleher, S.R. 8
Kelly, E.F. & R.L. Wettenhall, 49
Keynes, J.M. 19
Kirby Report, 103
Konrad, S. & I. Szelenyi, 12, 33, 35, 62, 64, 135–6, 138
Kranz, H. 49
Kress, G. 163–5, 166
Krieger, J. 124, 129, 130
Kundera, M. 149–50

labourism, 158
Laffin, M. 8, 37
Lane, L.M. 36
language
 bureaucratic language, 167
 conduit model, 162
 language politics, 155
 text-context dialectic, 163–4
leadership levels
 public bureaucracies, 9
Levine, D. 104
Liebow, E. 142
Life is Elsewhere, 150
line of command
 delegation, 25
Logue, J. 120–1
Logue, J. & Mishra, R. 123
Looseley, S. 33
Luhmann, N. 22, 43, 46–7

management improvement, 1–12
manageralism, 6–7
managerialist approach, 6
 social and political agendas, 7
managers
 autonomy, 11
management discourse, 332–5
 ACTU, 33
 Australian Labor Party, 33–5
 dominance in 1980s, 32–5
 Whitlam Government, 33
mandarins

INDEX

Commonwealth Public Service, 16–19
Department of Foreign Affairs, 17
Mannheim, K. 64
market orientation state administration, 5
Marklund, S. 127, 129
Marshall, N. 41, 43
Marshall, T.H. 116, 126, 142
Martin, B. 28
Martin & I. Szelenyi, 71
Marx, K. 69–70, 105
Massey, D. 106
Mauss, M. 102
May Economic Statement (1987), 122, 125
McCulloch, D. 69
McDonald, K. 104, 117–8
Meiskins, P.F. 26, 35
Melucci, A. 155, 170
Meyer, M. 43
Milibrand, M. & M. Liebman, 137
Mills, H. 89
minorities, 28
  exclusion of non-higher educated, 28
  inclusion on merit, 28
Mintzberg, H. 9
Mishra, R. 123, 125
Mosher, F. 49

Nash, J. 106
National Policy on Languages, 160
National Wage Case (1988), 82, 116
New Right
  demands for smaller government, 1

O'Donnell, & Hall, 94
O'Loughlin, M. & B. Cass, 75, 79
Offe, 35, 129–30, 171
Office of the Status of Women, 84–5
Olsen, 123
openness, 29–31
  expert-led value debate, 30–1
Orwellian doublethink, 172–3
Ostrander, S. 73

Panitch, 138
Parsons, 22
Pateman, C. 46, 128, 143
Patterson, M. & L. Engleberg, 72
Peattie, L. & M. Rein, 169
performance-indicators, 23
Peters, T.J. & R.H. Waterman, 9, 26, 43, 105
Piven, F. & R. Cloward, 129
policy discourse
  families, 155
  parents, 155
policy documents, 160, 167
politics of difference, 157
politics of claims, 170
politics of discourse, 149–174
  corporate management, 172
  discursive multiplicity, 163–5
  discursive closure/openness, 166
  discursive reality, 164
  generic closure/openness, 166
  global culture, 174
  higher education, 153
  invervention by state, 169–170
  language politics, 155
  multiculturalism, 153
  needs-based planning, 168
  power, 161–2
  politics of the state, 169–74
  private status, 170
  public status, 170
  rationing strategies, 171–2
  social heterogeneity, 166
  statecentric modes of management, 153, 168
  value-orientation, 161
Pollitt, C. 35
Pomeroy, J. 11
power
  politics of discourse, 161–2
Poynton, C. 86
Pratt, G. 6
public administration, 13–35
  changes, 13–14
    Western Australia, 14
  chief executive officers
    performance agreements, 14
  Commonwealth Public Service Board, 15–20

195

mandarins, 16–17
promotion by seniority, 16
promotion on merit, 20
Senior Executive
   Management Program,
   15–16
scientific management
   approach, 15–16
cost-benefits, 21
rational-legal authority, 20
Prime Minister's Department
   internal differentiation, viii
problem-setting, 159
Public Service Boards
   decrease in role, 8
   rational management style, 10
Pusey, M. 83–5

Radin, B. & B. Benton, 30, 50
Raymond, J. 76, 91
Redford, E. 49
Reich, R. 111
Reid, E. 68
Report of the Committee of Inquiry into the Labour Market Programs, 103
Roach, S. 72
Rosaldo, M. 85
Rosanvallon, P. 139
Ross, G. & J. Jensen, 137–8
Ross, R. 106
Ryan, L. 65

Sahlins, M. 102
Sassen-Koob, S. 107
Schacht, C. 33
Schon, D. 159
Schwartz, 129
Seccombe, 72
senior executive service
   creation, 8
   corporate consciousness, 10
Senior Executive Management Program (1987), 15–16
SEMP streams, 179
Sheriff, P. 12
Showstack-Sassoon, 65
Siim, B. 145
Skills in Australia, 86
social control techniques, 26–7

people-and process emphasis,
   26–7
South Australia
   Government Management
   Employment Act 1986, 20
Guerin Review, 20
Review of Public Service
   Management, Final Report, 7
Review of Public Service
   Management, Initial Report, 7
Spann, R.N. 9
state administration
   market orientation, 5
state invervention, vii–viii
Stack, S. 142
Stewart, J. & M. Clarke, 55
Stretton, H. 32
Summers, A. 65, 69
Szelenyi, I. & B. Martin, 62

technical flexibility, 31–2
technical intelligensia, 18–21
   characteristics, 22
   credentials, 18
   status, 24
technical promiscuity, 31–2
The Book of Laughter and Forgetting, 150
The Unbearable Lightness of Being, 149–50
Thompson, E. 11, 12
Thompson, G. 101
Threadgold, T. 149, 163, 166
Toward a National Agenda for a Multicultural Australia, 103

welfare state
   economic interaction, 104–8
   feminism, 119–48
   crisis of welfare state,
      119–30
   feminist relationship to
      crisis, 139–48
   post-welfare state, 130–5
   response of left to crisis,
      135–9
foreign investment, 108–110
Hawke Labour Government,
   131
higher education, 103

INDEX

immigration, 103
labour marker programs, 103
multiculturalism, 103
restructuring policy, 101–118
  Australian public policy,
    113–118
  centralised wage system,
    115–116
  citizenship, 116–117
  entrepreneurs, 113–114
  ethos, 113–118
  immigration, 103, 117
  nation-state responses,
    110–113
  skills formation, 103
  Whitlam Labor Government,
    131
Western Australian Government
  White Paper (1986)
  changing and improving
    government administration,
    13, 14, 23

Wade, I. 6
Walsh, P. 8
Ward, I. 33
Warwick, D.P. 52–3
Watts, R. 33, 40, 115
Weber, M. 12, 15, 17, 19, 103–4
Weir, L. 64
Western Australia
  White Paper, 23
Whitlam, G. 131
Wilenski, P. 3, 6, 49, 55, 161
Wilensky, H. & C. Lebeaux, 90
Wilson, E. 129
Wilson, E. 129, 140, 143
Winkler, J.T. 40–1
Wright, E. & B. Martin, 63, 70–7

Yeatman, A. 93, 97, 104, 123,
  125, 133, 170
Young, 28

Books of Related Interest

Accommodating Inequality
Gender and housing
SOPHIE WATSON

Australian Public Policy and Economic Vulnerability
FRANCIS G. CASTLES

Feminist Challanges
ELIZABETH GROSZ AND CAROLE PATEMAN (EDS)

Gender and Power
Society, the person, and sexual politics
R.W. CONNELL

Getting Equal
Labour market regulation and women's work
CAROL O'DONNELL AND PHILLIPA HALL

Government Administration in Australia
R.N. SPAN

Public Policy in Australia
GLYN DAVIS, JOHN WANNA, JOHN WARHURST, PATRICK WELLER

Secretaries Talk
Sexuality, power and work
ROSEMARY PRINGLE

Sexual Subversions
Three French feminists
ELIZABETH GROSZ

Short Changed
Women and economic policies
RHONDA SHARP AND RAY BROOMHILL

Sisters in Suits
Women and public policy
MARIAN SAWER

The Treasury Line
GREG WHITWELL

Women, Social Science and Public Policy
JACQUELINE GOODNOW AND CAROLE PATEMAN (EDS)

Women, Social Welfare and the State
BETTINA CASS